◆ The Two-Week Traveler Series ◆

THE BEST OF BRITAIN'S COUNTRYSIDE

♦ The Two-Week Traveler Series ♦

THE BEST OF BRITAIN'S COUNTRYSIDE

SOUTHERN ENGLAND
A Driving & Walking Itinerary

Bill and Gwen North

THE MOUNTAINEERS

The Mountaineers: Organized 1906 "...*to explore, study, preserve, and enjoy the natural beauty of the outdoors.*"

© 1991 by William Nothdurft
All rights reserved

8 7 6 5 4
5 4 3 2

No part of this book may be reproduced in any form, or by any electronic, mechanical, or other means, without permission in writing from the publisher.

Published by The Mountaineers
1011 S.W. Klickitat Way, Suite 107, Seattle, Washington 98134
Published simultaneously in Canada by Douglas & McIntyre, Ltd., 1615 Venables Street, Vancouver, B.C. V5L 2H1

Published simultaneously in Great Britain by Cordee
3a DeMontfort St., Leicester, England Lel 7HD

Manufactured in the United States of America
Edited by Nick Allison
Maps by Karen Gally
All photographs by the authors, except author photograph by Beth Wilson
Cover photograph: Burford
Cover design by Elizabeth Watson
Book design by Barbara Bash
Frontispiece: Dorset; page 5: Silbury Hill, by Avebury

Library of Congress Cataloging in Publication Data

North, Bill, 1947–
    The best of Britain's countryside : southern England : a driving and walking itinerary / Bill and Gwen North.
       p.   cm.—(The Two-week traveler series)
    Includes bibliographical references and index.
    ISBN 0-89886-264-7
    1. England—Description and travel—1971– —Guide-books.
2. Automobile travel—England—Guide-books. 3. Landscape—England—Guide-books. 4. Walking—England—Guide-books.
I. North, Gwen. II. Title. III. Series.
DA650.N59   1991
914.204′859—dc20   90-48755
                                                                         CIP

For Eric:

*What matters is not the heights you attain,
but that you attempt the climb.*

Contents

PART ONE Introduction
- About This Guidebook 11
- How This Book is Organized 13
- The Itinerary at a Glance 14
- Preparations 17
- Understanding Britain 24

PART TWO The Itinerary
- DAY ONE: Journeying to the Heart of a Nation 42
- DAY TWO: The Land of the "Cotswold Lion" 58
- DAY THREE: Footloose in the Cotswold Hills 68
- DAY FOUR: Steeping in Bath and Its Environs 86
- DAY FIVE: Across the Roof of Devon 101
- DAY SIX: A Day on the Cornwall Coast Path 114
- DAY SEVEN: Exploring the Lizard 125
- DAY EIGHT: The Secret Side of Cornwall 138
- DAY NINE: A Day of Contrasts: Dartmoor and Dorset 148
- DAY TEN: Exploring Hardy's Dorset 160
- DAY ELEVEN: Into the Land of Enigma 175
- DAY TWELVE: Time-traveling through Southern England 186
- DAY THIRTEEN: In the Realm of Sea and Sky:
  A Day in the South Downs 198
- DAY FOURTEEN: Among the Gardens
  of the Garden of England 214
- DAY FIFTEEN: A Flirtation with London 229
- DAY SIXTEEN: Home 240

Further Reading 245
Useful Addresses 247
Index 249

PART ONE

Introduction

A Note About Safety

Safety is an important concern in all outdoor activities. No guidebook can alert you to every hazard or anticipate the limitations of every reader. Therefore, the descriptions of roads, trails, routes, and natural features in this book are not representations that a particular place or excursion will be safe for your party. When you follow any of the routes described in this book, you assume responsibility for your own safety. Under normal conditions, such excursions require the usual attention to traffic, road and trail conditions, weather, terrain, the capabilities of your party, and other factors. Keeping informed on current conditions and exercising common sense are the keys to a safe, enjoyable outing.

The Mountaineers

About This Guidebook

Density of feature... is the great characteristic of English scenery. There are no waste details; everything in the landscape is something particular—has a history, has played a part, has value to the imagination.
—Henry James
The Art of Travel

There may be no more beautiful and varied countryside in the world than Britain's. There are surprises at every turn—both in the shape and form of the landscape itself and in the imprints left by thousands of years of human settlement—if only you know where to look.

Helping you discover the *real* England is the purpose of *The Best of Britain's Countryside: Southern England*, the second book in *The Two-Week Traveler Series*. After years of helping people find their way around Britain, we've learned that what they remember most fondly about their visits isn't this or that museum or city or castle, but the charming out-of-the-way nooks and crannies of the English countryside: verdant meadows bounded by hedgerows ablaze with wildflowers, timeless little stone villages clustered in the folds of the hills, enigmatic Stone Age monoliths amidst rippling fields of barley, soaring coastal cliffs, cozy country pubs, and warm, welcoming people—the kind of places you just stumble upon and remember forever. That's the *real* Britain, and the subject of this book. So the first thing you need to know is that the itinerary described here, while including carefully selected "famous attractions," aims principally to steer you clear of the tourist traps and off the beaten track.

In sixteen relaxed but richly varied days you'll experience:
- A dozen of England's official **Areas of Outstanding Natural Beauty;**
- Two of its **national parks;**
- Walks along three official **Long Distance Paths;**
- Six of its official **Heritage Coasts;**
- Nearly a dozen **prehistoric sites;**
- The most complete **Roman ruins;**
- Several magnificent **castles, abbeys,** and **cathedrals,** both ruined and intact;

- Three old and intriguing **cities;**
- Four grand **stately homes;**
- Britain's **oldest university;**
- Five stunning **gardens;** and
- Visits to many of the most charming **villages.**

The second thing you should know about this book is that it doesn't pretend to be objective. We know your vacation time is limited and that you can't afford to waste it trying to guess which places to visit and which to skip, so we try to provide unambiguous advice to help you make choices among several intriguing options each day. We also think you're likely to have a healthy curiosity about the things you see as you travel through England, so we describe not just what and where things are, but also *why*—with a wealth of details about people, places, and things along the way.

After opening sections on preparing for your trip and understanding British culture, each subsequent chapter covers a different day on your itinerary. You can follow closely the main route or activity of the day, use the suggestions simply as an outline and explore whatever takes your fancy, or choose one of the diversions we've designed to lead you happily astray or accommodate uncooperative weather.

You'll spend much of your time tooling along through the countryside in your rented car, but every other day we slow you down to walking speed, with half-day and all-day walks. And you don't have to be a seasoned hiker to enjoy them; they are well paced, include shortcuts, and offer so much visual variety you'll wonder where the time went.

On Day Sixteen, when you board the plane for home, you'll take with you memories of sweeping scenic vistas, winding country lanes, charming thatched villages, soaring cathedrals, ancient civilizations, and friendly people—in short, the best of Britain.

Bill and Gwen North

How This Book is Organized

Each chapter covers a different day in the itinerary and includes:

1. ORIENTATION. An opening page or two to set the scene—a description of the landscape through which you'll be traveling, a bit of history, and so forth—to give you a taste of what's to come.

2. THE ROUTE. Detailed directions to guide you through the day's drive (or walk), with a running commentary to illuminate the passing scene.

 This symbol indicates driving portions of a day's trip.

 This symbol indicates walking portions of a day's trip.

3. DIVERSIONS. Alternatives to the main route (or additions to it) so that whatever your mood, or the condition of the weather, you have more than one way to spend the day.

4. CREATURE COMFORTS. Guidance on where to spend the night (Daily Bed) and where to have dinner (Daily Bread).

The Itinerary at a Glance

DAY 1: Arrive in London and head west, up the **River Thames.** Visit prehistoric sites in the **Vale of White Horse,** then drive north, stopping at a restored **weaving mill,** and continuing to the picture-book town of **Burford.**

DAY 2: Drive through the prettiest villages in the **Cotswold Hills.** Lunch at an old pub. Explore **Warwick Castle,** England's grandest. Optional visit to a **rare breeds farm.**

DAY 3: Take a daylong walk along the **Cotswold Way,** one of Britain's scenic Long Distance Paths, visiting an **Iron Age fort,** flower-bedecked **villages,** and a **medieval manor house** en route. Optional shorter **river valley walk** and visits to **Blenheim Palace** and **Oxford University,** England's oldest. Then drive south to spectacular **Bath.**

DAY 4: Tour the extraordinary ruins of the **Roman Baths,** then take the **guided walking tour** of the city and its splendid Georgian architecture. Afternoon visits to nearby **Wells Cathedral** and the ruins of **Glastonbury Abbey,** legendary burial place of King Arthur.

DAY 5: Drive across the **Somerset Levels** to the medieval market town of **Dunster.** Then drive through **Exmoor National Park** along the **Devon coast.** Visit the picturesque villages of **Selworthy** and **Clovelly,** then drive down the rugged **Cornwall coast** to spend the next two nights in a tiny fishing village.

DAY 6: A day walking the breathtaking **Cornwall Coast Path,** high above the Atlantic. Optional visit to **Tintagel Island.**

DAY 7: Drive down to the south Cornwall coast for an afternoon walk around **Lizard Point,** graveyard of hundreds of sailing

Itinerary at a Glance

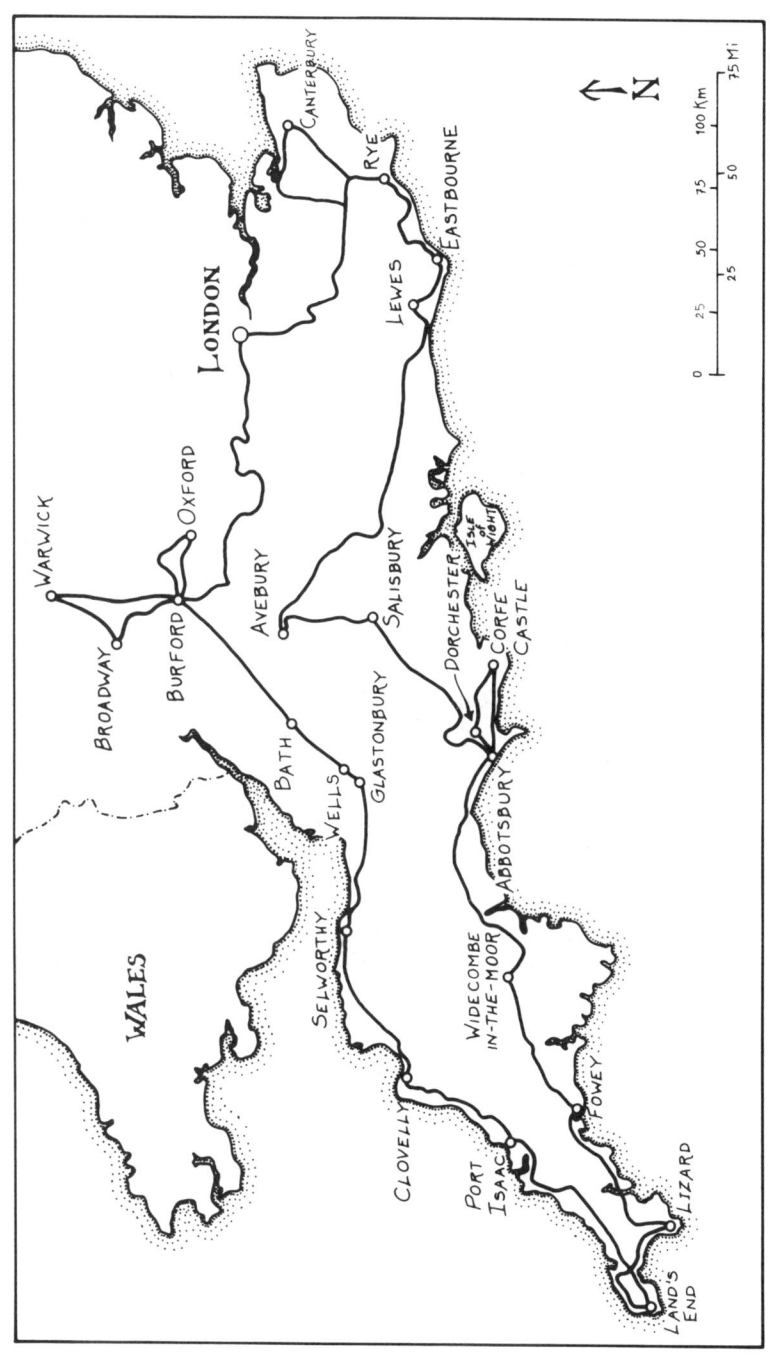

ships. Optional driving tour of Stone Age monuments on the **Land's End Peninsula.**

DAY 8: Drive through **smugglers' haunts** and **pirates' lairs** of the south Cornwall coast. Then drive northeast into the eerie heights of **Dartmoor.**

DAY 9: Morning guided walking tour in **Dartmoor National Park.** Optional driving tour of the park with three short walks to special sites. Short afternoon drive east into **Dorset** to settle in for two nights.

DAY 10: Daylong walk along the beach and coastal ridge above ancient **Abbotsbury,** including a stop at its medieval **swannery.** Alternative driving tour through the "**Wessex**" villages immortalized by Thomas Hardy.

DAY 11: A day of driving into **Wiltshire,** including stops to see the giant at **Cerne Abbas,** the cathedral in **Salisbury,** and the ruins of **Old Sarum, Stonehenge,** and **Avebury.**

DAY 12: A morning walk among the enigmatic Stone Age monoliths of **Avebury.** Afternoon drive east into **Sussex.** Optional visit to the **Weald and Downland Museum,** an open-air museum dedicated to preserving ancient buildings. Next two nights in East Sussex.

DAY 13: Full day's walk along two branches of the spectacular **South Downs Way,** including the white cliffs of the **Seven Sisters,** two medieval villages, the **Long Man of Wilmington,** and the beautiful **Cuckmere River Valley.** Alternative drive through Sussex to the Regency resort of **Eastbourne,** a **Roman castle,** and the site of the A.D. 1066 **Battle of Hastings.**

DAY 14: Morning visit to picturesque **Rye.** Afternoon drive through Kent, the "**garden of England,**" with visits to **Bodiam Castle,** the gardens of **Great Dixter, Sissinghurst,** and **Scotney Castle,** and the stately homes of **Penshurst, Hever Castle,** and Churchill's **Chartwell.** Alternative afternoon trip to **Canterbury.**

DAY 15: A whirlwind visit to **London,** including a window-shopper's **walking tour.** Alternative day in **Kent.**

DAY 16: Home.

Preparations

Remember that time-honored phrase, "Getting there is half the fun"? Forget it. Anytime you go anywhere unfamiliar, there's a certain unavoidable amount of anxiety: Did I pack the right things? Will the car be okay? What if I can't find a place to stay? Are the natives friendly? Will I be able to understand them?

Relax. The natives are most assuredly friendly, once you get through the formalities. They speak English (sort of) and you'll have no trouble understanding them (usually). The chapter that follows this one sorts out some of the mysteries of Britishness. As for the nuts and bolts of getting ready and getting there, here's what you need to know.

Cerne Abbas, Dorset

WHEN TO GO

Official British Tourist Authority policy: anytime. Experienced travelers' advice: late spring, early fall. Your boss's advice: sometime in the summer, and don't be gone long.

Winter is a magical time in Britain. There are limitless expanses of countryside that seem to be yours alone, cozy fires burning in ancient inns, and a warm welcome from people with plenty of time to cater to you personally. But you'll miss the extraordinary green of the English countryside, the masses of wildflowers in the meadows, and the profusion of countless cottage gardens. What's more, most important monuments, castles, and stately homes are closed until Easter. And, of course, the chances of sustained good weather are, to put it tactfully, slim.

In many respects, the finest time to visit is late spring (after April 1) and fall (before November 1). Virtually all attractions are open, the weather is most consistently good, and the crowds are weeks away. Spring flowers, set against a backdrop of freshly minted green, are breathtaking; fall colors have a sweetly melancholy beauty. (Remember that with daylight-saving time, it will get dark earlier after the last weekend in October and later after the last weekend in March.)

But summer's attractions are powerful: the gardens are at their zenith, the fields ripple with golden wheat and ripe barley, and the sun, while less reliable than in spring and fall, is warm and seems to make the old stone cottages glow. Then, too, there is the velvet softness of midsummer evenings, when the long rays of the setting sun coat the landscape in honey gold. In short, there really *are* attractions in every season; choose the one that suits you best... and be adventurous.

RENTING A CAR

The plain fact is that to find the very best of Britain, you really have no alternative to renting a car. Trains and buses, which used to go almost everywhere in rural Britain, have been sharply reduced. (**Note:** Most rental agencies require renters to be at least 21 years old and not older than 65 or 70.) For driving in Britain (and on the left), see the next chapter; for renting a car in Britain, here are some tips.

THE BEST RATES. You'll usually get a lower rate by reserving (and sometimes *paying for*) a car before you leave for Britain. Most major North American car-rental companies operate in Britain, either under their own name (Hertz, Avis, Budget) or the name of a European partner (Dollar is InterRent, National is Europcar-Godfrey Davis). Call their 800 numbers and ask for an unlimited mileage rate schedule for Britain. Some British car-rental ("car-hire") companies also have 800 numbers in the U.S., including Swan National, Town and Country, Kenning, and Guy Salmon. Compare rates and be sure they include tax and the collision damage waiver (see below). Some airlines offer promotional fly-drive packages through brokers who represent British firms (Kemwel is one such broker), and these generally represent the best bargains. Ask when you make your air reservations.

Whomever you choose, be sure they have a network of branches throughout the country in case you need a replacement car. If you intend to pick up the car in one place and leave it in another, be sure they won't add a hefty "drop charge." (**Note:** Unless you rent with a credit card, be prepared to pay a sizable deposit before you drive away.)

THE RIGHT SIZE. British cars, even large ones, may be smaller than you are used to and may have names you've never heard of before. In general, British cars are well appointed and a lot faster than you'd expect from their size. Most car-hire firms offer a full range of vehicles, from tiny two-seaters to station wagons ("estate wagons"). Unless you specify otherwise in advance, expect a manual transmission. Even a small car with an automatic will cost as much as a large standard-transmission car, but if you've never driven a manual-transmission car this is not the time to learn.

INSURANCE. Your rental car will come with on-the-road mechanical breakdown coverage from either the British Automobile Association (AA) or Royal Automobile Club (RAC), but you also will be encouraged to purchase insurance against collision, personal injury, and loss of personal effects. As at home, beware: the insurance can increase your rental rate significantly. You can avoid the collision damage waiver (CDW) if your own insurance company covers you for overseas rentals or by using an American Express card, a gold VISA card or MasterCard, or any Diners Club card. All three provide free overseas collision coverage, but check the fine print beforehand; terms vary. If you aren't otherwise covered, pay for the insurance. If you don't you will be liable for any damage, often up to the full value of the car. An accident, even a small one, can be costly and ruin your holiday.

VAT. Britain has a 17.5 percent value added tax (VAT) on all goods and services—including car rental. Unlike the tax on gifts you buy to take home with you, the VAT on car rental will not be refunded, since you "consumed" the service in Britain. When you're comparing rates, be sure you know whether VAT is included.

WHAT TO TAKE WITH YOU

OFFICIAL DOCUMENTS. If you're a citizen of the United States or any Commonwealth nation, you don't need a visa, just a valid passport. Others should check with the nearest British consulate. (**Note:**

Chatting up the natives, Cornwall

Photocopy the first page of your passport and keep it separate; if you lose your passport, this will simplify replacement.) To rent a car all you need is a valid driver's license from home. If you're interested in staying in a youth hostel, join the International Youth Hostel Federation (IYHF), either through the American Youth Hostel Association (P.O. Box 37613, Washington, DC 20013, telephone 202-783-6161) or by writing directly to the IYHF (Midland Bank Chambers, Howardsgate, Welwyn Garden City, Herts., England). In both cases, ask for the *YHA Accommodation Guide for England and Wales*.

MONEY. This one's simple: carry VISA/Barclays Bank traveler's checks *in pounds* (available in most large banks). Besides the safety of carrying traveler's checks in general, these particular checks will already be in local currency and therefore can be used as cash in most restaurants, shops, and hotels (though not B&Bs). And when you need cash, there are Barclays Bank branches in virtually every town of any size in England; you won't have to worry about exchange rates or pay a cashing commission. If you can't get these checks, buy American Express traveler's checks. In either case, keep the serial numbers separate from the checks and know how to report lost or stolen checks for a refund. Avoid cashing checks in a Bureau de Change or at Chequepoint branches; their exchange rates are poor and they charge high cashing commissions.

Credit cards are accepted in virtually all shops, hotels, restaurants, and gas ("petrol") stations—but, again, not in B&Bs. In addition, they come in handy if you suddenly need a cash advance.

How *much* money you should take depends on the style in which you are accustomed to travel. For a small rental car, expect to pay roughly $450 per week including tax and petrol. Hotels can run from as little as $18 per person per night to as high as $200, in the most exclusive country-house hotels. B&Bs range from $20 per person per night in rural areas to $30 in especially popular destinations (higher still in cities and in classier "country-house" B&Bs). Dinner for two, with drinks, at a good pub can be as low as $30; dinner for two, with wine, at a very good restaurant will run $50 to $75. Estimate your daily costs, then add a cushion for the occasional extravagance. (**Note:** Prudent guidebooks recommend a money belt; we've never felt the need in England, but there's always a first time.)

CLOTHES. Take one of everything—one bikini, one down jacket, etc. Seriously, English weather is notoriously fickle; even in midsummer it's just as likely you will spend some time huddled around a coal fire in a cozy country parlor as sunbathing on a Cornish beach. Since you're not backpacking and your bags will spend most of the time in the trunk ("boot") of your car, you might as well pack enough to be prepared. In general, dress comfortably on days you spend touring and visiting historic sites, and keep a lightweight sweater and rain jacket handy in the backseat. At dinnertime, remember that the British are a bit more formal; except in pubs, men should wear a jacket and tie, women a skirt. To keep the bulk down, coordinate around a single color scheme, layer light clothes as needed, spend an hour doing a wash at a coin-operated laundry halfway through the trip, and if you find you need a heavy sweater, buy it there.

WALKING GEAR. While there are occasional steep bits, none of the walks in this book is in particularly rugged terrain, so the current generation of walking shoes and sneakers will serve you well throughout the trip. If you don't already have such shoes, be sure the ones you buy have a lining of breathable, waterproof fabric. Remember, this is England; even if it doesn't rain while you're walking, the chances are good the grass will be wet. Really waterproof shoes will make a big difference. The same goes for rainwear: buy breathable, waterproof rainwear. It'll cost more, but without it your chances of being wet and miserable at some point are pretty high. As for walking socks, the best combination is still a wool or wool/polypropylene blend outer sock and a thin polypropylene inner sock to wick moisture away. In spring, fall, *and* summer, plan on layers of light clothes: a cotton T-shirt (plus turtleneck if it's cold), cotton (or flannel) overshirt or blouse, lightweight sweater, wind- and waterproof rainwear, and light- to midweight cotton or wool blend slacks (shorts in summer). A hat and gloves can make a difference in the fall.

A few other items, packed in the kind of small knapsack students use to carry books, can make your walks and picnics more pleasant: a small Swiss army knife with a can opener for tinned meats and a corkscrew for the occasional bottle of wine, a small tablecloth, collapsible cups (or just save some of the plastic cups from the flight over), and moleskin and adhesive bandages for blisters.

BOOKING ACCOMMODATIONS IN ADVANCE

If you're willing to be adventurous, you won't need to make reservations in advance for most of the stops on this itinerary, especially if you stay at B&Bs. If, however, you want to be free of the worry of deciding where to stay, the British Tourist Authority's Tourist Information Centre (TIC) network is poised to help. There are TICs in every town of any size in England, and regional centers to coordinate information dissemination. The address of the regional or local TIC is included in the Creature Comforts section of each day's itinerary. Write or call a few months in advance, ask for their accommodations brochures, and then write or call the establishments that interest you. When you reach England you can use the TIC "Book-a-Bed-Ahead" (BABA) service to arrange accommodations a day or two in advance (see "British Hotels, B&Bs, and Restaurants" in the next chapter). You *will* want to make advance reservations in London and Bath, which tend to be crowded; in any "resort" area you hit on a weekend; and wherever you plan to stay your first and last nights, when looking for a room is the last thing you'll want to be doing. See the applicable Creature Comforts sections for options. (**Note:** Beware public holidays, when the English take to the country: Good Friday and Easter Monday, the first and last Monday in May, and the last Monday in August.)

OTHER BOOKS TO READ

For detailed listings of accommodations, restaurants, and pubs, along with a selection of the best background books, consult the Further Reading section at the back of the book.

COPING WITH JET LAG

Jet lag is the transatlantic travel industry's dirty little secret. There are over-the-counter potions, theories about what not to eat or drink on the flight over, and behavior modification regimens before you leave, all designed to reduce jet lag. They don't work. No matter who you are or how you change your routine, you *will* have jet lag during the first day or two of your trip.

The only technique that works reliably to lessen the "breaking-in period" is to stay active the day you arrive, no matter how leaden your legs. Walk, sightsee, and rubberneck straight through the first afternoon, have a reasonable and perhaps slightly early dinner, take another after-dinner stroll, and then *and only then* head for bed. Tomorrow the worst will be behind you.

Sissinghurst, Kent

Understanding Britain

*E*ngland has an international reputation for lousy weather, warm beer, bad food, and unfriendly people. The first is often true, the second and third are exaggerations, and the last is grossly unfair.

The weather is actually quite predictable: wherever you go, it will always have been gorgeous *yesterday.* Hang about awhile and it can turn glorious in the wink of an eye. Beer—real ale, not the pale, thin stuff most countries produce—is pumped up from casks in pub cellars, arriving rich, cool, and amber in frothy mugs. Food *can* be dull, but even in the most remote parts of Britain today there are small restaurants with inspired chefs and pubs producing deeply satisfying, homemade, traditional pub meals.

As for the people, what some visitors take as aloofness in the English is simply politeness—a social grace nearly extinct in some countries and apparently unknown in others. Living as they do on an island buffeted by the brash Atlantic and the unpredictable North Sea, the English tend to be a bit insular themselves—reserved and careful, as if unwilling to rock the social boat for fear of swamping it. They will in-

stantly blurt, "Oh, sorry..." when you blunder into them on the street, as if it were their fault. They chant "Please" and "Thank you" repeatedly and often incongruously in a kind of frenzy of politeness. And, of course, they *queue*—lining up habitually to wait their turn for everything. Stand still briefly on any English street corner and there will soon be people queueing behind you, assuming in their quietly polite way that you, at least, must know what you're doing.

And then there is this: how can you label "aloof" the country that gave us "The Goon Show," "Monty Python's Flying Circus," "Fawlty Towers," and "Eddie the Eagle," the delightfully loopy English Olympic ski jumper? Eccentric, yes. Outrageously silly, certainly. But hardly aloof.

So persist gently through the formalities; you'll soon be on your way to warm, often hilarious, and certainly memorable experiences.

THE LANGUAGE

George Bernard Shaw described America and Britain as "two nations separated by a common language." Certainly a lot of words used frequently are either completely or subtly different (see box). Sometimes conversations you think are being conducted in the same tongue simply drift off into confusion; a Devonshire dialect, for example, can be as dense and impenetrable as a hawthorn hedgerow. And words often are pronounced differently from how they're spelled—ask three residents of Cirencester how to say their town's name and you're likely to get three different answers ... all, apparently, correct.

A Practical Guide to British English

BRITISH   **U.S. EQUIVALENT**

At Hotels/B&Bs:
twin   = two single beds
double   = one double bed
bathroom   = little room with a bathtub in it
loo, toilet, w.c. (water closet)   = bathroom
flannel   = washcloth
torch   = flashlight
fortnight   = two weeks
porridge   = hot oatmeal
fully cooked breakfast   = fried egg, bacon, sausage, etc.

BRITISH	U.S. EQUIVALENT
At Restaurants:	
cream tea	= tea with scones, jam, clotted cream
clotted cream	= a bit like whipped cream
jam	= jelly, preserves
jelly	= Jell-O
chips	= french fries
crisps	= chips (potato)
sweet, pudding	= any dessert
bill	= check
Shopping:	
chemist	= drugstore
plaster	= bandage
jumper	= sweater
pinafore	= jumper (dress)
tights	= pantyhose
braces	= suspenders
suspenders	= garters
waistcoat	= vest
vest	= undershirt
pants	= underpants
trousers	= pants
plimsolls	= sneakers
trainers	= running shoes
first floor	= second floor
ground floor	= first floor
off-licence	= retail liquor store
Transportation:	
queue ("cue")	= line
return	= round-trip ticket
single	= one-way ticket
Underground	= subway
subway	= underground walkway
Miscellaneous:	
football	= soccer
American football	= football
redundant	= laid off, idled
cheers	= thanks/good-bye
"a nice cuppa"	= tea, solution to all ills

DRIVING IN BRITAIN

Repeat the following: "We have nothing to fear but fear itself." Good. Now let's talk about driving on the left. Rule 1 is: Know the car. Ask the car-hire company representative for a complete run-through of your car's features (including the radio, which is remarkably confusing given how few stations there are). Be sure there's a good spare tire ("tyre") and jack in the trunk ("boot") and an owner's manual to show you how to do tricky things—like releasing the gas ("petrol") tank lid. Rule 2 is: Practice. Drive around the lot a bit to get used to things. Ironically, the safest place to learn driving on the left is a high-speed highway ("motorway"). With limited access, a slow lane, and few decisions to make, you have time to adjust. The itinerary that follows puts you on motorways first, no matter which airport you arrive at. Soon, you'll be driving like a native. Trust us.

DRIVING ETIQUETTE. British drivers are well trained and aggressive. They drive accurately and fast (usually over the limit, except in towns), will pass ("overtake") on curves and blind hills, and never use their horns (they blink their lights instead, which—somewhat confusingly—can mean either "move over" or "come ahead").

On the other hand, they are punctiliously correct about important things: coming to a full stop as lights turn red; stopping for pedestrians at crossings with blinking yellow lights, "beeping" walk signals, or white "zebra" stripes on the road; yielding unfailingly at traffic circles ("roundabouts") to cars already in the circle or approaching from the right; and backing up into the last passing place when confronted by an oncoming car on a one-lane minor road (you're expected to show similar courtesy; blink your lights to signal you're yielding). They also give wide berth to cars with red L (Learner) signs in the windows, so the faint of heart may wish to stop at a garage or hardware store and buy a pair. (You can buy a Highway Code brochure at bookstores.) **Note: Seat belts are mandatory in the front seat. Also, police check for drunk drivers and use breath analyzers. Punishment in both cases is swift and stern.**

BRITISH ROADS. There are four classes of roads in Britain, three identified with the prefixes **M, A,** and **B,** and the fourth simply **unclassified.** "M" roads are motorways—six-lane, high-speed, limited-access freeways, which cut across all but the most remote regions of the country. On road signs they are numbered with single or double digits (e.g., M4, M25) in blue and white. "A" roads are the major "arterials"; you can tell how major they are by how many digits follow the letter (e.g., A4, A34, A343). The fewer the digits, the more important the road. "B" roads connect smaller villages with nearby market towns and are generally two lanes wide. Unclassified roads, with no letter or num-

ber, run through rural areas, are by far the loveliest, and may only be one lane wide with passing places. *All* roads, no matter how minor, are well maintained; after all, the inventor of macadam paving was a Scottish civil engineer named McAdam!

Speed limits typically are not posted because the rules are simple: on motorways and divided highways ("dual carriageways"), 70 mph (112 km/h); on other open roads, 60 mph (96 km/h); and in built-up areas, 30 mph (48 km/h).

Some other tips: (1) road signs tell you not just what road you are on, but what other roads (indicated in parentheses) that road will take you to; (2) when you come to an unmarked fork in a very rural area, the *less* important branching road will have a dotted white line painted across its entry; (3) to keep ugly overhead road lights to a minimum, reflecting "cat's eyes" are set into the pavement along the dividing line. Your lights will illuminate them far ahead. In the daytime, you'll be warned when you stray over the midline by the sound of your tires bumping over the reflectors.

PARKING. On-street parking limitations are indicated by yellow lines on the pavement and corresponding signs. A dotted yellow line indicates that parking is permitted, except as posted on the sign. A single solid line generally means no parking during working hours, also indicated on signs and usually 8:30 A.M. to 6:30 P.M., Monday through Saturday. A double yellow line generally means no parking anytime, period. Parking at white zigzag lines, pedestrian crossings, and within 25 yards of a traffic light is also prohibited. In most towns, follow blue-and-white P signs to parking lots. Most have "pay and display" machines from which you buy a stick-on parking stamp.

GASOLINE. The bad news: gasoline is expensive (roughly two to three times the U.S. price per gallon). The good news: British cars get great gas mileage, and the imperial gallon equals 1.2 U.S. gallons (about 4.5 liters). Use only 4-star (97 octane) leaded or premium unleaded in your rental car, as appropriate.

CAR TROUBLE. Before you drive out of the lot, get instructions from your rental agency about how to handle accidents, and use the AA or RAC breakdown coverage that comes with your car. If you experience major mechanical trouble you should expect to get a replacement car promptly (this is why it's wise to rent from a firm with many branches).

The way to Maiden Newton... and other helpful English road signs

A Driver's Glossary

bonnet	= hood	*lay-by*	= pull-over place
boot	= trunk	*lorry*	= truck
car park	= parking area	*petrol*	= gasoline
cul-de-sac	= dead end	*roundabout*	= traffic circle
diversion	= detour	*silencer*	= muffler
dual carriage-way	= divided highway	*tailback*	= traffic jam
		windscreen	= windshield
estate car	= station wagon	*zebra*	= crosswalk
flyover	= overpass		
give way	= yield		

BRITISH HOTELS, B&BS, AND RESTAURANTS

The best accommodations in Britain are at the extremes of the cost spectrum: lavish and expensive country-house hotels, and charming and inexpensive bed and breakfast (B&B) accommodations in private homes and, even better, on farms. In between is a wide range of hotels and guesthouses, which often offer no more than a B&B and cost much more. In a special category are historic old inns, which will cost a bit more than a B&B, may have terrific atmosphere, but may also have a noisy pub downstairs. Choose inns with care (write for the British Tourist Authority's booklet *Stay at an Inn;* see Useful Addresses).

FINDING A NICE ROOM FOR THE NIGHT. If chic country-house hotels are your preference, book months in advance; they're exclusive in part because they have so few rooms. The same is true for the nicest inns, and for almost any place in a popular city like Bath.

For B&Bs, there's a kind of art to finding the best ones. Begin looking between 4:00 P.M. and 5:00 P.M. (earlier in the fall and winter, when it gets dark sooner). B&B establishments, whether in cities or out in the countryside, identify themselves with a small sign hung out at the roadside or in a front window. The more popular the area (near famous sites, national parks, beaches, etc.) the more choice there will be. In towns and cities, B&Bs mysteriously cluster in distinct neighborhoods.

The English, Welsh, and Scottish tourist boards have a "Crown Classification Scheme" to identify the level of facilities that accommodation establishments offer. The more "crowns" on the plaque displayed outside the door, theoretically, the better the facilities. But it

The Dower House, a B&B on Weshall Hill, Burford

doesn't help much: it tells you whether there will be a TV or tea- and coffee-making facilities in your room, but it tells you nothing about the charm of the place, the tastefulness of the decor, the quality of the food, or the hospitality of the hostess/host. A new, quality award system is just being introduced.

To identify the nicest B&Bs (see Further Reading for listings), adhere religiously to this rule: *If it looks well cared for, you'll be well cared for.* Because they're in private homes, B&Bs are as different as people. There are both wonderful B&Bs and duds. The B&B idea started out as a way for hospitable grannies to make a few bob (pounds) by letting out the rooms no longer needed by their grown children. But today, especially in the most scenic parts of Britain, offering B&B accommodations may be the primary source of income for a young couple restoring a big country house or farmstead. Whatever the situation, this is a case where you really can "tell a book by its cover." When you see a B&B that intrigues you (fresh paint, flourishing garden, handsome sign), knock or ring and ask if they have the kind of room you need (single, double, twin, family). If there's a vacancy, you'll be asked if you'd like to look at the room. The answer to this question is "yes," no matter how desperate you are. This is your chance to "case the joint" (screaming infant? odd smells? bizarre furnishings?) and to begin framing a gracious exit line, just in case. You should expect a clean (often quite charming) room, with drawer and hanging space, and sometimes a sink and mirror. In most cases toilet and bathroom will be down the hall, not *en suite*. Sit on the bed; there is nothing quaint about an antique mattress, and in any event you can use it (too soft, too hard) as an excuse to beat a hasty retreat, if necessary. If you like what you find, settle in, inquire about local dinner options, and set a time for breakfast (you pay the bill, in cash, in the morning).

THE UBIQUITOUS BREAKFAST. Somewhere back in the dark recesses of B&B history (post-World War II? Middle Ages?) the word went out that the second *B* in *B&B* would include: juice and cereal, fried eggs (two for men, one for women—watery scrambled eggs are an inedible alternative), bacon (sometimes fried, sometimes steamed), grilled sausage (often local and varying widely in texture and taste), possibly grilled tomatoes and mushrooms, toast (well cooled in little holding racks), marmalade, and tea (with an extra pot of hot water) or coffee. Massive and sustaining, it's a terrific bargain and may last you all day. Thankfully, the rigidity of the menu is changing; the more contemporary your hostess, the more likely you are to be offered a more imaginative breakfast.

B&B EVENING MEALS. Some country and "upscale" B&Bs offer evening meals—often a superb alternative and an excellent value, though you usually need to let them know in advance (easier for the two-night stops on the itinerary). Ask what's on the menu and choose accordingly. You can purchase wine to accompany dinner at an "off-licence" (liquor store), wine merchant, or supermarket in town.

RESTAURANTS. It is still possible to eat badly in Britain, but you have to work at it. During the last decade, superb little restaurants and country inns have sprung up even in the remotest corners of Britain, many run by chefs lured to the countryside from London by the higher quality of life (see Further Reading for listings). Using fresh and seasonal local ingredients, these restaurants have created a kind of "new British cuisine," which is imaginative without being fussy. Eating, at last, is one of the joys of Britain's countryside.

Understanding Britain **33**

Warm and welcoming, pubs are your best bet for affordable lunches and, increasingly, excellent dinners

PUBS AND "PUB GRUB"

> *There is nothing which has yet been contrived by man by which so much happiness is produced, as by a good inn or tavern.*
>
> —Dr. Samuel Johnson

Hundreds of years ago, ale making was done at home, and people who made especially good ale were licensed to sell pitchers of it from a "public room" in their house. Soon these public houses—*pubs* for short—became freestanding businesses. Inevitably, the most ambitious ale makers grew beyond their public houses and became brewers. By the 1800s the first *tied houses*—pubs owned by breweries—emerged. Today, some 80 percent of all pubs are owned by large breweries; only 20 percent are *free houses* (where the proprietor, not the beer, is free).

There is nothing comparable to the pub outside of Britain. An English pub is a neighborhood's or village's communal living room, where folks go to spend the evening together, not to get drunk. Until recently, there were two faces to a pub, preserving class distinctions: a "Public Bar" with bare floors and walls and simple furnishings for workingmen, and a "Saloon" or "Lounge Bar" for gentlemen and ladies, with comfortable chairs and tables, carpeting, and the decorative flourishes that today are traditional—little lamps lending a warm glow, shiny horse brasses, hunting prints, and so forth (jukeboxes and slot machines surged briefly but seem to be fading). Except in the most remote areas, the Public Bar largely has disappeared, often to be replaced with a restaurant offering more ambitious (though not always better) meals than those available in the bar. (**Note:** Children under fourteen may be barred from pubs, except those with a "family room" without a bar.)

THE MYSTERIES BEHIND THE BAR. In any pub, but especially in free houses, the number of beers on tap—not to mention the bottled beers arrayed behind the bar—can be bewildering. The names, brands, even the colors—from amber to dark brown—are all unfamiliar. In general, British ales (technically, they're not beer) fall into four categories: *bitter,* the traditional cool, mildly carbonated, light brown ale (which tastes nutty, not bitter); *best bitter* or *special,* ostensibly a brewery's premium product, with a slightly higher alcohol content and a slightly higher price; *strong,* which, as its name suggests, is a bit stronger still and may have a slightly sweet aftertaste; and *mild,* a dark brown, malty, creamy ale less alcoholic than the others (and called *brown ale* when bottled). All four are made strictly from malted barley, hops, water, and yeast and are neither warm (they're kept at 55 degrees) nor flat (all have varying degrees of natural or artificial carbonation).

Behind the bar, the taps with the long handles are for fresh, unpasteurized, traditional "real ales" that are drawn up from their cellar casks by the vacuum created when the long handles are pulled down. The taps with little flip levers deliver "keg beer"—pasteurized, artificially carbonated, and less distinctive ales kept in pressurized aluminum kegs. By the late 1960s the big breweries had very nearly replaced the traditional ales with the easier-to-keep "keg beers," until a consumer rebellion led by the Campaign for Real Ale (see their guide in Further Reading) turned back the tide. Not only were the big breweries forced to bring back their traditional ales, but dozens of new, small breweries have sprung up as well, with loyal followings.

Also available in most pubs are bottled *pale* or *light ale,* stronger, more carbonated, and less distinctive than drafts; *stout,* the strong, black, malty drink favored in Ireland; and European (and sometimes Australian or American) *lagers,* thin, pale, and uninteresting. Alcoholic cider, dry and quite refreshing, may also be on tap, and local versions in Somerset and Devon are renowned for their sneaky impact. Beers, ales, and ciders come by the pint or the half (never "half pint") and are served in either dimpled glass mugs or straight-sided "jars" (glasses).

Many British women favor lagers sweetened with either lemon soda (called a "shandy") or Rose's Lime Juice. Both drinks are disgusting.

There are, of course, hard liquors. When ordering Scotch, ask simply for "whisky," specify a brand, and indicate whether you want it "neat" (plain), with ice, or with water (there are no other respectable options). Martinis are popular in Britain, but here it means a glass of Martini-brand vermouth, so be specific (ask for a "gin martini"). A gin and tonic will come with lemon, not lime (no one knows why), and all mixed drinks, as well as soft drinks, will come with only a single ice cube, as if ice were being rationed, unless you request more.

PUB HOURS. The somehow charming after-lunch ritual of "Last orders!" and "Time please, gentlemen!" is no more—at least not by law. Since World War I, when pubs were closed in the afternoon to improve quality control in munitions plants, pub hours have been 11:00 A.M. to 3:00 P.M. and 5:30 P.M. to 11:00 P.M. A couple of years ago, however, afternoon closing was abolished and pubs were permitted to remain open from 11:00 A.M. to 11:00 P.M. Monday through Saturday (and noon to 3:00 P.M. and 5:30 to 11:00 P.M. Sunday). But don't depend on it; the English are traditionalists, and many country pubs still close in the afternoon. Even those that remain open generally stop serving lunch after 2:00 P.M.

PUB GRUB. There may be no better bargain than eating at a pub, daytime or night. Sandwiches, "ploughman's lunches" (fresh cheese, bread, salad), hearty soups, and meat pies of various types can generally be had for less than a "fast food" lunch in the States. But dinner can also be a treat: steak and kidney or shepherd's pies, roasts, game dishes, fish, regional specialties, and often more sophisticated meals are increasingly available in England's pubs. True, there are still dreadful dinners, but the good food campaign has spread almost as fast as the real ale campaign, and travelers are the main beneficiaries. (**Note:** City pubs sometimes offer lavish lunch menus, when they get the biggest crowds, but may serve no food in the evening.)

Some pubs, many inns, and most hotels have separate dining rooms with more involved menus. Check the menu (and the crowd); while some of these dining rooms have inspired chefs, many others are simply more expensive than their more popular pubs (and about as lively as mausoleums).

THE CURRENCY

The coin of the realm in England is the pound sterling—think of them as fat dollars, worth between U.S. $1.50 and $2.00 in recent years. Bank notes come in denominations of £5, £10, £20, and £50. There are 100p (pronounced "pee" and short for *pence*) in a pound.

Coins come in denominations of 1p, 2p, 5p, 10p, 20p, 50p, and £1. The 1p and 2p coins are copper, the 5p and 10p are silver, the 20p and 50p are silver and six-sided, and the £1 coin is thick and brassy. To make life interesting, the 20p coin is much smaller than the 10p, and the £1 coin is smaller than either the 10p or 50p coins. You may still come across 1 and 2 *shilling* coins, equal to 5p and 10p respectively, left over from before the decimal system was introduced.

THE PHONE SYSTEM

You are likely to encounter two kinds of public phones: those that are coin operated (keep a handful of 10p, 20p, 50p, and £1 coins) and those that take Phone Cards (which you buy at post offices for between £2 and £20). At coin-operated phones, you put money in first (10p is the minimum) and then dial. When your party answers, a digital readout on the phone tells you how much money you're using up as you talk (creating remarkable levels of anxiety). When the readout reaches zero you either add another coin, hang up, or get abruptly cut off. If the readout shows you still have credit and you want to make another call, don't hang up (you'll lose the credit if you do); press the "follow on call" button and dial the next number. The subtraction process continues when you are connected.

Most British phone numbers are composed of a regional dialing code of several numbers, usually printed in parentheses, and the specific local phone number (which may be from three to seven digits). If all you have is a town name and the specific phone number (e.g., Anytowne 123), dial the operator (100; no coin needed) and ask for the regional dialing code for that town. If you need a phone number anywhere in Britain, dial Directory Enquiries (also a free call); the number is 192 outside London and 142 within the city. The International Operator is 155. Emergency (police, fire, ambulance) is 999—a free call and one which sometimes can be made even from nonworking phones. (**Note:** Some public phones cannot receive incoming calls, but they're not marked as such.)

If you wish to make a long-distance call from a private phone in Britain and want to know the cost so you can pay the phone owner, dial the operator and ask to place an *ADC* call (for "advise duration and charge"). The operator will place the call, then call you back a few minutes after you've finished to report the charge. (**Note:** The British are a bit wary of letting strangers use their phone, so be formal in your request.) As anywhere, most hotels in Britain charge a usuriously high per-minute fee for placing overseas calls (ask before you call). To call overseas cheaply, ask the operator for the Home Country Direct dialing code for the country you're calling.

Understanding Britain   **37**

WALKING IN BRITAIN

A nation of walkers, Britain has more than 120,000 miles (193,000 kilometers) of maintained footpaths, and guards these protected rights-of-way jealously. Since virtually all land is privately owned, the system depends upon cooperation: landowners agree to let walkers pass, while walkers agree to stay on the footpaths and follow the Country Code (see sidebar). Half-day and all-day walks are included at least every other day in this itinerary because, frankly, there is no better way to experience the best of Britain's countryside. The walks include national

Waymarker along the Dorset Coast Path, Abbotsbury

parks, official Areas of Outstanding Natural Beauty, Heritage Coasts, official Long Distance Paths, Forestry Commission lands, National Trust properties, and private farmlands and meadows. If you're a hiker at home—or "walker," as they say here—you'll find Britain a paradise for pursuing your hobby. If you're not (we're not either), you're in for a treat: stunning scenery, fragrant wildflowers, charming villages—scenes you'll remember for the rest of your life.

DIFFICULTY. Though designed to provide a lot of variety in both terrain and natural features, all the walks in this book can be made by reasonably fit folks, including retirees. Long walks—four or five hours—either include shortcuts or have shorter alternative walks in the same chapter. Walks described as *easy* involve level or gently undulating ground along well-maintained paths. Walks described as *moderate* involve some steady climbs or generally easy terrain with occasional steep slopes, again on well-marked paths. There are no *difficult* summit climbs or areas of especially rough terrain in this itinerary.

MAPS AND TRAILS. The maps included in each chapter, and the narratives that accompany them, are really all you'll need to negotiate these walks. For those who prefer a bit more detail, however, recommended Ordnance Survey maps (available in local bookstores and newsstands en route) and locally produced walking guides are also listed. Virtually all paths are marked with either signposts or *waymarkers*—posts painted with either yellow arrows for public footpaths, blue arrows for public bridlepaths ("bridleways"), or the acorn symbol of the Countryside Commission's official Long Distance Paths.

SAFETY. None of these walks is dangerous, but accidents happen. Except in Dartmoor (where, in any event, you'll probably be following a guided walk), you'll seldom be far from a public phone (dial **999** for police rescue). As a general rule, tell the people with whom you're staying what your plans are (they may have useful suggestions anyway). As an extra precaution you may want to carry a whistle or flashlight (six whistle blasts or flashes is the International Distress Signal; three is the answering response). As for weather, while none of the areas covered by these walks is subject to extremes, it always pays to layer your clothing to stay warm or cool. Thoroughly waterproof outerwear, however, will make the difference between a miserable or memorable walk.

THE COUNTRY CODE. Much of Britain's countryside, while privately owned, is looked after by the Countryside Commissions of England and Wales. Ultimately, however, *you* are responsible for its upkeep. Most of what you need to remember is common courtesy and common sense and is covered by the official **Country Code.**

The Country Code

- Enjoy the countryside and respect its life and work.
- Guard against all risk of fire.
- Fasten all gates.
- Keep dogs under close control.
- Keep to public paths across farmland.
- Use gates and stiles to cross fences, hedges, and walls.
- Leave livestock, crops, and machinery alone.
- Take your litter home.
- Help to keep all water clean.
- Take special care on country roads.
- Make no unnecessary noise.

PART TWO

The Itinerary

♦ DAY ONE

Journeying to the Heart of a Nation

LONDON ♦ THAMES VALLEY ♦ COTSWOLDS

- ♦ Coping with London's airports
- ♦ Meandering through the historic Thames Valley
- ♦ Into prehistory in the Vale of White Horse
- ♦ Getting settled in the Cotswolds

Glide gently, thus for ever glide,
O Thames! that other bards may see
As lovely visions by thy side
As now, fair river, come to me.
—William Wordsworth, 1789

On the gently rounded edge of the Berkshire Downs, high above the softly billowing green carpet of the Thames River Valley, childhood stories return to reclaim your heart. Among the patchwork fields at your feet, the thatched villages of *Tom Brown's Schooldays* cluster within a latticework of hawthorn hedgerows stretching to the horizon. Away across the meadows, you can just make out the lazy bends of the Thames itself and hear the faint rustlings of *The Wind in the Willows*. If the day is misty and still, you may hear the echoing hoofs of a knight's horse and the clash of steel against steel, for it was very near here that the legendary King Arthur fought off Saxon invaders and, centuries later, Alfred the Great repelled the Danes and preserved the Kingdom of Wessex. Along the top of the chalk ridge just behind you is the footpath, worn deep by the ages, that prehistoric pilgrims used on their way to worship at Stonehenge.

The heart of England is a geography of the imagination, a place where fairy tales, legends, and history merge. It is a landscape at once changeless and constantly changing, like imagination itself. Roughly bounded by the swell of the chalk downs on the south, the Cotswold escarpment on the west, and the Chiltern Hills on the east, this region—

also called the "Home Counties"—is the very essence of England, what the English themselves think of when they think of home. The Thames Valley and the Cotswold hills are an ideal introduction to southern England—a rich tapestry of ancient stone villages with rose-covered cottages, venerable parish churches, vast country estates, crenelated castles, and enigmatic stone circles, all set in a lush landscape of astonishing visual variety. There are high, swelling downlands, verdant water meadows, wildflower-strewn pastures enclosed by dense hedgerows, dry-stone walls of amazing artistry, leafy valleys and hushed beechwood forests, and soaring escarpments from which you see, if not forever, then very nearly. Misty moors and tangy coastal cliffs will come later; but first, unwind awhile in England's tranquil heartland—you can be there in just a little over an hour from London's airports.

ARRIVING IN BRITAIN

It's wise to keep these pastoral images in mind this morning, because your first hour in Britain is likely to be a bit harried. For reasons that have more to do with airline convenience than common sense, virtually *all* international flights to London arrive early in the morning, simultaneously disgorging huge crowds of cranky, jet-lagged travelers to the city's two international airports: **Heathrow,** just west of the city, and **Gatwick,** to the south on the Surrey/West Sussex border. Heathrow is larger, and therefore busier and more crowded, than Gatwick (except in July and August, when British charter flights cause chronic delays at Gatwick). Neither has any advantage over the other for this itinerary, so pick your destination by whichever airline gives you the best fare.

The arrival process has three steps: (1) immigration (after a long walk, or shuttle ride in the case of Gatwick, and a long wait); (2) baggage retrieval (grab a free baggage cart and prepare for another long wait); and (3) customs (mercifully expeditious, unless you're either too shabbily or too well dressed). If your patience begins to wear thin, remember that airport officials are trying to distinguish terrorists, drug runners, and other lunatics from garden-variety disgruntled passengers. On especially busy mornings, this isn't easy.

LOCATING YOUR RENTAL CAR

Unless you're planning a detour to London for a few days (see below), your next task is locating your rental car so you can reach the peace and quiet of the English countryside as soon as possible.

Most international flights to **Heathrow** arrive at Terminal 3. After you pass through the doors into the arrivals hall, you'll find an airport information desk, a Bureau de Change (which will charge a fee for any currency transactions), and check-in desks for several of the major international car-rental companies. Other companies can be called from public phones located near the MEETING POINT sign (dial 192 for Directory Enquiries if you don't know the number). Then, go out the doors in the left front corner of the hall and your car-rental company will pick you up, at the designated area, in a well-marked minibus.

The international-arrivals hall at **Gatwick** has a handy tourist information booth, along with a Bureau de Change and check-in desks for several major car-rental firms. Again, there are banks of public phones nearby from which to call other car-rental companies. Then, to get to the designated pickup area, head for the right front corner of the hall, and follow the signs. (For Hertz, Avis, Budget, and National/Europcar, walk to your car just downstairs.)

DETOURING TO LONDON

If you choose to postpone the pleasures of the countryside for the attractions of the city, you have two transportation choices to London from Heathrow, but only one practical choice from Gatwick. From Heathrow, a cab ride into the city will cost nearly £40, plus tip. The cabs are spacious and driven by unfailingly polite, and often quite friendly, cab drivers. If you have a lot of baggage, and especially if three or four people are traveling together, it's the best bet. If your baggage is manageable and your budget a bit tight, take the subway—called the **Underground** or, more colloquially, the "Tube." Just push your baggage cart down the ramp marked for the Underground and in minutes you'll be in the Tube station beneath the airport. What's more, there's a British Tourist Authority Information Centre in the station. Buy the official BTA London Map here, while you have the opportunity. Then, when you get to the subway ticket counter, ask for a free Tube map and buy a "single" (one-way) ticket to the stop closest to your hotel. However, if you plan to use the Tube again today, buy a one-day pass instead; for just a few pence more you'll ride free for the rest of the day. And if you plan to stay for several days, ask about other tourist passes; several are available, so check terms and restrictions.

From Gatwick to London, the only practical route to the city is the **Gatwick Express,** BritRail's direct train service between the airport and Victoria Station (cabs from Gatwick take forever and are very expensive). The train runs every 15 minutes, the trip takes less than half an hour, and it's a bargain at £8 at this writing. When you get to Victoria Station, take a few minutes to browse through the excellent British Tourist Authority Information Centre and Book Store (and buy the official BTA London map). Also, if you don't already have your hotel booked, the tourist authority offers an excellent accommodation booking service for a modest fee. Then, walk out to the cab queue and head for your hotel.

Journeying to the Heart of a Nation **45**

But this is a book about the countryside, and while we offer a brief taste of London at the end of this itinerary (see Day Fifteen), pastoral England is our objective today, and the sooner we get there the better.

🚗 UP A LAZY RIVER

Distance: 120 miles/193 kilometers (from Gatwick)
Roads: From motorways to narrow country lanes
Driving Time: 3 hours, including lunch; 3.5 hours from Gatwick
Map: Michelin Map #404

London and its suburbs are cupped within a bowl of chalk hills. In through one crack in the bowl's rim, and out another, flows the **River Thames.** To trace its course upstream from its estuary east of the city is to move through time: through the city's high-tech heart in the Docklands, past Victorian factories and government buildings, along banks lined with elegant Georgian townhouses, past the gardens of Kew and Hampton Court Palace, beneath the massive walls of Windsor Castle and along the emerald playing fields of Eton, through medieval riverfront villages with their ancient half-timbered walls leaning this way and that, past feudal fields plowed and planted for centuries, and back further still, near the river's source, where it flows in the shadow of Iron Age forts and even earlier and more mysterious monuments. The Thames is more than a river; it is England's collective memory.

Following the river's meanders deep into the English countryside is our objective this morning. From **Gatwick** (for Heathrow, see below), follow the blue-and-white motorway signs to the **M23** north. After about 12 miles on the M23, you'll reach the **M25,** the "London Orbital" or outer ring road around the metropolitan area. Stay to the **left** and follow signs for the M25 west (clockwise).

The M25 is like any urban bypass—crowded, but convenient. In fact, it was obsolete the day it was completed. The traffic load is so heavy that scientists recently claimed that the lead from auto exhausts deposited in the soil along older segments of the highway (unleaded gas is new) was dense enough to be mined commercially!

Almost exactly a half-hour after you get onto the M25, you'll encounter the **M4,** the main east-west motorway from London to South Wales. Stay to the **left,** and follow signs for **The West,** Slough, and Reading. In moments, you'll be on the M4. If you landed at **Heathrow,** this is where you come in. Just follow signs from your rental agency for the M4 west, just outside the airport. Soon thereafter, as you approach Exit 6, the great gray eminence, **Windsor Castle,** rises up in the haze off to your left on a rocky bluff above a bend in the Thames (leave the M4 at Exit 6 if you want to visit Windsor). Quite soon thereafter, leave the M4 at **Exit 7,** go around a long curve, and, at the roundabout junction, turn **left** onto the **A4** toward **Maidenhead** (originally

46 ITINERARY: DAY ONE

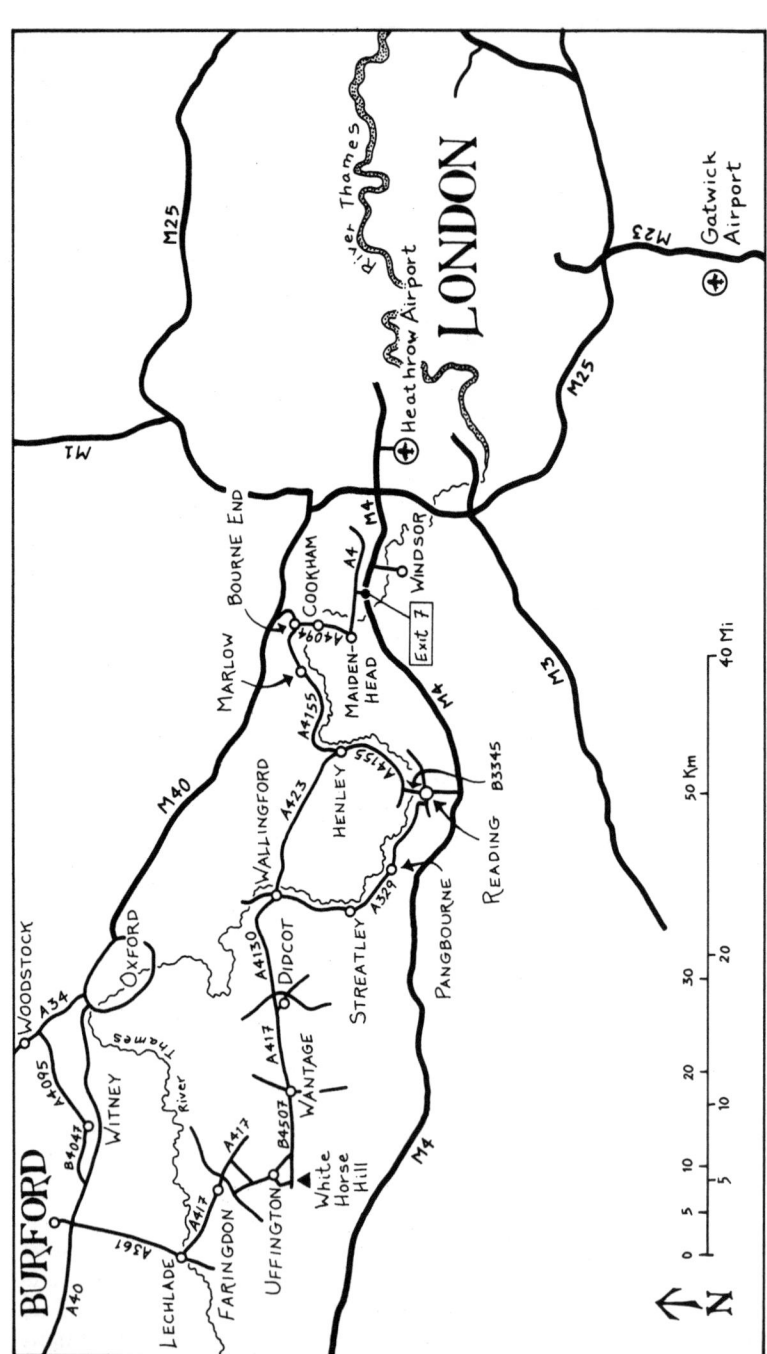

Maydenhythe, or "maiden's landing place").

You enter the town by crossing the placid Thames on a stone bridge trimmed with balustrades and Victorian-style street lamps. On the other side, turn **right** (three-quarters of the way around the circle) onto the **A4094** in the direction of **Cookham.** Almost instantly, the hurly-burly of twentieth-century suburban London vanishes, replaced by the leafy riverscape, with its weeping willows, river cruisers at anchor, and the broad green lawns of riverfront houses. You may want to stop and uncurl your fingers for a while at **Boulter's Lock,** just up the road from the bridge. The lock keeper's cottage is ablaze with flowers throughout the summer and the chaotic business of getting boats into the lock will make your unsteady driving skills look positively accomplished.

"Messing about with boats" at Boulter's Lock, on the River Thames at Maidenhead

> ### Slow Boating through Britain
>
> The Thames, over 200 miles long and a major commercial artery for centuries, was made more easily navigable by the construction of locks and weirs during the heyday of canal building, in the late eighteenth and early nineteenth centuries. The river was connected to the west by the Kennet-and-Avon Canal (currently being restored) and to the north by the Oxford and Grand Union canals. Before the canals were rendered obsolete by the railroads, it was possible to travel from the Lake District, near the Scottish border, to Littlehampton, on the south coast, entirely by inland waterways. You can go almost as far today, for many of the old canals have been restored for recreational use. Dozens of canal-boat rental companies have sprung up throughout central Britain to meet the growing demand. There is nothing quite so idyllic as chugging along through the English countryside at a stately three miles per hour with only one decision to make all day: which riverside pub to tie up to for the night. River cruisers and old-fashioned canal "narrowboats" come equipped with every modern convenience, from hot showers to refrigerators. And for the truly indolent, there are "hotel barges" to cater to every whim. For information, contact the British Tourist Authority (see Useful Addresses).

Beyond Boulter's Lock, the A4094 cuts across wildflower-speckled meadows to Cookham, one of the loveliest little villages on the Thames. Cookham's Bel and the Dragon pub, on the side street on your left, is one of the oldest in Britain ("Bel" was a Babylonian deity). Small as the village is, Cookham has more than its share of notables: the painter Stanley Spencer (1891-1959) lived here, as did *Wind in the Willows* author Kenneth Grahame, who invented the stories of Ratty, Mole, Badger, and Toad to lull his son, nicknamed "Mouse," to sleep at night. Cookham is also home to the current Swan Keeper to Her Majesty the Queen, whose job is to preside, every third week in July since 1295, over the "Swan Upping"—marking and apportioning the swans and cygnets of the Thames between Sunbury and Pangbourne among their three traditional owners: the Crown, the Vintners' Company, and the Dyers' Company.

On the other side of the village the road crosses the river at another weir and lock. Cliveden House, the riverfront stately home thought to be one of the inspirations for "Toad Hall" in *Wind in the Willows*, is just out of sight beyond a bend in the river to the right (access to Cliveden and its gardens is ahead on the right near Bourne End). At **Bourne End,** follow the road around to the left and, at the roundabout, take the **A4155** toward **Marlow.** The scene changes from water meadows to rich farmland, much of it fresh vegetables for London. Marlow itself is a busy market town with a handsome mix of Georgian and Victorian townhouses and an elegant nineteenth-century suspension bridge. It was in this picturesque, if unlikely, town that the poet Percy Bysshe Shelley's wife, Mary, wrote *Frankenstein*.

Stay on the A4155 and follow signs for **Henley,** slicing first through an ancient beechwood forest (the "Wild Wood" in *Wind in the Willows*) and then flattening out along a lovely sinuous stretch of the river, edged with iris in spring, the opposite hillsides dotted with fluffy sheep. As you enter Henley-on-Thames, with its graceful Georgian architecture, a one-way traffic pattern turns the route sharply left toward the straight stretch of river where the Henley Regatta has taken place every July since 1839. Stay in the right lane, go **straight** past the bridge, and continue on the A4155 around the back of the town, then **left** again along the river. (**Note:** If you're in a hurry to head north or want to avoid the traffic in Reading, turn right here and reenter Henley; then take the **A423** north to **Wallingford** and pick up the itinerary again there.)

Approaching **Reading,** high above the river, watch for a **left** turn off the A4155 (which goes on to Caversham) onto the **B3345.** Follow signs for "Town Centre" and cross over the river into the city. This next bit is a little complicated, but take it carefully and you'll be out of town before you know it. At the roundabout on the other side of the bridge, go three-quarters of the way around and then **left,** following signs for the **M4 West.** Pass the large shopping center on your left and then turn **left** again at the next roundabout, continuing in the direction of the M4 west. At this point the road dips below ground. Head down the ramp, move to the left lane, and take the first **left,** again marked for the M4 West. Then go **right,** cross over the underpass, and continue up the hill. Eventually you'll see a sign for a **right** turn toward **Oxford** and the **A329.** Follow these signs through the western suburbs of Reading and soon you will begin to see signs for **Pangbourne.**

North of Pangbourne, you ride high above the river as it twists through the hills, its banks edged with flowering fruit trees and yellow-green willows in the spring and the river itself alive with boaters. The river valley narrows gradually as you approach **Goring Gap,** the place where the Chiltern Hills on the right encounter the Berkshire Downs on the left. At **Streatley** (whose cheese shop is reputed to be the finest in England), you may wish to turn right at The Bull pub and drive down to the river and busy Goring Lock. Just beyond is a handsome old pub with a good reputation for lunch, should that time have finally arrived. (Remember: pubs are *reliably* open for lunch only between 12:30 and 2:00.)

The Uffington White Horse

Then go back up the hill to the A329, turn **right,** and continue along the river valley, through billowing grain fields, toward **Wallingford**—the first place William the Conqueror was able to cross the Thames as he pressed north after the Battle of Hastings in 1066. Enter Wallingford and turn **left,** at the intersection by the Lamb Arcade, onto the **A4130** toward **Didcot.** From Didcot, follow signs to **Harwell Village** (past the somewhat jarring interruption of the cooling towers at the Atomic Energy Research Establishment) and take the **A417** to **Wantage.** At the first roundabout as you approach Wantage, turn **left,** following signs for **Ashbury,** the **B4507,** and the **Uffington White Horse.** At the intersection with the **B4001** continue straight ahead for "White Horse Hill."

THE TIMELESS VALE OF WHITE HORSE

You are riding along the edge of the Berkshire (pronounced "bark-*shur*") Downs, a splendid landscape of softly rounded slopes, rolling ahead of you like great green ocean swells. The Berkshire Downs are part of a vast chalk plateau composed of the skeletons of minute marine organisms deposited 150 million years ago on the floor of a shallow prehistoric sea to a depth of hundreds of feet. Today, the remnant ridges and plateaus of England's chalklands reach from the white cliffs of Dover and the even whiter cliffs of the "Seven Sisters" in Sussex (see Day Thirteen), around London, and then west far into Wiltshire and Dorset. What rivers there are in the downlands have long since cut through the soft rock to lower levels, lowering the water table and rendering these hills dry and relatively infertile. As a result, the Downs are used primarily as pasture, although intensive farming has converted some of the slopes to grain production.

A few miles past the intersection with the **B4001,** a clear sign to **White Horse Hill** points the way straight up the steep slope of the Downs along a narrow lane to a small car park on the left. Here is a place of ancient magic. A mile and a quarter to the southwest is **Wayland Smithy,** a Neolithic tomb made of massive standing stones and dating from 3500 B.C. It gets its name from a legend stretching back through Nordic mythology to Wayland, god of the blacksmiths. According to tradition, if a horse has thrown a shoe its rider should tether it to one of the stones, leave a coin, turn away, and whistle three times, and the horse would be shod (and the money gone, thank you very much). A few steps away, the **Ridge Way,** thought to be the oldest path in the country (estimates range from 5,000 to 10,000 years old), strides across the windy top of the downland ridge some 40 miles (65 kilometers), from Goring Gap to Avebury to the southwest. Routes like the Ridge Way, part of a network of ancient migratory and commercial paths that tended to follow ridge lines high above the thickly wooded valleys, give us a term we use even today: *highway.*

Straight ahead from the explanatory sign in the northeast corner of the car park is the **White Horse** itself, graceful and abstract, as if created by Matisse, racing along the northern slope of the Downs. Some 360 feet (110 meters) long, cut deep into the turf to expose the brilliant white chalk below, the White Horse is the oldest such monument in Britain. Just how old is a matter of conjecture. It may have been cut to commemorate Alfred's victory over the Danes at nearby Ashdown in A.D. 871, but the similarity between its shape and horse-cult art from the Iron Age lead some historians to conclude it was created as early as 500 B.C. as a representation of the goddess Epona, protector of horses. This theory gains credence from **Uffington Castle,** the huge oval earthen fortification, dating from the same period, that stands just to the right of the White Horse. Finally, downhill from the horse's tail is flat-topped **Dragon Hill**, where St. George, England's patron saint, is said to have slain his dragon. A patch of ground where grass never grows is alleged to have been poisoned by the dragon's blood.

Legends aside, the spectacular view from White Horse hill is also a window on more recent history, if you know how to read the clues. The plain stretching north from the foot of the Downs, checkered with fields in every imaginable color of green and brown, edged with hawthorn hedgerows, and broken from time to time with beechwood copses and clusters of thatched cottages, seems a storybook picture of everything English. And yet this timeless landscape is actually quite new.

Take the villages, for example. Before about the eighth century A.D., there were no "English villages" per se; the settlement pattern was widely dispersed, with isolated farmsteads and the occasional cluster of crude wooden buildings. The traditional English village, with its central green, orderly building arrangements, and neat cottage gardens emerged quite suddenly, between the ninth and twelfth centuries, in response to improving economic conditions, rapid population growth, and a somewhat more organized political situation (especially after the Norman Conquest). The "replanning" of the landscape was spontaneous in some parts of the country, but more often it was driven by the large landowners—lords, and those who "served the Lord": the bishops and abbots of the major churches, which owned vast tracts of land. Another revolution occurred in the sixteenth and seventeenth centuries, when house after house, village after village, was converted from predominantly wooden construction to stone and brick. Again, prosperity and the decisions of major landowners appear to have been the driving forces.

The picturesque patchwork fields, set off with stone walls and dense, flowering hedgerows, are an even more recent phenomenon. Up until the mid-1700s, the landscape at your feet was bleak and bare—vast areas of common grazing land, unbroken by walls or hedges, along with arable fields, laid out in long raised strips. Then, in the span of just 100 years, between 1750 and 1850, some 2,500 **Acts of Enclosure** were passed, subdividing the whole of central and southern England into the small, square fields we now think of as the defining elements of the English landscape. The enclosure movement began when the major landowners realized that livestock were more profitable than arable farming and that land was more efficiently grazed when livestock were rotated through small tracts of intensively managed land. And however one may feel about the impact these changes had on tenant's lives, the result of the enclosure movement was a richly varied visual landscape, generally better land-use management, and the creation of a superb network of wildlife habitats in the hedges and copses developed to define the enclosures. And so the scene before you, "olde worlde" as it may seem, may well be only 150 years old.

A Word about Hedgerows

When the Acts of Enclosure were passed, landowners needed something durable and dense to delineate new fields. Where stone was not readily available, they turned to hawthorn, used as a boundary plant for centuries—in fact, *haw* means "hedge." The shrub is tough, impenetrable, and beautiful when it blooms in the spring, and you can grow a hawthorn bush simply by shoving a cut branch into the soil. Farmers typically use only one or two species of plants to create hedgerows; the rest fill in by chance. Terrific wildlife habitats, hedgerows also were the source of a variety of medicinal herbs. Even the stinging nettle had a purpose: it was hung in dairies to keep witches from curdling milk! Naturalists have discovered that you can determine the age of a hedgerow by counting the number of woody species in a 30-meter (98-foot) section. It takes approximately one century for one new species to be established naturally per 30 meters of hedge.

🚗 NORTH INTO THE COTSWOLDS

Distance: About 20 miles/32 kilometers
Roads: Mix of narrow lanes and primary roads
Driving Time: 30 minutes; more with stops
Map: Michelin Map #404

The gently rising hills on the hazy horizon to the north are the **Cotswolds,** home for the next two nights. Head back down the steep lane from the car park, across the B4507, and into the tiny hamlet of **Woolstone,** a splendid little collection of thatched cottages and barns, a Victorian mill with decorative brickwork, and a picture-book pub called, inevitably, the White Horse (which will no doubt be closed, since it is likely to be midafternoon at this point). Turn **right** at the pub, toward **Uffington,** down a hedgerow-lined lane that zigzags around property lines but makes generally for the tower of Uffington's church. Turn **right** at the next intersection and enter Uffington, a village rich with thatched, half-timbered Tudor houses, then turn **left** and wander through the unclassified lanes that cross the flat meadows of the Vale of White Horse, following signs for **Faringdon**. After a few minutes you'll encounter the **A420** Swindon-Oxford road. Turn **right** in the direction of Oxford, and after a mile or two, turn **left** onto the **A417** through Faringdon to **Lechlade**.

As you enter Lechlade, you cross over an old stone bridge spanning the Thames, little more than a placid stream at this point. And as the half-timbered and brick cottages of the Thames Valley give way to soft gray-gold stone, mellow in the afternoon sun, the buildings themselves signal that you have entered the Cotswolds. (The other giveaway is the disproportionate number of antique shops, art galleries, and obviously thriving real estate agents.) At the center of town, turn **right** onto the **A361**.

A few miles north of Lechlade, you may want to turn off the A361 into **Filkins** to visit the **Cotswold Woolen Weavers Exhibition and Mill** (see Diversions below). Otherwise, continue north on the A361. At the roundabout intersection with the **A40** you want to go **straight ahead**—that is, halfway around and then left down the steep hill that plunges into the magnificent little Tudor market town of **Burford**, your home base for the next two nights.

There may be no more memorable introduction to any English village than this approach to Burford. You emerge from the dark shade of overarching trees to a breathtaking panorama: Burford's broad High Street scrolls away beneath you, elegantly clad on both sides with Tudor, Elizabethan, Georgian, and Victorian homes, inns, and shops, their rooflines zigzagging downhill to a one-lane, three-arch stone bridge over the Windrush River, the whole picture set against a backdrop of billowing green and gold hills.

Burford, long the gateway to the Cotswolds, has been "discovered," but so far it has resisted commercialism and cuteness. Despite its charms, it is still a functioning town (more a village, really), and makes a splendid base for exploring the region. This afternoon, after you've gotten settled, take a stroll down the narrow back streets. Peek into the lush cottage gardens and wander past the almshouses with their tiny doors. Drift through the grounds of the graceful Norman Church of St. John the Baptist with its lavender-trimmed cemetery. Stroll down to the bridge and the languid reach of the winding Windrush with its swans drifting in the current. Then walk back up the hill to Sheep Street, as the long rays of the afternoon sun burnish the yellow Cotswold limestone a rich gold. Burford is a deeply gentling place.

Journeying to the Heart of a Nation 55

Part of the loom exhibition at Cotswold Woolen Weavers

DIVERSIONS
Cotswold Woolen Weavers Exhibition and Mill

In **Filkins,** just off the Lechlade-Burford road, artisans have renovated a group of ancient stone barns and installed a museum of wool making and a busy mill, complete with throbbing, clanking, clattering Victorian carding, spinning, and weaving machinery. In addition to creating a fascinating little museum, the founders have also been responsible for bringing back from near extinction the Cotswold sheep breed. Garments made of its creamy fleece, and of many other English wools, are available in the small shop. Elsewhere in the complex are a gallery, a woodworking shop, and a stonemason's yard where you can see the golden Cotswold limestone shaped into graceful lintels and mullions.

CREATURE COMFORTS
Daily Bed

The almost impossibly picturesque villages of the Cotswolds have been destinations for travelers for centuries, so lichen-covered stone inns, hotels, and pubs abound. Burford was a favored overnight stop in the days of coaching and a few of its half-dozen first-class small inns, scattered along High Street and Sheep Street, still have archways leading to coach courtyards. There are also a handful of discreetly identified bed-and-breakfast establishments. Two or three B&Bs are on the left side of High Street as you enter town, one or two on Whitney Street, a side street on your right, and one just over the arched bridge at the bottom of the village. Others are at the Dower House on Weshall Hill (directly opposite the town on the other side of the bridge), at the Forge in Fulbrook (down the road to the right after you cross the bridge), and at a farm in the same village. Listings for some of Burford's inns can be found in the accommodation guides listed in Further Reading, but not the B&Bs. If you are willing to take "pot luck," simply wander through the little town and try the establishments that catch your eye (and suit your pocketbook), or stop in at the little Tourist Information Centre in the old brewery building on Sheep Street and ask for help.

But be forewarned: the direct M40/A40 highway from London makes this area a preferred destination for weekend visitors, so accommodations may be difficult to find late on a Friday or Saturday afternoon. For most of the stops on this itinerary, you really need not make reservations in advance. But for Burford on a weekend you may want to. Use our recommended accommodations guides (see Further Reading), or simply write or call the Tourist Information Centre, The Brewery, Sheep Street, Burford, Oxfordshire, telephone (099 382) 3558.

Daily Bread

The pub in the middle of High Street serves dinner both in its charming bar (get the romantic table close to the fireplace if the weather is cool) and in a lovely restaurant upstairs. In addition, most of the small hotels in town have dining rooms and the cuisine ranges from good to inspired (with prices to match). In short, it's hard to go wrong in Burford. It would be wise, however, to make reservations at the better restaurants as soon as you get into town.

After an early dinner, jet lag having finally overtaken you, collapse into bed. In the morning you'll find yourself in one of the most charming villages in all of Britain.

♦ DAY TWO

The Land of the "Cotswold Lion"

BURFORD ♦ NORTHLEACH ♦ THE SLAUGHTERS
STOW ♦ BROADWAY ♦ CHIPPING CAMPDEN
HIDCOTE MANOR ♦ WARWICK ♦ BURFORD

- A leisurely excursion through the Cotswolds' prettiest villages
- An optional visit to a rare-breeds farm
- Strolls in the most charming market towns
- Exploring one of England's grandest castles

Even when the sun is obscured... these walls are still faintly warm and luminous... as if they knew the trick of keeping the lost sunlight of the centuries glimmering about them.

—J. B. Priestley, 1934

Torn asunder, slammed together, submerged, elevated, eroded, and glaciated over the millennia, the British Isles have perhaps the most complex geologic structure of any nation on the face of the globe. One result of all this turbulence is that the rock underlying England's green mantle varies dramatically over very short distances. Consequently, you can tell where you are simply by looking at buildings and stone walls. The distinctive greenish-black slates of the Lake District are dark and brooding in that region's inevitable rain. The thick granite walls of Cornwall lean stolidly into the teeth of Atlantic gales. Glittering chunks of knapped flint cover Sussex houses like sequins. And generations of craftsmen have turned the clays of the Midlands into bricks laid in clever houndstooth and checkerboard patterns.

But nowhere is the relationship between local geology and regional mood more evident than in the Cotswold hills, famous for their honey-hued limestone (called *oolitic* because of its tiny egglike grains, and golden because of the presence of iron). Even on the bleakest winter

The trout-filled River Eye as it slips through Lower Slaughter

days there is an almost palpable warmth that radiates from the cozy villages in this hospitable patch of English countryside.

The Cotswolds, formally designated an "Area of Outstanding Natural Beauty," are like a vast rumpled counterpane spread out over some 640 square miles (1,700 square kilometers) of English countryside. Just a few inches beneath this coverlet of patchwork greens and browns is a giant slab of limestone, tilted up along an escarpment, some 60 miles (100 kilometers) long, that rises above the Severn River Valley from Bath and runs northeast almost to Stratford-upon-Avon. From its highest point, at Cleeve Hill (elevation 1,083 feet/330 meters) just north of Cheltenham, the slab dips gently eastward into Oxfordshire. The land in between is deeply folded, with softly rounded hills called *wolds*, velvety sheep-sheared meadows, and tranquil hollows cut by meandering, crystal-clear streams. Sheltering in the lee of the hills are settlements of unsurpassed charm—quintessential English villages with some of the finest vernacular architecture in the land: perfect parish churches, grand country manors set in manicured gardens, ancient cottages with steep peaks supporting lichen-encrusted stone roofing, gabled dormer windows with carved stone casements, and, always, a welcoming pub.

But while the warm limestone of the Cotswolds creates the mood of the region, credit for the markedly "upscale" character of its architecture—even the almshouses are handsomely proportioned—is due to sheep. Some 500 years ago, the rolling Cotswold hills swarmed with the "Cotswold Lion," a sheep with a fleece so long and silky that it dominated the international wool market (the *cots* in Cotswold is old Saxon for a sheep enclosure). The huge fortunes made by the region's landowners and wool merchants account for the elegance of the villages sheltered in the folds of the landscape, the large number of sprawling Tudor country house estates, and the stateliness of the parish churches. Even the churchyards honor sheep: many tombs have barreled tops in the shape of wool bales.

But by the mid-1800s, with the introduction of Merino wool (originally from Spain and later from New Zealand and Australia), the passage of the Acts of Enclosure, the shift of the weaving industry to the mechanized North, and the effects of wool taxes (the lord chancellor of the House of Lords sits on a woolpack for a reason!), the preeminence of Cotswold wool had declined. The villages and the Cotswolds are well preserved today largely because they were bypassed by the Industrial Revolution. The result, clusters of Cotswold cottages with their doorways and diamond-leaded windows softened by vibrant clematis, towering hollyhocks, and cabbage-size roses, is almost too beautiful and perfect to be true.

"POTTERING ABOUT" IN THE COTSWOLDS

Distance: About 95 miles/151 kilometers
Roads: Mostly secondary and unclassified roads
Driving Time: Plan on spending all day
Map: Michelin Map #404

The most rewarding thing you can do today is get lost as soon as possible. An itinerary through some of the prettiest villages and market towns in this region follows, but you may be just as happy simply wandering down one narrow country lane after another, past green and gold seas of barley and wheat, and through timeless little hamlets. There are visual treats around virtually every bend in the Cotswolds. One other piece of advice: if the weather report for today is good, but tomorrow's is iffy, take one of tomorrow's walks today while the sun shines; then tomorrow, in the shelter of your car, do today's driving tour. Sun can be a precious commodity in England at any time of year.

We begin today by taking our own advice: plunging down a narrow country lane into the heart of England. Drive down Burford's High Street and over the narrow bridge. At the miniroundabout on the other side, turn **left**. Then, just a few yards ahead, where the main road turns sharply right, go **straight** ahead instead, down the narrow lane paralleling the lovely Windrush River. Drive through **Taynton** and continue

The Land of the "Cotswold Lion" 61

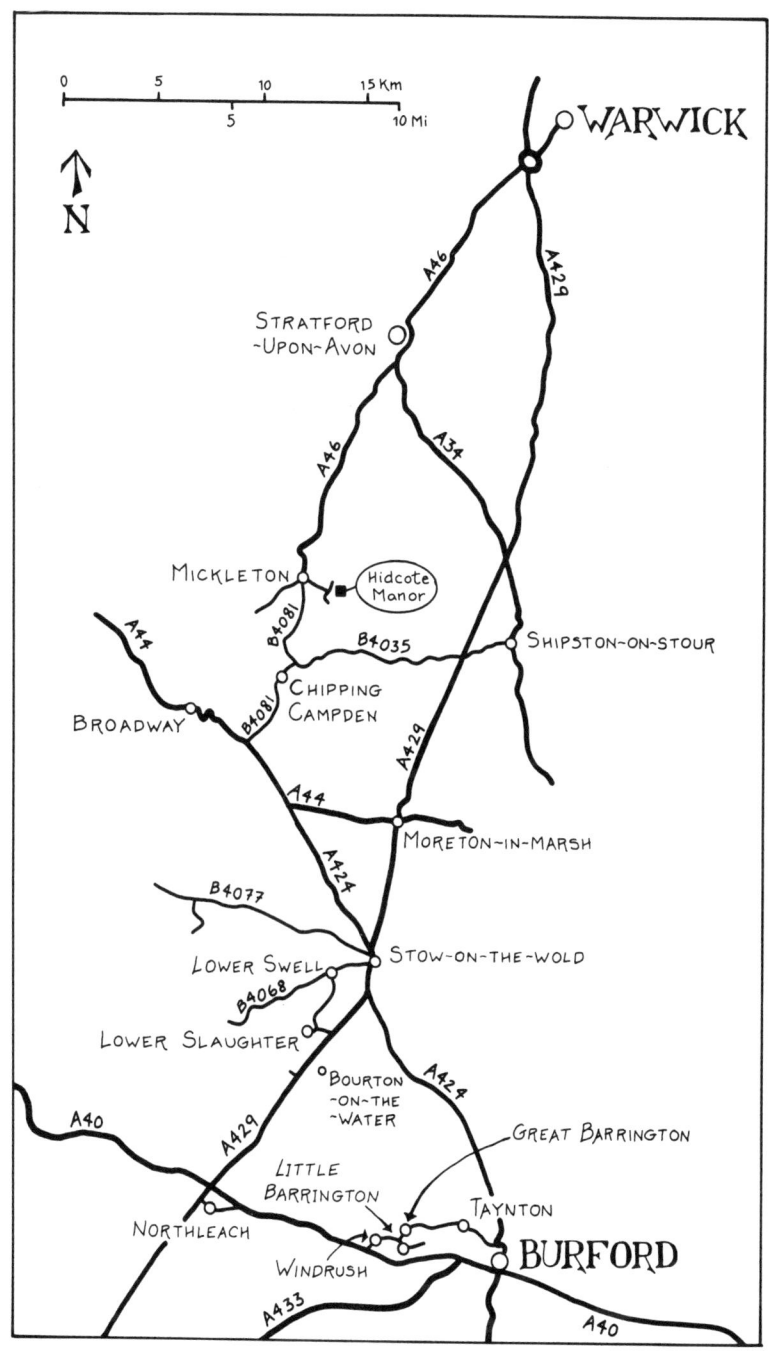

up the valley to **Great Barrington.** Great Barrington and its sister, **Little Barrington,** across the narrow river, are quarry towns, and the limestone blocks carved out of the hillsides here can be found as far away as St. Paul's Cathedral in London. Indeed, Thomas Strong, Sir Christopher Wren's master mason at St. Paul's, came from the Barringtons. Next, cross over the river, turn **right** at the pub, and continue upriver to tiny **Windrush,** gathered about its triangular green. Either here or at Sherborne, just upriver, turn **left,** away from the river, drive up the ridge to the **A40,** and turn **right.**

One of the fascinating things about the Cotswolds is the secretiveness of its settlements. Here on the ridge traversed by the A40, you can see for miles in both directions, but there is little sign of habitation; the villages are all huddled in the folds of the landscape, out of the wind.

A few miles to the west, bear **left** into **Northleach.** As you wander into the east end of this splendid market town it will become obvious that it is only a latter-day backwater, having recently been rescued from the thundering traffic of the A40 by a bypass. The main street is dense with stately limestone homes, inns, and shops, as befits the major wool center it once was, and there are few places in this region that display the craft of the Cotswold stonemason so well. Continue west through the center of town and, at the intersection with the **A429,** turn **right.** At the roundabout intersection with the A40 go **straight** ahead, toward **Stow.** Immediately on your left is an award-winning museum of English rural life called the **Countryside Collection.**

If you take a look at your road map at this point, you'll notice that the A429, with few exceptions, races straight as an arrow from crest to crest across the hills. This is a dead giveaway that you are on an old Roman road—as indeed you are, the *Fosse Way,* the principal highway of Roman Britain. You can trace the original road, built soon after the Roman invasion in A.D. 43, from south of Cirencester, site of a major fortress, northeast all the way to Leicester (*cester* is another Roman inheritance, meaning "fort") and beyond toward Lincoln.

After a few miles, a sign points off to the right to the village of Bourton-on-the-Water. Ignore it. At one time in the not-too-distant past, Bourton must have been a lovely place, its broad central green cut by the peaceful Windrush River, spanned by several graceful little bridges. But today, this self-styled (and absurdly named) "Little Venice of the North" is too cute for its own good. On sunny weekends cars and buses choke the village's narrow streets and throngs of tourists fill its many gift shops. The good news is that it's the only place tarted up like this in the whole region.

So instead of turning into Bourton, continue straight ahead on the A429 past the pub on the right and take the first **left,** onto a treelined unclassified road signposted for **Lower Slaughter.** The Slaughters, Upper and Lower, are the essence of Cotswold serenity, what Bourton must have been like before tourism took over. Their unfortunate name is a corruption of the Saxon word *slohtre,* or "marshy place." After making a sharp **right** turn, you enter Lower Slaughter along the little River Eye. Park here and wander among the gardens that front the cottages on either side of the shallow, trout-filled "river," then stroll upstream to the flour mill with its huge water wheel (a gentle one- to two-hour circular walk to Upper Slaughter is described in the next chapter).

Back in your car, turn **right** in the center of the village (turning away from the bridge) and continue on the main road, bearing **right** at the next two intersections, and finally turning **right** onto the **B4068** on the edge of sleepy **Lower Swell.** Drive through Lower Swell and continue to the handsome hilltop village of **Stow-on-the-Wold.** The highest village in the Cotswolds (800 feet/244 meters), Stow stands at the intersection of some eight roads, testimony perhaps to the importance of its great sheep fairs, held twice a year, at which some twenty thousand sheep were traded. The trading today, however, seems principally to be in antiques, for which there are a number of shops gathered around the paved central square (there's also a sinful bakery, if breakfast is wearing off, and a Tourist Information Centre).

From the village square, head north to the main road, the combined **A424** and **A429,** turn **right,** and then bear **left** at the fork and follow the **A424** north along the tops of the wolds, joining the **A44** north. After another few miles the road pitches over the edge of the Cotswold escarpment and zigzags down into the picture-postcard town of **Broadway.** Like Bourton-on-the-Water, Broadway is a favorite stop for tourists (and a good place for a pub lunch). Unlike Bourton, Broadway has maintained its dignity in the face of the onslaught; it is elegant where Bourton is cute. The homes that face its chestnut treelined "broad way" are, if anything, a bit self-consciously "above it all." Built of a warmer limestone than the houses of Stow, some days nearly peach in color, they are grander in scale than those in many other Cotswold villages. There are neatly trimmed lawns running down to the curbside and the flowers are a bit more formal than elsewhere. Broadway eschews overstatement.

Like Burford, Broadway was a coaching way station, which explains both its wide main street and its overall air of prosperity. Today, it maintains that prosperity by catering to upscale tourists, with antique shops and tastefully presented gift shops. When you've had a chance to poke around Broadway, head back up the long, progressively steepening main street—giving a moment's thought to the horses that had to pull coaches up over the escarpment here—and, after negotiating the hairpin bends and running along the ridge top for awhile, look for a **left** turn signposted for the **B4081** to **Chipping Campden.**

The *chipping* in Chipping Campden is Old English for "market," and the busy streets and shops make it clear that folks here are not simply waiting for the next tour bus to arrive. Curving High Street is a marvelous hodgepodge of tawny façades, built from the fourteenth to

seventeenth centuries, punctuated with deep-set doors, multipane windows framed with carved stone mullions, bay windows, and steeply pitched gables. There are shops plain and fancy, a handsome Jacobean Market Hall in the center of High Street, the Church of St. James, and the ancient Woolstaplers Hall, now a museum and information center. Despite all the bustle, there is a timelessness here that prompted British poet John Masefield to write: "In Campden Town the traveller finds the inward peace that beauty brings...." You will want to linger.

But press on; further delights await. Continue through town on the **B4081** (now joined by the **B4035**) and, where they fork, follow the B4081. On the outskirts of **Mickleton,** just before the intersection with the **A46,** turn **right** onto an unclassified road. A little less than a mile farther, turn left and follow signs for **Hidcote Manor Gardens,** the first garden of outstanding merit presented to the National Trust. Hidcote, created during this century by horticulturist Major Lawrence Johnston, is, in fact, a "garden of gardens"—a formal complex of individual gardens each focusing on a specific theme or flower (the herbaceous perennial borders and old roses are especially striking), each divided by extraordinary sculpted hedges and linked by terraces and paths (open daily except Tuesday and Friday, April through October). Next door is **Kiftsgate Manor,** also famous for its roses (open Wednesday, Thursday, and Sunday, April through September).

As you exit Hidcote, turn **left** at the T-junction and then **right** to return to Mickleton. Then turn **right** onto the **A46** heading north toward **Stratford-upon-Avon.** Do not, under any circumstances, be tempted to detour into Stratford proper. No opportunity to cash in on the immortal Bard has been overlooked here in Shakespeare's birthplace, and the town has become a tourist trap of historic proportions. Instead stay on the A46, following signs through a series of roundabouts for **Warwick.**

Every trip to England should include a castle, and **Warwick Castle** may well be the finest in the land. As you approach Warwick, follow signs for "Town Centre" and the castle. Park where indicated by the blue-and-white P signs; then walk up the narrow approach, cut deep into solid rock, to the castle entrance. Built on a bluff above the lovely River Avon on what is thought to have been the site of a Saxon earthen fort, Warwick Castle—a soaring confection of towers and crenellations, protected by a dry moat (now partially filled) and a fiendishly complex gate—was begun by William the Conqueror in 1068 and given to a supporter, dubbed the earl of Warwick. Various earls lived here for the next 900 years until they could no longer afford the upkeep. Today it is owned and run by the Madame Tussaud's organization. Dismaying as that may sound, the truth is they've done a wonderful job: the grounds

Chipping Campden, from the Jacobean Market Hall

Warwick Castle: soaring, stately, and deadly serious, it may be the finest castle in the land.

are lovely, the rooms, from the dungeon to the Great Hall, are well signed, the guides are engaging and informative, and the living quarters have been done with wax figures to recreate a turn-of-the-century weekend party (including a young Winston Churchill). It's all done tastefully and you come away with a rich sense of what life was once like in such a spectacular environment.

Save some time to wander the narrow streets of old Warwick, in the shadow of the castle. Then return home by driving **south** again on the **A429** (the Fosse Way) all the way to **Stow,** and then bear **left** onto the **A424** all the way into Burford—a ride of about 45 minutes in all.

DIVERSIONS

You could happily consume your entire holiday in the Cotswolds and still feel you hadn't taken its measure fully. You'll explore more of the area tomorrow, but one diversion is especially notable for lovers of the countryside: the **Cotswold Farm Park,** on a minor road branching south from the B4077 a few miles west of Stow. The Farm Park is part of the Rare Breeds Survival Trust and there are extraordinary examples of nearly extinct breeds including the Cotswold Lion, brilliantly plumed poultry, huge spotted pigs and tiny striped piglets, vicious-looking boars, plodding oxen, multihorned, multihued Jacob sheep, fringe-footed shire horses, and cattle breeds dating back to medieval times—literally a living museum. There are interpretive facilities and even a place for children to play with some of the younger animals. Open daily from April through September, it is a thoroughly entertaining and illuminating glimpse into the past.

CREATURE COMFORTS

See yesterday's listings.

About Your Morning Marmalade

Orange marmalade is as essential to an English breakfast as hot tea and cold toast. How this came to be, in a climate hardly conducive to orange growing, is a curious story. Back in the Middle Ages the Portuguese made a kind of candy from honey, spices, and quince—called *marmelo* in Portuguese. It became popular in England, so naturally the government slapped a high import duty on it; housewives retaliated by making their own. Over the years, any cooked fruit-and-honey mixture became known as "marmalade." In the eighteenth century, James Keiller, a grocer in Dundee, Scotland, imported a large shipment of Seville oranges from Spain, but they were so bitter they didn't sell and his wife made them into the first real orange marmalade. It was an immediate sensation. Marmalade arose in England in 1870 when another grocer's wife, a Mrs. Cooper of Oxford, made a batch and found she couldn't keep up with the demand. Frank Cooper's marmalade shop has been a fixture of Oxford—and marmalade has been on the tables of every B&B in England—ever since.

◆ DAY THREE

Footloose in the Cotswold Hills

BURFORD ◆ COTSWOLD WALKS
BIBURY ◆ BATH

- ◆ A daylong ramble on the Cotswold Way, including an Iron Age hill fort and three secretive villages
- ◆ An alternative two-hour river valley walk
- ◆ A rainy-day visit to Blenheim Palace and Oxford
- ◆ Through the southern Cotswolds to Bath

---

*A*s pleasant as it may be to drive through the Cotswold hills, you cannot truly capture their essence without slowing down to walking speed. How else to smell the perfume of wild roses in the hedgerows, or listen to the lazy buzz of bumblebees in the clouds of cow parsley along a dusty lane, or watch the brook trout idling in a crystal stream, or hear the larks high above the windswept wolds? The Cots-

The "splash" at the center of peaceful Upper Slaughter

wolds are a feast for the senses, but one you can really appreciate only if you leave your car behind.

The generations before you have made this task easy. Long before there were cars and roads there were footpaths—from village to town, home to church, farm to pub. In fact, there are an estimated 1,600 miles (2,575 kilometers) of protected footpaths and bridleways in the Cotswolds alone. In addition, there is the **Cotswold Way,** a 100-mile (161-kilometer) official Long Distance Path running virtually the full length of the Cotswold escarpment from Bath to Chipping Campden.

Today's itinerary begins with a walk—either a daylong walk or a shorter ramble—and ends with a drive south to that masterpiece of Georgian architecture, Bath. If you choose either walk, you may wish to put together a picnic lunch in the shops in Burford before you leave this morning. Finally, there's a tour of Blenheim Palace and the colleges of Oxford (see Diversions) if the weather proves uncooperative.

𐂂 STRIDING THE COTSWOLD ESCARPMENT

Distance: About 11 miles/18 kilometers; allow 6 hours. Shorter option: 8 miles/13 kilometers
Difficulty: Easy to moderate; two short uphill grades
Gear: Walking shoes/sneakers, rain gear, a lot of film
Map: Ordnance Survey Landranger #150

A good walk should have variety—so you remember not how far you've gone but how much you've seen—and today's meets this test. There are leafy woods carpeted with bluebells and pale yellow primroses; breezy ridge tops with views across several counties; the haunting remains of an Iron Age hill fort; a pub with good local beer, hearty lunches, and one of the best views in Britain; a feudal village with superb Jacobean architectural details; and classic English meadows ablaze with buttercups and daisies and hedged with hawthorn and blackthorn, fragrant in springtime.

Begin by taking the fast drive north from Burford to **Broadway,** along the **A424** and **A44.** At the bottom of the town, just beyond the Lygon Arms Hotel, the main road turns sharply right and a minor road turns **left** toward **Snowshill.** Take the minor road for about 0.5 mile to the tiny hamlet of Bury End, with its lovely old homes, and then take the first **right.** After this minor road bends right and passes the second house, the **Cotswold Way** crosses from the right. Park off the pavement (if the lane is crowded, park in Broadway and walk across the meadow opposite the church to this spot).

The hardest part of this generally easy but often breathtaking walk is immediately before you. Follow the footpath straight up the steep

70 ITINERARY: DAY THREE

meadow toward the gate on the edge of the wood at the top of the hill. Then bear slightly **left** and follow the path—occasionally muddy here—through the wood and out the other side, across a meadow, finally reaching an unpaved road above the village of **Buckland**. Turn **left** and walk up the road toward the farm roughly 0.5 mile ahead. Just beyond the farm buildings, go through the gate and turn **right** at the signpost pointing to Shenberrow Hill and Stanton. Here the Cotswold Way is a farm track, rough but obvious, which climbs up the closely cropped slope to the very edge of the Cotswold escarpment.

The view here, and all along the ridge top, is nothing less than spectacular, sweeping across the fertile Vale of Evesham, to the broad Severn River valley, the Malvern Hills, and, on a clear day, the Cambrian Mountains of Wales beyond. Tiny farming communities dot the patchwork pastures stretching out at your feet under a sky of palest blue, puffed with clouds tracing shadows across the fields below. In the spring, the Vale of Evesham—the "Fruitbasket of England"—is a gentle sea of white and pink orchard blossoms. In summer and into the autumn, the arable fields are a constantly changing Impressionist canvas of greens and golds.

Follow the ridge-top farm track through several gates until, a mile or so farther, you reach a T-junction with another farm road, leading off to the left to Great Brockhampton Farm. Cross this road and continue roughly **straight ahead,** with an evergreen wood edged by a wall on your right, until you reach the weathered earthen ramparts of the Iron Age settlement of Shenberrow Hill. Then, follow the yellow waymarker posts curving down the side of the escarpment, over a couple of stiles, and past a small pond, finally turning **left** onto another farm track and descending into **Stanton**. This is one of prettiest villages in the Cotswolds, thanks to the protection of the architect Sir Philip Stott, who owned the estate and village in the early 1900s. The only pub for miles, the Mount Inn, is back up the hill a bit on the first road you come to on the right. The view from its terrace, with the village below basking in the sunshine, is splendid (and so is the beer at this stage). The building stone here is a deeper gold than elsewhere, and the weathered walls seem to be made of a crumbly old cheddar.

Walk downhill along Stanton's long main street (little more than a lane) past the carefully restored, close-set Elizabethan and seventeenth-century homes, some thatched, some with stone shingles, and all ablaze in midsummer with a profusion of climbing roses and clematis. At the T-junction in the middle of the village, bear **left** and follow the road until it turns right again. On your left, a short farm lane passes the edge of the last house and climbs the hill beyond. Turn up this lane for a few yards, then turn **right** over the stile and follow the signposted Cotswold Way across a broad, sloping pasture punctuated by massive old oak trees, their understory branches all neatly trimmed at nibbling height by grazing cows.

After about 0.75 mile (1.2 kilometers), the path joins a paved minor road lined on both sides with oak trees. Turn **left** and follow the road around the edge of what is obviously a substantial estate. Rounding another bend to the left you come upon a magnificent confection of Jacobean architecture: the gatehouse of **Stanway Manor**, its massive oak doors surmounted by an arch capped with three curved gables embellished with carved scallops. A walk through tiny Stanway is a step back into feudalism, for the entire village—the cottages, the rectory, the lovely little Church of St. Peter, the superb tithe barn, and the Tudor manor house itself (open Tuesdays and Thursdays, June through August)—are owned by Lord Neidpath, whose family has lived here continuously since Henry VIII dissolved the monasteries and the estate passed out of the control of the abbots of Tewkesbury. The building stone here has higher levels of iron than elsewhere in the Cotswolds, and in the right light the gatehouse and manor glow with an inner fire.

With your back to the gatehouse, walk straight ahead a few yards, and then bear **left** up a track and then along a path paralleling a small stream, eventually reaching the **B4077**, which runs between Stow and Toddington. Here you have a choice. If you prefer a shorter walk today, cross the road, pick up the Cotswold Way on the opposite side, and follow it across another pasture to **Wood Stanway**. Turn **right** in the village, then **left** and **right** up a small lane, and take the footpath (not the Cotswold Way) west across the fields past **Didbrook** and on to **Hailes** to visit the ruins of Hailes Abbey, maintained by the National Trust. Then, when you are ready to return to Broadway, walk out to the **A46**, turn right, and either hitchhike back to Broadway, take the bus, or simply call a cab (there are pay phones in Didbrook and at the intersection of the A46 and B4077).

For the longer walk back to Broadway, turn **left** on the A4077 at Stanway, walk past several flower-bedecked cottages, and, where the road turns sharply to the right to begin its climb up the escarpment, walk **straight ahead** instead, up a lane into Lidcombe Wood. After entering the forest, take the first lane branching off to the **left** and climb up the long hill on the edge of the forest. Stay to the **left** at the fork. After zigzagging left and right, the forest track leaves the pasture border and plunges into the wood and up a narrowing ravine. If the day has been a warm one, you'll welcome the cool silence of the forest, broken only occasionally by the raucous screech of a pheasant or the rustle of a rabbit in the undergrowth.

At the top of the ravine, the track levels out and approaches the edge of the wood. Here, turn **right** onto another forest lane, staying in the wood until you reach the opposite edge, a hundred yards or so farther. While this forest lane turns to the right to stay inside the forest boundary, take instead the footpath to the **left** that runs along the edge of a field, with the wood on your left. When the wood finally ends, continue **straight ahead,** sloping uphill across the field toward a stone

The magnificent Jacobean gatehouse at Stanway Manor

Footloose in the Cotswold Hills

wall. At the corner of the stone wall, take the footpath **left** a few yards, then turn **right** and head downhill to the peaceful little village of **Snowshill**, nestled in a fold in the hills and clustered about its little green-cum-cemetery. At the fork in the center of town, stay **left** past the Manor House (maintained by the National Trust). From here it is an easy 2-mile (3.2-kilometer) walk along the minor road (first uphill, then down) through gently rolling farmland and along blackberry-filled hedgerows to Bury End and the minor road (left) where you parked your car. If you parked in Broadway, simply continue straight ahead.

A Less Strenuous Alternative: Windrush River Drive and Stroll through the Slaughters

If jet lag still has you down, or you simply aren't up to a full day's walk, here is a lazy day's alternative: a meandering tour through the Windrush Valley and a pastoral stroll through the meadows of the little River Eye between Lower and Upper Slaughter.

Begin by driving east out of Burford on narrow Whitney Street (off High Street at the Andrews Hotel). Almost immediately, Burford's bustle is left behind and you find yourself in a wide pastoral valley, the Windrush River wandering serenely through water meadows to your left. Bear **left** after about a mile (1.6 kilometers) and continue along the river past the bridge to tiny Widford ("wide ford"). At the crossroads by the cricket ground, continue **straight** into **Asthall**. At the T-junction, turn **right** to climb the hill and then turn **left** onto the **B4047**. After a little less than 2 miles (about 3 kilometers), turn **left** onto a minor road for **Minster Lovell**. Bear **right** as the road slides down to the Windrush River. At the 500-year-old Swan Inn, follow to the right signs for ruined **Minster Lovell Hall**, its gaunt remains casting long shadows across the emerald grass along the riverbank. This is a haunting, and haunted, spot. In 1485, Francis Viscount Lovell, a supporter of an unsuccessful pretender to the throne, hid from his pursuers in a secret chamber in the manor house. Only one servant knew where Lovell was hiding and the servant died suddenly. Some two hundred years later, during a renovation, the room was discovered—along with the skeletons of a man at a table and a dog at his feet.

On this melancholy note, return to the Swan, turn **right,** and head uphill away from the river. Turn **left** ahead onto an unclassified lane to **Asthall Leigh.** Then turn **left** again toward **Swinbrook**, riding now along the slope above the opposite bank of the river. At Swinbrook, wander down to another beautifully sited Swan Inn, right on the river, then turn around and climb up out of the picturesque hamlet, bear left at two forks, and follow the course of a tiny stream up a long narrowing valley.

Footloose in the Cotswold Hills

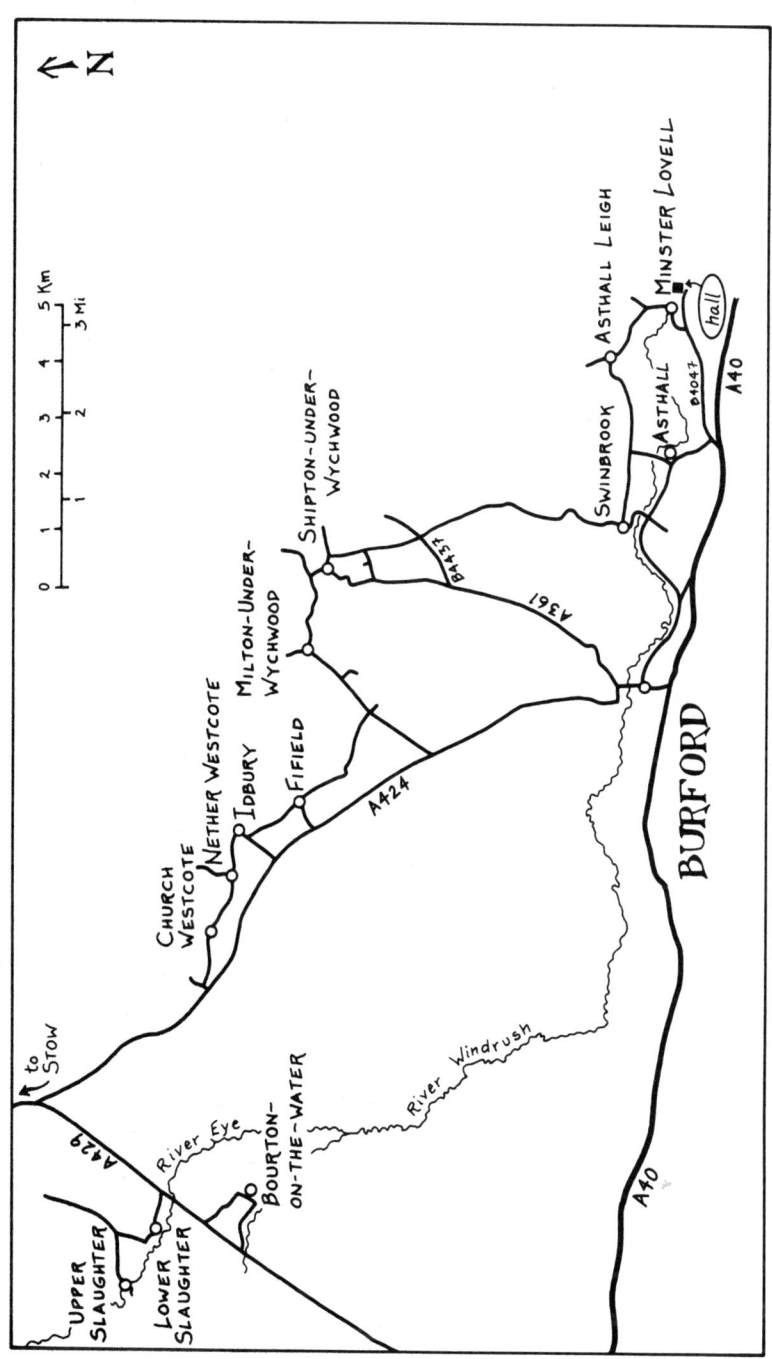

At the point where you crest the ridge, continue **straight** across the crossroads (the **B4437**) and follow the minor road for another 0.5 mile or so (about 0.75 kilometer) toward **Shipton-under-Wychwood**. Entering the village, take the first **left**, then the second **right**, turning onto the **A361**. The road twists through the center of the village, passing some remarkable Tudor mansions. At the point where it turns sharply right at the end of town to cross the river, turn **left** instead, in the direction of **Milton-under-Wychwood**. The "Wychwood" was one of the five great forests recorded in the Domesday Book, the real-estate survey William the Conqueror undertook in 1086 to take stock of what it was, exactly, he had conquered. Over the centuries, the forest has been gradually carved, cleared, and enclosed into nothingness, and only sparse patches remain today.

At the T-junction in Milton, turn **left**, rising gently uphill, and then, at the next T-junction, **right**. This minor road connects the little villages of Fifield, Idbury, Nether Westcote, and Church Westcote, all perched on the hillside along roughly the same plane—the point at which springs bubble out of the limestone ridge that rises to the west above them. Drive along through these "springline" hamlets and finally, a 0.5 mile (0.75 kilometer) or so beyond **Church Westcote**, turn **left** and, at the junction with the **A424**, turn **right** and drive north about 2 miles to the junction with the **A429**. Take care at this busy intersection and turn **left**. Then, after about 1.5 miles (2.5 kilometers), turn **right** onto the narrow, treelined approach to **Lower Slaughter**.

Park on the roadside opposite the hotel, don your walking shoes or sneakers, throw your picnic fixings into a knapsack, and begin this easy two-hour stroll by walking up the path along the right side of the tranquil "River" Eye through the village to the flour mill, with its great water wheel. Just beyond the little shop by the mill, turn **left** down the alley and pick up the footpath to **Upper Slaughter**. The route is really less a path than a series of small buttercup-filled meadows along the river, connected by "kissing gates" set into the walls. The route then slants gently uphill across a pasture in which medieval ridge-and-furrow plowing patterns are still visible, passes a few stiles and gates, and enters what is obviously a manor "park," with huge maple and spreading oak trees dotting the meadows and a pretty round pond off to the left graced by an old willow. Then the route starts downhill, through another kissing gate, into a shady lane opposite the manor house. When you reach the road, follow the footpath along the left side of the road down into the village and turn **left** at the fork.

Less formal and perhaps even more enchanting than its prim sister, Upper Slaughter is a loose collection of clematis-draped Cotswold cottages with luminous limestone façades and steeply pitched gables. They front onto a wildflower-bordered bit of the River Eye with a "splash"— a place where the road goes *through* rather than over the stream (if you

Footloose in the Cotswold Hills

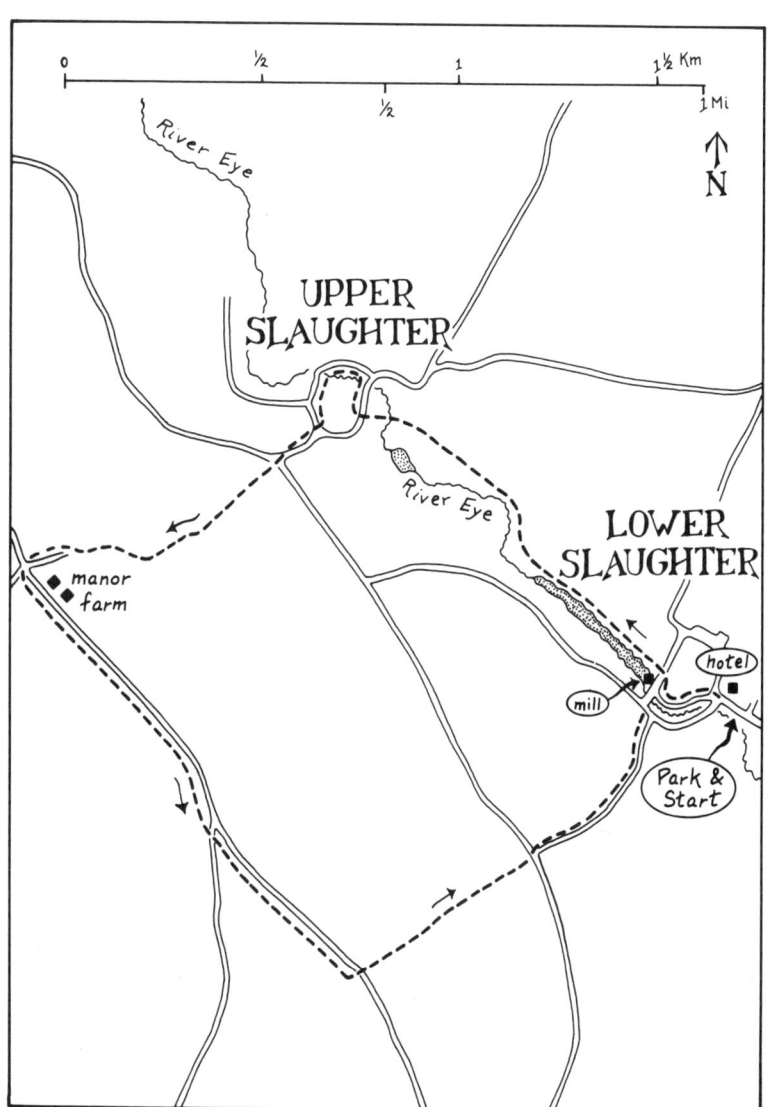

haven't eaten already, this is a lovely place for a picnic). A footbridge carries the path over the river and back up the hill, past the church, to the main road. On the other side of the road ahead, a gate leads to a bridleway running uphill. At the top you pass through a gate and across a field to the lane running around to the right of the manor farm. Reaching a minor road, turn **left** and walk along the roadside, edged in midsummer with frothy clouds of Queen Anne's lace and bordered by

hedges rich with red campion, daisies, wild rose, and honeysuckle. At the fork, stay to the **left** following the road until, a few hundred yards farther, a clearly marked bridleway cuts **left,** uphill toward Lower Slaughter. At the top of the ridge, on the last leg of the walk, the view across the wolds is stunning. Bouton-on-the-Water is visible below, surrounded by billowing fields of green barley studded with brilliant orange poppies, and wheat as gold as Cotswold stone in the sun. The bridleway ends at a minor road. Continue **straight ahead,** following a lane downhill 0.25 mile (0.4 kilometer) into Lower Slaughter once again.

🚗 THROUGH THE COTSWOLDS TO GEORGIAN BATH

Distance: About 70 miles/108 kilometers, from Broadway
Roads: Mostly primary roads
Driving Time: 2.5 hours with stop at Bibury
Map: Michelin Map #404 or #403

Having completed either walk, it's time to head south for Bath, perhaps Britain's most beautiful city, a living essay in sumptuous Georgian architecture and site of some of the best Roman ruins outside of Rome. From Lower Slaughter take the **A429** (or, from Broadway, the **A44** and **A424** to Stow and then the **A429**) south through Northleach to **Fossebridge.** Here, turn **left** onto a minor road through the pastoral valley of the **Coln River** as it winds southeast to join the Thames. In **Coln St. Dennis,** turn **right** over the bridge to begin a series of skips from one side of the river to the other. Drive southeast along the narrow lane paralleling the river to **Coln Rogers,** then across the river and back again to **Winson.** Further downriver cross yet again into **Ablington,** and turn **right** down the narrow river valley into picturesque **Bibury.**

Among the most photographed of England's small villages, Bibury on a weekday can be tranquility itself, a comfortable old jumble of stone, stream, woods, and flowers (even on a busy weekend, it seems to absorb visitors with equanimity). Bibury shelters in a narrow swale on a bend in the Coln. As you enter the village, the ivy-clad Swan Hotel is on your left and ahead is a reedy expanse of marsh called Rack Isle. Now a conservancy area frequented by wildfowl, its name dates from the 1600s, when this was a busy weaving center, and fabric fresh from the fulling mill (on your right, now a museum) was hung on racks to dry in this open area. The exquisite weavers' cottages, called Arlington Row and owned now by the National Trust, are straight ahead. The vil-

The weavers' cottages at Bibury, in the valley of the little River Coln

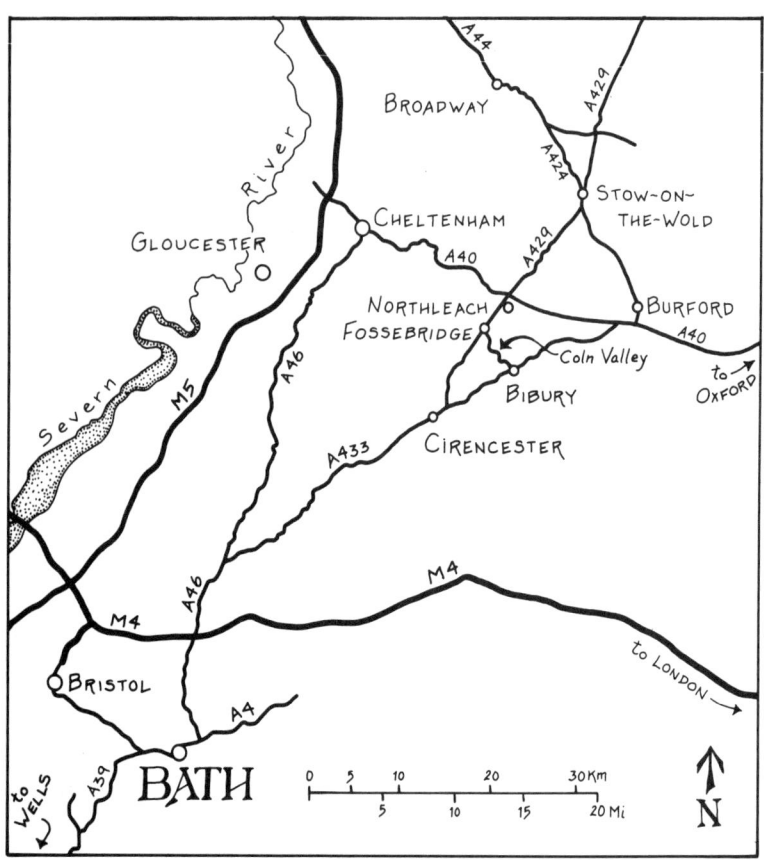

lage proper, all gables and peaks, is just around the bend beyond the cottages and includes a Jacobean manor house (now a hotel) and a fine little church with Saxon details.

Leave Bibury by the **A433** south, up the hill by the mill. Drive through **Cirencester,** staying on the A433 another 18 miles (29 kilometers) until it joins the **A46.** Continue through the Cotswold hills an additional 15 miles (24 kilometers) toward **Bath.** About 9 miles (14.5 kilometers) beyond the intersection with the M4 motorway, after winding through the gently folded countryside, the A46 curves sharply to the left and pitches diagonally down the slope of a deep valley. On the opposite side, row upon row of yellow stone Victorian and Georgian townhouses appear, marching down steep streets toward the Avon River in the valley bottom. The tall, rectangular tower of the Bath Abbey defines the city center ahead. At the intersection with the **A4,** turn right, following signs for Bath, past a steady succession of graceful homes, with tall first-floor windows and beautifully detailed doorways, and richly painted Victorian shop fronts right out of Dickens.

At the fork ahead, you must make a choice. If you want the help of the Tourist Information Centre to find a place to stay tonight, continue straight ahead, bear left onto one-way Walcott Street, turn left at Bridge Street, and go around the Guildhall building, then turn right alongside the abbey. Follow the blue-and-white "i" signs; the informa-

Pulteney Bridge and the terraces of Bath

tion center is a few steps away from the entrance to the Roman Baths on the plaza next to the abbey. If, however, you intend to stay in either of the neighborhoods recommended in Creature Comforts below, turn left at the fork and go over the bridge trimmed with four little Greek temples. Then, at Sydney Gardens, either turn left onto Beckford Street and left again up Warminster Road (the **A36**), or right around the edge of the garden to Pulteney Road. Either way will offer many options.

DIVERSIONS
A Rainy-day Alternative:
Blenheim Palace and Oxford University

If the weather is uncooperative for today's walks—after all, these hills are green and lush for a reason—here is a (mostly) indoor alternative nearly as memorable as the Cotswold countryside itself.

From Burford, drive up the hill to the roundabout and turn **left** onto the **A40** toward Oxford. At the next roundabout, bear **left** onto the **B4047** (detouring to **Minster Lovell Hall,** if you wish; see details above) and drive through **Witney,** famous even today for its wool blankets. Then take the **A4095** through **Long Hanborough** to the roundabout intersection with the **A34** and turn **left** to the handsome village of **Woodstock.** Bear **left** into the village proper, drive to the end of the street, and turn left into the forecourt of the gate to **Blenheim Palace** (park open year-round, 9:00 A.M. to 5:00 P.M.; palace open daily 11:00 A.M. to 6:00 P.M., mid-March through October).

You pass under the arch of a massive stone gatehouse and far ahead, across a vast manicured lawn, stands the palace—an awesome pile of

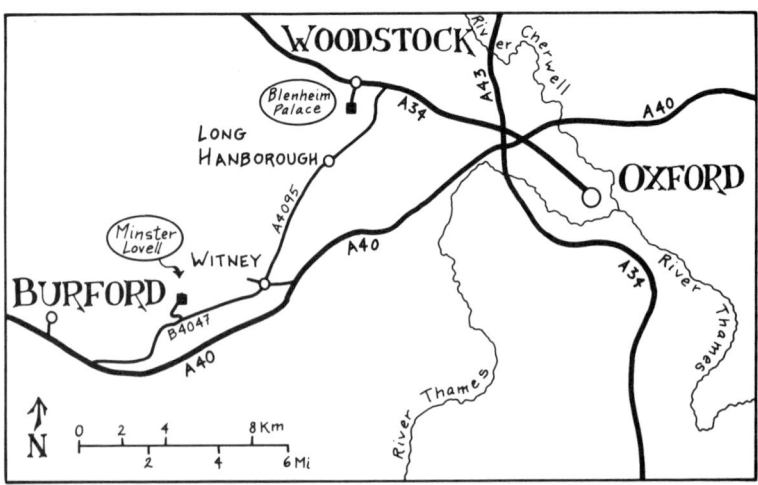

Cotswold stone fashioned into an Italianate vision by the architect Sir John Vanbrugh. The palace was a gift of the Crown to Sir John Churchill, first duke of Marlborough, in recognition of his victory over the French at the Battle of Blenheim in 1704. A perfectly proportioned central structure topped with a classical pediment supported by six massive pillars is flanked by two elegant mirror-image wings enclosing a huge courtyard. One-hour tours of the palace depart every half-hour. Out the "back door" is a formal garden of fountains and pools and, beyond, the 2,000-acre park and lake, created by perhaps the most famous English landscape architect, Lancelot Brown—called "Capability" because of his unerring sense of the "capability" of a bleak landscape to be converted into something pleasing. Frankly, there is about the sheer scale of Blenheim something just a bit beyond human comprehension, but no visit to England would be complete without a visit to one of these monuments to excess.

From Woodstock, head south again on the A34 to **Oxford.** The city of "dreaming spires" sits in a flat plain between the Chiltern Hills on the southeast and the gradually rising Cotswolds to the northwest. Like most major population centers in Britain, Oxford is encircled by a ring road, but the direction signs are good: just look for the **A4144** (Woodstock Road) into the city center. Approaching the center of town, the Woodstock Road becomes St. Giles, then Cornmarket, then St. Aldates. At St. Aldates, keep an eye peeled for the **Oxford Information Centre,** across from the Town Hall. Park nearby (follow the P signs) and return to the center for background brochures and the guided walk through the colleges. Even if your taste does not run to the scholastic, Oxford's timeless quadrangles, cloisters, towers, shops, and gardens, like anything with the patina of great age, are beautiful—and best appreciated on foot. For a quick audiovisual orientation back to medieval days, go to the **Oxford Story** museum near the Sheldonian Theatre on Broad Street, back up Cornmarket and to the right.

Oxford is the oldest university in England and the second oldest in Europe. Merton, oldest of the thirty-five colleges, was founded in 1264 (but only moved to Oxford ten years later). Christ Church is the grandest, its chapel serving as the city's cathedral. Magdalen (pronounced "maudlin") is certainly the loveliest, with its fifteenth-century cloisters and lawns running down to the River Cherwell (pronounced "charwell"). Its colleges aside, however, the charm of Oxford is due in no small part to its gardens—including the incomparable Botanic Garden, founded in 1621 on the banks of the Cherwell, and the war memorial garden, a small gem just off St. Aldates—and its medieval layout, a delightful maze of lanes and alleys. You can capture a bit of the flavor of another age by "grazing" for your lunch today among the dozens of stalls in the **Covered Market,** built in 1774 to neaten up the open-air market that had already been there for centuries. You'll find it at the

ITINERARY: DAY THREE

The cloistered confines of Magdalen College, Oxford

corner of High and Turf streets.

By midafternoon, however, it will be time to head south to Bath. Take the **A40** due west and, just beyond the Burford roundabout, turn **left** onto the **A433**. At **Bibury,** pick up the itinerary described above.

CREATURE COMFORTS
Daily Bed

Bath has been catering to visitors since the Romans established their now-famous baths, and the range of choice—from luxurious to modest—is wide. But this is also one of the most popular tourist destinations in this itinerary. While you need not book accommodations in advance, you may gain substantial peace of mind—and save a good bit of time—by doing so. The simplest way to do this (besides the guidebooks in Further Reading) is to write in advance to the Tourist Information Centre (Abbey Church Yard, Bath BA1 1LY) and request a copy of their color *Accommodation Guide*. With a locator map and color photos, as well as facility and price-range information, you'll know what you're getting into in advance. What's more, this guide includes several attractive and less expensive farmhouse B&Bs a few minutes out in the countryside.

Alternatively, if you're getting the hang of B&B picking, try cruising one or two neighborhoods where there is a good selection of them. Remember the rule: *If it looks well cared for, you'll be well cared for.* Among the best areas are those along the terraces above Pulteney Road and along the high, scenic slopes above the river on Warminster Road north of Sydney Gardens (see directions above). For the budget-minded, there is a Youth Hostel out Bathwick Hill Road in the direction of the American Museum (left at the roundabout south of Sydney Gardens; Raby Place becomes Bathwick Hill). Remember that in a popular city like Bath, the B&B rates will be a few pounds higher per person than out in the country.

Note: After spending the morning and early afternoon tomorrow in Bath, you'll be heading south to nearby Wells and Glastonbury. You can either plan on spending just tonight in Bath and stay near Glastonbury tomorrow night or, if you find you particularly like the place you discover tonight, stay there for two nights.

Daily Bread

There are a lot of pubs and lovely small restaurants to choose from in the center of Bath. Two locations with interesting options in a range of price categories are the edges of the pedestrian district north of the information center and the narrow streets around the Theatre Royal. For more details, check the pub and eating guides in Further Reading.

♦ DAY FOUR

Steeping in Bath and Its Environs

BATH ♦ WELLS ♦ GLASTONBURY

- ♦ A subterranean tour of the Roman Baths
- ♦ A free guided walking tour of Georgian Bath
- ♦ A walk around magnificent Wells Cathedral
- ♦ A stop in "Arthurian" Glastonbury

Bath is the dear old lady of Somerset... one of those old ladies who have outlived a much-discussed past, and are now as obviously respectable as only old ladies with crowded pasts can be.

—H. V. Morton
In Search of England, 1935

There is about Bath a faint air of having "seen it all." There is a stateliness in its sweeping Georgian terraces, but there is also something else... a certain worldliness, a hint that more than just therapeutic water bubbles beneath its serene surface. It's as if old Beau Nash, the eighteenth-century dandy who made Bath chic, still haunts the city's soul. Perhaps all spa towns have this slightly dissolute characteristic. If so, Bath has had plenty of time to develop it—some 8,000 years of living with the vicissitudes of fashion.

Taking a stroll through the centuries is this morning's first adventure, and it begins at the **Roman Baths,** directly opposite the Tourist Information Centre on the plaza in front of the abbey (the most convenient parking is the large lot just north of Pulteney Bridge on Northgate Street).

THE BATHS OF BATH

Bath has been a hot attraction ever since primitive tribes first found its hot springs here in the narrow, twisting valley of the River Avon sometime around 6000 B.C. But it was the Romans, arriving in A.D.

Victorian ironwork and classical colonnades compete for attention at the entrance to the Roman Baths.

43, who made it a tourist destination drawing their sybaritic compatriots from as far away as Londinium. Be up early this morning so you can be at the entrance to the baths when they open at 9:00 A.M. That way you can take the first guided tour and be out in time for the free city walking tour at 10:30 A.M.

The Roman Baths are simply extraordinary. Exploration and excavation goes on constantly (a major renovation was completed in 1988). The result is an archaeological site almost eerily perfect—as if the Romans had left only recently, not two millennia ago. The guided tour begins at the King's Bath (a relatively modern creation that is, frankly, a bit on the slimy side). Then you walk down several feet and 2,000 years into a vast complex of bathing pools of varying temperatures, saunas, and steam rooms all connected by beautifully engineered passageways and water systems. Archaeologists have burrowed around underneath the heart of the city and discovered temples, markets, villas, and more baths, but they are faced with a dilemma: further excavation of the Roman ruins threatens the stunning Georgian architecture on the surface.

The main hot spring feeding the baths gushes a steady 280,000 gallons of 116° F. (46.5° C.) sulfurous water per day and is completely unaffected by rain and surface runoff, leading hydrologists to conclude that its source is ancient and deep within the earth's crust.

The Romans frolicked about here for some four centuries before the implosion of the empire forced them to withdraw, and one cannot help concluding that England would have been a far more comfortable place had the Romans—and their central heating—survived. The remarkable state of preservation of the baths today is due to the fact that they have been covered for centuries by layer upon layer of silt from the repeatedly flooding river. Indeed, it was only about a hundred years ago that the ruins were discovered. According to one story, a house simply collapsed one day into a hole; when excavators dug down to discover the cause and begin the process of rebuilding they hit an inch of solid, hammered lead—the lining of the Great Bath.

When the tour is completed, wander back through the museum and out into the courtyard—pausing perhaps to listen to the string trio playing in the elegant Pump Room—and look for the free official city walking tours, which assemble just in front of the information center. The walk is really a stroll, is wonderfully entertaining, and takes about two hours, depending on the whim of the guide.

A WALKING TOUR OF BATH

Distance: About 1.5 miles/2.4 kilometers; allow 2 hours
Difficulty: A leisurely stroll
Gear: Comfortable shoes/sneakers, rain gear, camera
Map: Take the free guided tour or use a free city map
from the Tourist Information Centre

In the mist of the centuries that followed the Roman retreat, Celtic and Saxon kings battled across the landscape. Meanwhile, the hot water continued to bubble to the surface. Settlement of some kind is likely to have existed here almost continuously after the Romans, but Bath really reemerged from the silt of history in A.D. 973, when the Saxon lord Edgar was crowned first monarch of all England in an abbey that had been built by the Benedictines years before. A century later, in 1088 af-

TRIM ST. → TRIM BRIDGE
- ASSEMBLY ROOMS
Guildhall Banqueting Room

Steeping in Bath and Its Environs   **89**

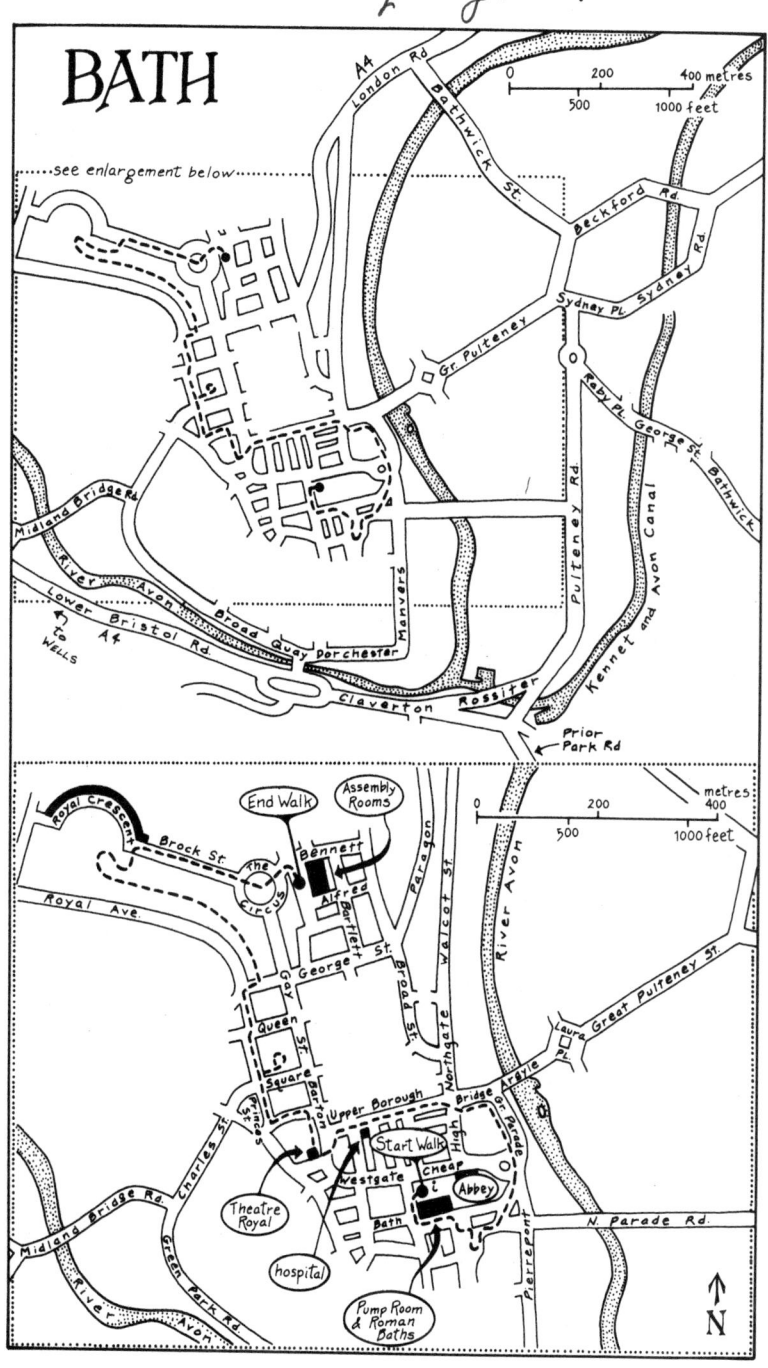

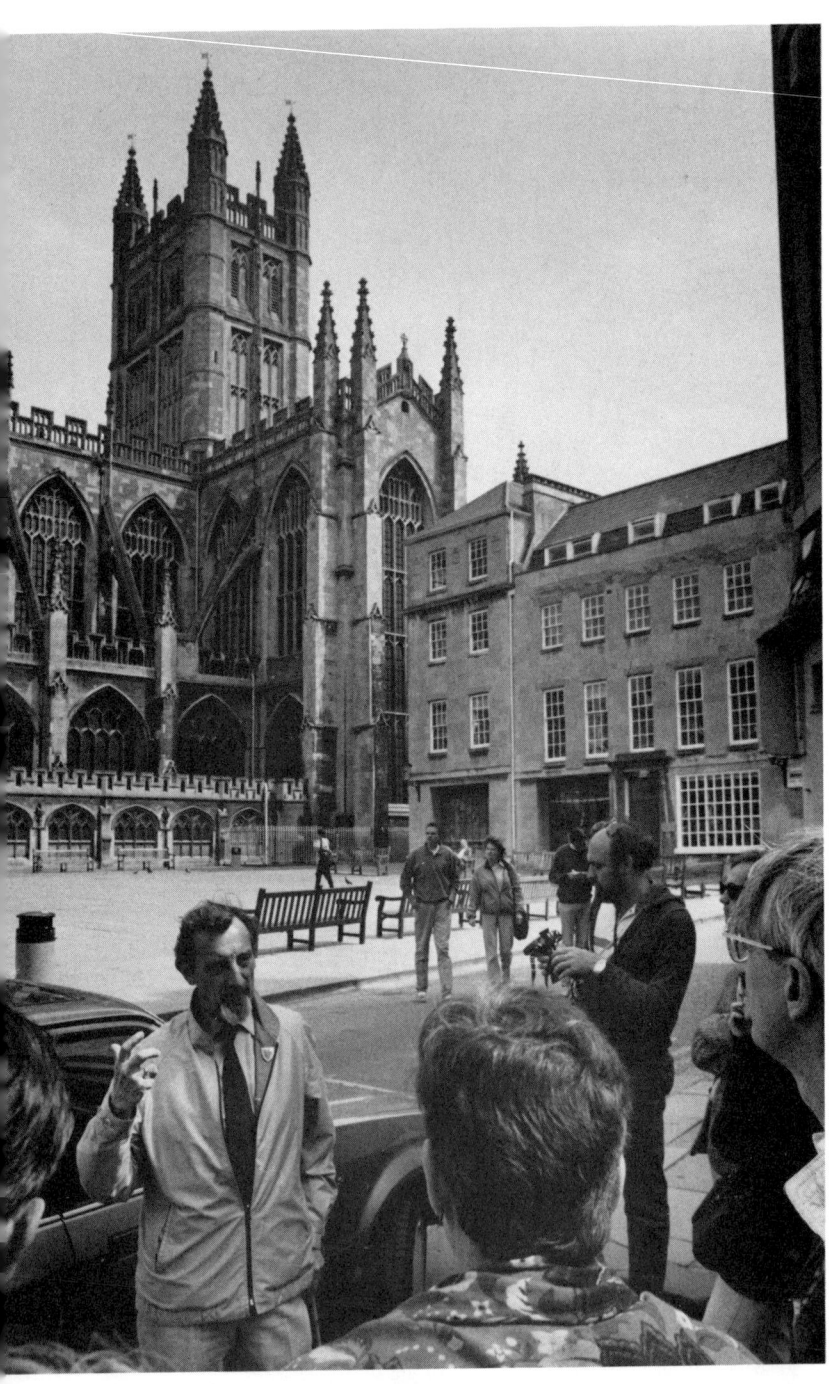

ter the Norman invasion, a new cathedral was built—one so enormous that the entirety of the present **Abbey Church of St. Peter and St. Paul** (begun in 1499) sits in what was only the nave of the original. In subsequent centuries the seat of the see of the cathedral was moved to Wells and the site was downgraded to an abbey. The abbots who built much of the current Abbey Church became rich—and corrupt—in the wool and health-services trades. Still, this must be one of the few churches in England that evidences a sense of humor: note that among the angels climbing ladders to heaven on both sides of the west front one is falling earthward again.

After Henry VIII dissolved all the monasteries (ironically, soon after the church was completed), the city degenerated into one of the most notoriously squalid and crime-ridden spots in England until Queen Elizabeth I, who visited during one of her "royal progresses," established a secular corporation to run the city and ordered it to clean up its act. It must have worked, because in the first few years of the 1700s Queen Anne visited to "take the waters" twice and dedicated followers of fashion immediately followed suit.

The walking tour, which next passes through the columned gateway at the western end of the Abbey Yard and around to gracious **Abbey Green,** is really about what happened next: the creation, in the span of only twenty-five years, of the most beautiful city in Britain.

The folks who flocked to Bath to "take the cure" and enjoy the emerging social scene came for months at a time with their entire families in tow, servants and all. Sallying forth to the baths each morning in sedan chairs (precursors to taxis), they rested in the afternoon, took tea, then prepared for a nearly endless round of parties and balls in the Assembly Rooms built for the purpose. When they arrived, they sought elegant rental accommodation, much like what they were used to in London. But what they found, at least at the beginning of the 1700s, was a typical medieval town: a jumble of timber, mud, and stone houses lining narrow streets with raw sewage running down the center.

With an unerring sense of market demand, two men—an architect and a wealthy businessman—made the city habitable. A third, a dandy and brilliant social organizer, made the place fun. It was an unbeatable combination.

The architect was John Wood, a Bath native who adapted the classical designs of Palladio into the graceful terraced townhouses that characterize Bath today: five stories high, but with the first floor in the basement and the top floor set back from the roofline out of sight. They were built in rows so that the overall impression was palatial even though each individual dwelling was relatively modest. It was John Wood and his son who were responsible for designing most of Bath's

Bath's volunteer guides dish up a splendid mix of history, architecture . . . and period gossip.

greatest buildings: the Royal Crescent, the Circus, the Assembly Rooms, and more.

The businessman was Ralph Allen, impeccably honest, civic-minded, and an efficiency expert. He made his first fortune creating the modern postal service and his second by systemizing the quarrying and delivery of building stone to the town's burgeoning construction industry. Allen and the Woods created the Georgian masterpiece that is Bath today.

The man who put Bath on the eighteenth-century social map was Richard "Beau" Nash. A failure at Oxford, at the law, and in the army, Nash—a notorious rake and gambler—found his niche as the tastemaker and official master of ceremonies of the Bath social whirl. With nothing but the sheer force of his character, Nash established the "rules" for taking the cure, set the social calendar, greeted arriving families with fanfares, fixed them up with doctors and shopkeepers, regularized the sedan chair runners who ferried "patients" to the baths, and—most important, since it was his principal source of income—institutionalized the gambling houses. Eventually, not content with the challenges of being "King of Bath," he accepted an invitation to do the same for the spa being developed at Tunbridge Wells, nearly 200 miles (325 kilometers) away in Kent, commuting between the two in the largest coach that had ever been built.

Having set the architectural and social context, the walk now curves down to the banks of the Avon, past Bath's own *Ponte Vecchio*, the lovely shop-lined **Pulteney Bridge.** This is not, by the way, the same Avon that flows through Shakespeare's Stratford; there are some six major Avon Rivers in England; *avon* means "river" in Celtic. Next you walk up to the corner of the enclosed **Guildhall Market** on Bridge Street, along Upper Borough Wall Street past the **hospital**—the first purpose-built hospital in Britain (designed by Wood and built with stone donated by Allen)—to St. John's Court, site of Nash's home. Then the walk continues past the newly restored **Theatre Royal,** through **Queen Square,** ringed with gracious mansions (designed, again, by John Wood), to the extraordinary **Royal Crescent**—a colonnaded curve of thirty-three townhouses overlooking what once was open countryside and today is Royal Victoria Park. Designed by John Wood's son and completed in 1778, the austere crescent is said to be the finest example of Georgian domestic architecture in Britain. Number 1 Royal Crescent is a museum with period furnishings from kitchen to attic (open Tuesday through Saturday, April through October).

From the crescent, you walk east along Brock Street to the **Circus,** a perfectly circular expanse of Bath townhouses built by the Woods, senior and junior. The trees, which block the full impact of the design and its wonderful classical details, were planted by the Victorians, who never did know when to leave well enough alone. If you look carefully at the perfectly regular exterior of the Circus, you begin to notice that the modest front doors are not evenly placed. This is because what one contracted for with the Woods was a certain number of feet of frontage on the circle; behind the façade the living space you sought could be two, three, or more "units" wide.

Finally, the walk ends at the **Assembly Rooms**—*the* place to see and be seen in Bath's heyday—a block from the Circus between Bennett and Alfred streets. The site of the grandest affairs (figuratively and literally) of the late 1700s, the building today is the home of the Costume Museum, an illuminating look at fashion through the centuries.

For lunch, you can either retire to the nearest pub or café or walk back to the Guildhall Market, near Pulteney Bridge, and put together a picnic lunch from among the dozens of purveyors of cheeses, meats, breads, and vegetables, and then enjoy it from the banks of the river. For shoppers, Bath is rich with specialty stores of all kinds, including a number of antique shops along Bartlett Street.

🚗 A PILGRIMAGE TO WELLS AND GLASTONBURY

Distance: About 25 miles/40 kilometers total
Roads: Well-signed primary roads
Driving Time: Less than 45 minutes to Wells
Map: Michelin Map #403

The plan for this afternoon is a journey from the secular to the sacred, from opulent Bath to the bare, broken bones of legend-haunted Glastonbury Abbey, with an intervening stop in Wells to visit one of the finest cathedrals in Britain.

From the center of Bath, follow signs for the **A4** toward **Bristol**. After crossing to the south bank of the Avon River and passing under the railroad, you'll begin to see signs with the **A39** in parentheses (ignore signs for the **A367**). After about 10 minutes the **A39** branches off the A4 to the **left** for **Wells**, some 17 miles (27 kilometers) away. A few miles farther on, the A39 merges with the A37 for a while, zigzagging through the village of **Farrington Gurney,** and then separates from it again. Then the A39 climbs up a long ridge of the Mendip Hills to Pen Hill and a panoramic view opens below you, with cone-shaped Glastonbury Tor, crowned by St. Michael's tower, rising like a ghost from the flat, hazy Vale of Avalon. Immediately below you is the tiny city of Wells, clustered around the spring from which it takes its name, its grand cathedral rising from a sea of medieval rooftops. The road plunges steeply down into the city, bending around the cathedral precincts. After passing the cathedral, keep an eye peeled for the little market square off to your left just at the point where the road turns sharply

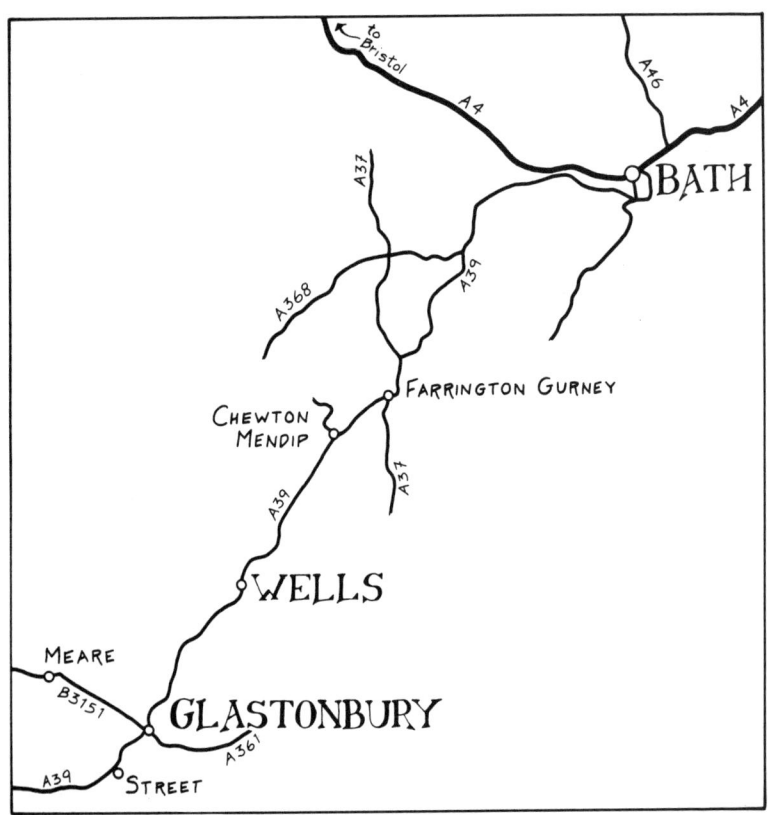

right in the middle of town. Park in the small "pay and display" parking area in the square near the Town Hall and Tourist Information Centre.

Henry James visited Wells in 1872 and wrote: "Wells is in fact not a city with a cathedral for central feature; it is a cathedral with a little city gathered at its base." What strikes you as you stand in the turreted archway between the market square and the broad lawn of the cathedral close is that Wells the cathedral and Wells the city are all of a piece: a harmonious medieval relic (with occasional Georgian and Victorian flourishes) somehow surviving—indeed thriving—in the twentieth century. The **cathedral,** built between the twelfth and fourteenth centuries and serving both Wells and Bath, is the focal point. Its towers are short and stumpy, in the early English manner; its greatest glory is the elaborately carved (and newly restored) west front—a kind of vast vertical sculpture gallery composed of nearly 300 ecclesiastical statues. The limestone of which the cathedral is built has a curious chameleonlike

The intricately carved west front of Wells Cathedral

The peaceful precincts of Vicars' Close, Wells

character. Under a cloudy sky the west front is a somber gray. But it is in its glory in the afternoon, when the lowering sun turns the façade to luminous gold and each statue stands out in sharp relief. The interior is lovely, especially the fan-vaulted ceiling, the Lady Chapel, the elegant Chapter House, and the inverted arches added in 1338 when the central tower threatened to collapse. But somehow the outer precincts are even more evocative of the period.

Vicars' Close, through Chain Gate opposite the North Porch of the cathedral, is a good example. Built in the fourteenth century to house a community of lesser clerics, the enclosed and peaceful cobbled street—allegedly Europe's oldest complete street—is lined by handsome medieval row cottages with lush front gardens, gas lamps, and tall, graceful chimneys. It is not difficult to imagine the contemplative comings and goings of medieval priests.

On the other side of the cathedral, back through the gate to the market square and left through yet another stone gate, is the **Bishop's Palace.** Begun in the thirteenth century, the palace was fortified with its high turreted wall, moat, and drawbridge in the fourteenth century after a quarrel between the bishop and the town fathers. The bishop of Bath and Wells still lives in the palace, but today the atmosphere is more tranquil: the moat (filled with water bubbling up from St. Andrew's Well) is lined with daffodils and iris and populated by swans and mallards. A peek through the gate to the inner courtyard reveals a handsome manor house trimmed with roses and other perennial flowers (grounds and chapel open Thursdays, Sundays, and Bank Holiday Mondays from 2:00 P.M. to 6:00 P.M., Easter through October; Wednesdays 11:00 A.M. to 6:00 P.M., May through September; and daily in August).

Back at the market square, take a moment to enjoy the shop fronts, their handsome façades a rich mix of the colors of another era: olive green with sage trim, burgundy and white, chocolate and red, navy blue and gold, hunter green and cream, their names all hand-painted in flowing script or bold block letters in gold. Then hop back in your car and take the **A39** south again to **Glastonbury.**

Only 10 minutes away, the town of Glastonbury sits on rising land above the flat **Somerset Levels.** Once an arm of the sea, the Levels were still being flooded seasonally as recently as 1607. As far back as 4000 B.C. there were human settlements here, perched on wooden pilings and connected by roads made from cut timbers and brush. The county name, Somerset, means "the summer people" and comes from the practice among local farmers, dating from prehistoric times and continuing until quite recently, of moving livestock down to the flatlands during the dry summer months to graze the rich water meadows. While the Romans and medieval abbots each made an effort to drain the area, it was not until the eighteenth and nineteenth centuries that a comprehensive system of drainage channels (called *rhynes* and pronounced "reens") was developed. And even today, the Levels, with their iris-edged canals, contented herds of Fresian cows, humpbacked bridges, and sleepy villages, seem to have escaped the depredations of the twentieth century.

The misty Levels have been a fertile breeding ground for legends—Christian, Arthurian, and a curious but commercially attractive mix of both—for centuries. Joseph of Arimathea, a disciple of Jesus on a divinely directed journey to find a suitable resting place for the chalice used at the Last Supper, is said to have disembarked here, stuck his staff in the ground, and when it took root and blossomed built the first Christian church in Britain in A.D. 37 (a thorn tree alleged to have been grown from a cutting of the original tree grows today in a corner of the grounds of Glastonbury Abbey). He is also said to have buried the chalice—the Holy Grail—beneath what today is Glastonbury Tor, from which a spring flows that stains red (a matter of iron content, actually).

King Arthur is said to have received his sword Excalibur from the

Lady of the Lake at nearby **Meare** and to have been brought to the Isle of Avalon (later Glastonbury) to die after the Battle of Camlan in A.D. 542. In 1190, the Abbey announced that the remains of a man and woman were discovered within the grounds of the abbey and with them a lead cross inscribed with Arthur's name (the "discovery" came just after a major fire).

There is no reliable evidence of either Joseph or Arthur, but there may have been a primitive church here in the fifth century and there was certainly an abbey founded in Glastonbury in A.D. 688. It is to visit the awesome ruins of the last great abbey, begun early in the thirteenth century, that we come to Glastonbury this afternoon. (The abbey is open daily 9:30 A.M. to 6:30 P.M. in December, successively later as the year progresses, and until 7:30 P.M. in June, July, and August.) To reach the entrance, follow the A39 through town, down High Street, and left onto Magdalene Street. The entrance is on your left.

Like some stupendous bleached and ravaged skeleton, the abbey ruins are moving evidence of the brutal thoroughness of Henry VIII's dissolution of the monasteries. After having the uncooperative abbot hung, drawn, and quartered on the tor, the king had the huge church, then one of the richest and most powerful in Britain, sold as an attractive source of precut building stone. What remains is well excavated and displayed, and provides an illuminating look at medieval abbey life (see

Glastonbury Abbey: what Henry VIII destroyed, the imagination rebuilds.

a model of the abbey before destruction in the Gatehouse Museum). Rent the portable tape cassette at the gatehouse for the best tour.

The best time to see these ruins is late on a summer afternoon, with the sun low in the sky, casting long, dark shadows across the emerald lawns—a more romantic, mystery-shrouded vision no legend could ever evoke.

DIVERSIONS

Off the beaten track for centuries, Somerset has managed to retain many of its traditional **crafts.** If you find you have had enough of baths, crescents, and cathedrals, you can spend a delightful afternoon (or part of tomorrow morning) visiting some of the craftspeople who are thick upon the ground in this quiet county. Somerset is the last place in England where willow is still grown commercially for the *withies* and *osiers* needed for **basket making.** Fresh shoots are harvested from the tops of those odd chopped-off (*pollarded*) old willow trees you see lining the drainage ditches in the Levels (Stoke St. Gregory, southwest of Street, has several basket makers and a Willow and Wetlands Visitor Centre, closed Sundays). There are **potteries** throughout the region, but one of the most intriguing is Muchelney Pottery (south of Langport, near the ninth-century Muchelney Abbey), run by John Leach, grandson of Britain's most famous potter, Bernard Leach, and possessing one of the few wood-fired kilns in England. **Cider** is another traditional Somerset product, from dry and mildly alcoholic to sweet and powerful scrumpy. It's still made at Rose Farm, site of the book *Cider with Rosie,* southwest of Wincanton on the A357. For a brochure on Somerset crafts, stop in at the information centers at Wells or Glastonbury, or write in advance to the West Country Tourist Board, 37 Southernhay East, Exeter, Devonshire EX1 1QS, or to the Somerset Guild of Craftsmen, Yard End, Carters Lane, Crowcombe, Taunton TA4 4AA.

CREATURE COMFORTS

If you chose to spend a second night in Bath, home is only a short ride back from Glastonbury on the A39, and you already know how many choices there are for dinner in Bath. If you decided instead to spend the night in Somerset, here are some suggestions.

Daily Bed

Pilgrims have been trooping through Wells and Glastonbury for centuries and folks here have been catering to their needs just as long. You will already have noticed plenty of farmhouse B&B choices along the A39, and there are more on some of the side roads, for example the

B3151 to Meare (with its own Levels and Moors Information Centre). In addition to recommendations in the accommodations guides listed in Further Reading, consider writing directly to the Tourist Information Centres in Wells (Town Hall, Market Place, Wells BA5 2RB) and Glastonbury (1 Marchant's Buildings, Northload Street, Glastonbury BA6 9JJ). They produce their own brochures with local accommodations listings and can provide you with Somerset Tourism's brochures: "Where To Stay In Somerset" and "Farm and Country Holidays in Somerset."

Daily Bread

The relatively steady stream of tourists through this region tends to help spawn delightful small restaurants and pubs that go far beyond the average. Both Wells and Glastonbury are well endowed, Wells perhaps more so. Ask for recommendations where you are staying or simply stroll through these tiny towns and find something that fills the bill. And while you're in Somerset, try some of the local specialties: fresh and smoked **trout,** mildly alcoholic apple **cider,** sinful **Bath buns** (sweet pastries packed with currants and a bit of citron, with a brown glazed crust dusted with crushed rock sugar), and *real* **cheddar** cheese.

Cheddar... but Not from Cheddar

At the beginning of World War II, there were some 1,600 farms making country cheese in Britain. By the mid-1970s, there were 68, and fewer than 30 used traditional methods. Cheddar, the greatest name in British cheeses—crumbly, tangy, yet buttery, and just right with a pint of Somerset cider—isn't even made in Cheddar (just northwest of Wells) anymore. But great English cheeses, like real ale, are making a comeback, and there is one dairy, Priory Farm, just off the A39 at Chewton Mendip, where you can still see real cheddar curd mixed, spread out on long tables in thick yellow slabs, then cut, folded, drained, and pressed into great round *truckles* to age nine months to maturity. Once you've seen the final product, crusty and dark, you'll never be able to buy that strange, chewy, plastic-wrapped orange stuff in the supermarket again.

♦ DAY FIVE

Across the Roof of Devon
SOMERSET ♦ EXMOOR
DEVON'S NORTH COAST ♦ BOSCASTLE

- ♦ A drive across the Somerset Levels to medieval Dunster
- ♦ Picturesque Selworthy and breathtaking Exmoor
- ♦ The Victorian coastal resorts of Lynton and Lynmouth
- ♦ The sheltered fishing villages of Devon and Cornwall's Atlantic coast

---

[North Devon is] the most delightful place for a landscape painter this country can boast....
   —Thomas Gainsborough

Exmoor is sneaky. One minute it's all soft green meadows, wildflowers, and creamy thatched cottages cradled in deep, tranquil valleys. The next minute it's wind-blasted moorland, gnarled and stunted scrub oak, and acres of rugged heather and thorny yellow gorse stretching to the horizon. Another moment later it's a breathtaking expanse of angry ocean tearing at tortured cliffs that have been the graveyards of ships for centuries. You can't take your eye off it for a second.

Part Somerset, part Devon, Exmoor is a place apart. A 265-square-mile (690-square-kilometer) national park (that is neither "national" nor a "park") and royal forest (that was never forested), Exmoor is an ancient and deeply eroded sedimentary plateau that ripples across the roof of the southwest peninsula, peaks at Dunkery Beacon (1,704 feet/519 meters), then plunges into the Bristol Channel from some of the most dramatic cliffs in Britain. Only about a quarter of Exmoor is true moor at all; the rest is coastal ridge and wooded inland valleys where red deer, descendants of the herd that avoided the ice sheet that covered the rest of Britain during the last Ice Age, still roam. Even at the height of tourist season, Exmoor seems empty; people simply disappear into its deep combes—as did the Doones, the seventeenth-century

ITINERARY: DAY FIVE

The woolen industry is gone, but Dunsters' gabled Yarn Market remains—a quiet counterpart to the castle at the other end of town.

band of outlaws romanticized in R. D. Blackmore's novel *Lorna Doone*.

Today's itinerary is a drive through the northern reaches of Exmoor, before turning south toward Cornwall. You'll spend most of the day in your car, but the constant scene changes will make the day pass all too quickly.

🚗 ACROSS THE LEVELS, OVER THE MOORS, AND DOWN THE COAST

Distance: 123 miles/198 kilometers Glastonbury to Crackington Haven; 136 miles/219 kilometers Glastonbury to Port Isaac
Roads: A39 all but the last few miles
Driving Time: All day
Map: Michelin Map #403

We begin deep in Somerset. Whether you stayed in Bath or near Glastonbury last night, take the **A39** west through **Street** and out along the high ridge above the Somerset Levels, with curious lumpy bits of the Mendip Hills—called "tumps" locally—poking out of the flat, drained meadows and fields. As you approach **Bridgewater,** the texture

Across the Roof of Devon **103**

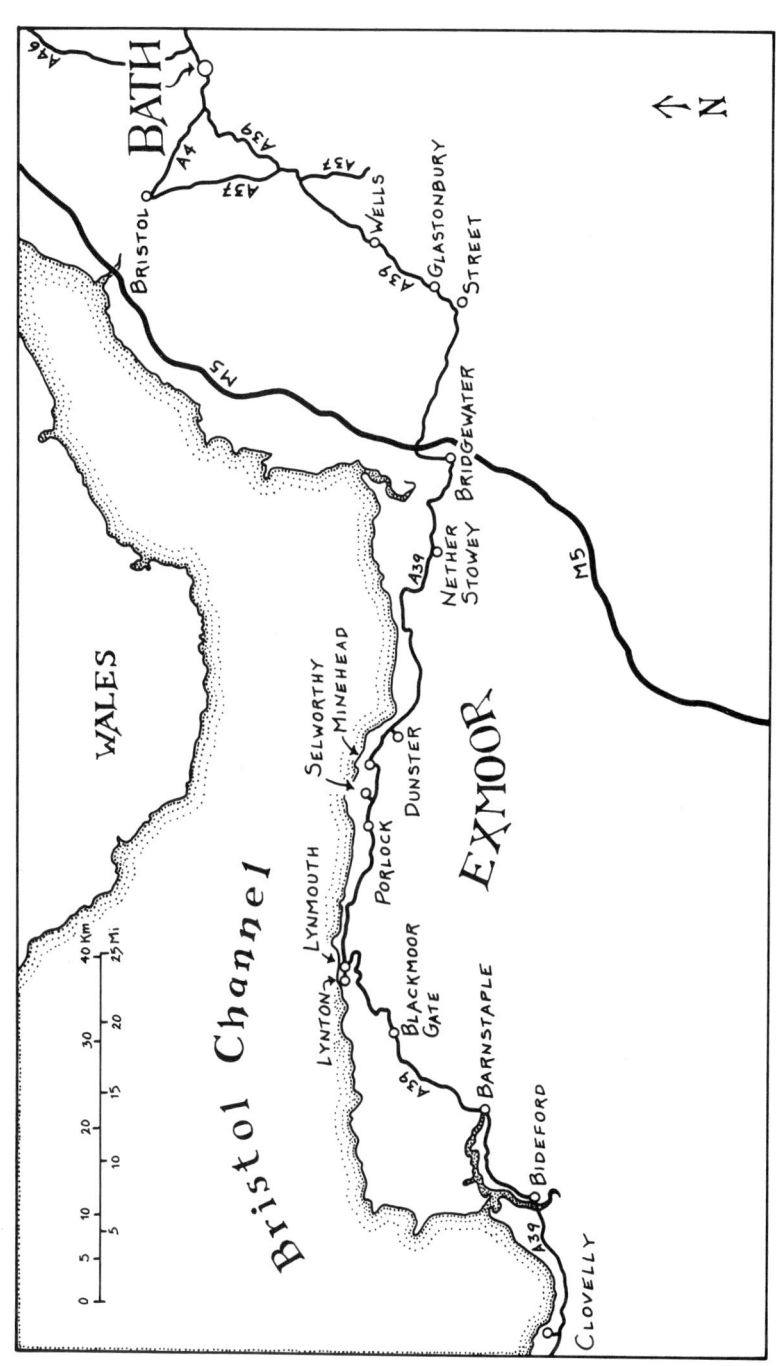

Picturebook-pretty Selworthy, tucked away in a fold of the Exmoor hills, is protected by the National Trust.

of local buildings begins to change from the pale limestone of the Mendips to a rusty red sandstone and, increasingly as you head west, to half-timbered and thatched cottages. In the spring, the A39, winding through the villages of **Nether Stowey** (where Coleridge wrote "The Rime of the Ancient Mariner") and **Holford** (where Wordsworth lived with his ever-present sister Dorothy), is lined with thousands of wild daffodils, their sunny heads bobbing in the gusts of passing cars.

Beyond **Williton,** the Brendon Hills begin to rise in great green swells on your left, precursors to the higher plateau of Exmoor yet ahead. And just beyond **Carhampton,** high on a wooded promontory above a lush meadow also on the left, you can see the towers of Dunster Castle. **Dunster,** a handsome medieval village, is worth a short detour at the next **left.** The broad main street is crowned by the castle, a nineteenth-century replacement of the original, which, in 1,000 years of history, was owned by only two families. The Luttrells, who owned it from the Middle Ages, have since donated the castle to the National Trust. At the other end of town is an eight-sided seventeenth-century Yarn Market, testimony to the strength of the weaving industry that once supported the region before the Industrial Revolution concentrated mill production in the north. When you finish exploring the village, come back out to the A39 and turn **left.**

Beyond the western limits of **Minehead,** a typically boisterous English seaside resort with broad sandy beaches, you pass the boundary marker for **Exmoor National Park.** Exmoor is one of ten national parks in Britain, but the title is misleading. The land here and in the other parks is mostly privately owned and in active economic use; the "national" designation acknowledges the importance of the area to the nation, while the "park" designation indicates that the land is managed by the Park Authority to preserve its unique natural characteristics. The impact of that special management is clear the moment you cross the boundary: the suburban landscape of Minehead gives way immediately to a long, lush valley of mixed forest and meadows and a riot of roadside wildflowers.

A little over a mile farther on, watch for an abrupt **right** turn into a deep lane almost completely enclosed by its overarching hedge. A few hundred yards uphill is **Selworthy,** a tiny picture-book cluster of thatched cottages built in the early 1800s by Sir Thomas Acland, tenth baronet of Holnicote, to house retired estate workers. Selworthy, now owned by the National Trust, shelters in the lee of Selworthy Beacon, which rises more than 1,000 feet (over 300 meters) above the sea and is the site of an Iron Age fort. From the steps of the whitewashed fifteenth-century church, high above the little village, you can see deep into the folds of Exmoor all the way to the barren moor tops of Dunkery Beacon to the south.

A word of warning: Selworthy is almost impossibly pretty, which means that it attracts crowds on sunny summer weekends. But if you've lucked into a light day, by all means take a few minutes to walk down to the little hamlet, gathered around a tiny green invisible from the road. Park above the church, walk around the front, turn right up a lane along the left side of the church, then left through a gate and down to the cottages themselves, deeply thatched, with thick cob walls (a mix of mud, gravel, and hay, covered with plaster) painted the color of rich Devon clotted cream and trimmed with rambler roses, clematis, and blazing border gardens. The National Trust has a small visitor center and the tea shop was voted the best in the nation in 1989.

From Selworthy continue west on the A39—upon which you'll be driving all day—to **Porlock.** Stay to the left through the winding, narrow streets of this pretty village and take the steep switchback road up over Porlock Hill (in springtime, the orchards on the hillside are carpeted with thousands of daffodils and narcissus). Toward the top, risk your life and glance back over your shoulder for sweeping views of Porlock Bay. After running through a dense thicket of scrub oak, the road emerges to a different landscape entirely: miles of high, heather-clad moorland rolling off to the horizon on your left, a deep purple carpet when it blooms in late summer. If you pull off the road for a moment you may see Exmoor's largest birds of prey, the graceful and unfortunately named buzzard, drifting effortlessly on the wind and, closer to the ground, a tiny kestrel hovering like a miniature British "Harrier" fighter plane, poised to attack.

The road clings to the high coastal ridge for several miles before the landscape begins to break up again, the combes becoming deeper as Exmoor's north-rushing streams sense the sea below. Then, after you cross the boundary from Somerset into Devon and pass through **Countisbury,** the road turns toward the coast and simply drops out from under you, plunging down the side of the cliff toward Lynmouth, far below by the sea. There are several rather ominous sand-filled "escape route" pits for runaway cars and trucks on your left as you descend.

Lynmouth is a charming old fishing village tarted up to look like a Victorian resort (if you managed to refuse tea and cakes at Selworthy, this might be a good place to stop for lunch). Wedged into a narrow valley cut by the fast-flowing River Lyn, it is connected to its sister **Lynton,** high above on the ridge, by a funicular—from the top of which there is a breathtaking cliffside walk (part of the Somerset and North Devon Coast Path) to the Valley of Rocks, a mass of pinnacles and headlands above the sea a mile to the west.

From Lynmouth the A39 twists upstream, clinging to the steep side of the gorge above the River Lyn. It's a spectacular ride, the road narrowing almost to one lane where its engineers were unable to cut any more room out of the red sandstone cliff face. The mood of the land-

Thatched Roofs: Pretty and Practical

Lightweight, an excellent insulator against cold, heat, and noise, and adaptable to almost any roof shape, thatch was once widely used for roofing in England. Today it persists in Devon and Dorset (where longstraw is available) and in the lowlands of East Anglia (where Norfolk reed is grown). The complicated craft of bundling, pegging, trimming, and crowning a thatched roof takes great skill—a skill that was dying until it was revived recently with the help of a craft guild and England's Rural Development Commission. A decline in the availability of thatching materials (a casualty of intensive farming) and the time involved in gaining the skill make thatch roofs expensive, about four times the cost of slate or clay tile. But straw roofs can last more than twenty years, Norfolk reed more than eighty, so it's a long-term investment. When the thatching is completed, the entire roof is covered with wire mesh to discourage birds and rodents from setting up house under the eaves, and the ridge line (which takes the greatest beating) is thickened and trimmed with each thatcher's signature pattern.

scape, once again, is completely different from what it was only moments ago: the hillside is thickly forested and you climb through a leafy tunnel broken occasionally by heart-in-mouth glimpses of the sheer drop to the rocky river floor below and "Watersmeet," the rapids where the East Lyn River and Hoar Oak Water collide (a National Trust property).

Then abruptly, another scene shift: the A39 gains the crest of the Exmoor plateau again and runs along its western edge, a softer rolling landscape with velvety green meadows, hedgerows thick with pale yellow primroses and lemon yellow daffodils in spring and red campion in summer, masses of creamy sheep, cows knee-deep in buttercups, and widely dispersed farmsteads. *Be forewarned, however, about those hedgerows:* they are not what they seem. Centuries ago, the technique for delineating property lines in this part of England was to dig a deep ditch, heaving the removed dirt and rock into banks along both sides. That's why Devon's country lanes are so deep. It's also why, in a squeeze or emergency, you don't want to swerve into the "hedges" hoping to get by with only scratched paint. Those "hedges" are as unyielding as the earth and rock of which they are composed; the lush foliage is just a disguise.

A few miles ahead, at **Blackmoor Gate,** the A39 appears to dead-end. Simply turn **right** here, then **left** almost immediately and continue on the A39 south through **Barnstaple,** a bustling market town at the mouth of the River Taw, around the Taw estuary to **Bideford** (literally "by-the-ford"), then south a further 10 miles (16 kilometers) to the turnoff for **Clovelly,** on your **right.**

"Turnoff" may well be the right word here. For years, Clovelly was—and still is—the kind of romantically picturesque fishing village that appeared on English biscuit tins and candy boxes. It is an extraordinary place, a jumble of whitewashed cottages tumbling some 400 feet (120 meters) down a cobbled and stepped "street" so steep that the chimney of one cottage may be level with the basement of its uphill neighbor. Supplies are delivered by wooden sledges. Not a place for the faint of heart or short of breath. Almost an anagram of "lovely," Clovelly is a perennial winner of England's "Best in Bloom" contest, with hedges of purple and red fuchsia, roses and clematis climbing to rooftops, geraniums and lobelia cascading from window boxes, and orderly little cottage vegetable gardens. Far below, a postage-stamp harbor, protected by a massive stone jetty, is home to a small, colorful array of fishing boats, and an ancient pub offers real ale to fortify you for the climb back uphill. That's the good news. The bad news is that someone, presumably the latest lord of the manor, has deemed these attractions insufficient (or simply insufficiently profitable), and has built an enor-

The fractured cliff face of Hartland Point, on Devon's wild Atlantic coast

mous "Visitors' Centre" at the top of the hill, through which everyone must pass. Admittedly, the audiovisual program is a good introductory history and the view from the terrace is terrific, but the gift shop and café scream "tourist trap." Close your eyes until you're out the other side and then relax and enjoy this remarkable village.

Another caution: like Selworthy, Clovelly can be overrun with visitors—as many as 3,000 on a peak midsummer Saturday. On the other hand, at midweek you may have it nearly to yourself. If you find the car park jammed with tour buses and decide to turn back, an attractive alternative awaits—the short drive out to **Hartland Point,** just around the bend. Drive back out to the A39, turn **right,** then after a few hundred yards take the next **right,** onto the **B3248** signposted for Hartland. This narrow road winds through high-walled fields into the main village of Hartland. Here, carry on straight ahead in the direction of **Hartland Stoke** (whose parish church is one of the prettiest in Devon) and, beyond that, down to **Hartland Quay**—a tiny cluster of weather-beaten stone cottages and one plucky little hotel stolidly confronting the Atlantic gales. Weather permitting, take a few minutes to see the spectacular cliffs on either side of the settlement. The rocks in these bizarre cliff faces were laid down as sand and mud on a sea floor 320 million years ago, then buckled and repeatedly folded back upon themselves 30 million years later by some unimaginable geologic force. The cliffs themselves are actually quite young, created 3,000 years ago when the glaciers of the last Ice Age melted and sea levels rose over 300 feet (100 meters).

Time now to head south into **Cornwall.** Return to Hartland village and bear **right,** following the B3248 out to the A39. At the main road, turn **right** and drive another 20 to 30 miles (32 to 48 kilometers) or so through the rolling farmland sheltering behind the coastal ridge, past **Bude** to the area of coastal Cornwall between **Crackington Haven** and **Port Isaac** to find a home for the next two nights (see Creature Comforts below).

DIVERSIONS
Dartington Glass Works

In a day with as many attractions as this one, you may find you have no need of further distractions. But if the weather has been poor and you find yourself approaching Bideford with plenty of time left in the day, consider a visit to the **Dartington Glass Works** in Great Torrington, 7 miles (11 kilometers) east up the valley of the River Torridge (watch for the sign just before you go over the soaring new bridge to Bideford). The glassworks is part of a complex of activities—industrial, agricultural, artistic, and educational—initiated 25 years ago by a Tontes-based family to help diversify and strengthen Devon's strug-

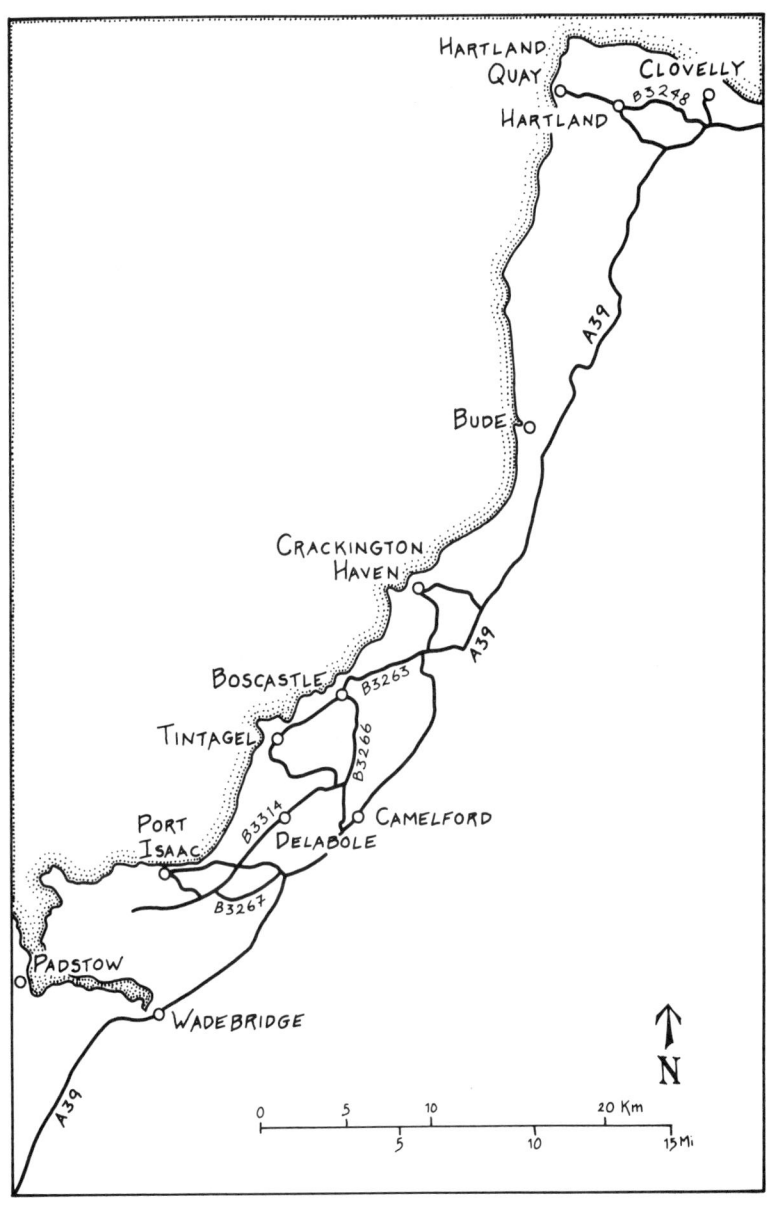

gling rural economy. The glassware produced in Torrington—24 percent lead crystal—is simple and contemporary, in contrast to the elaborately cut crystal from Ireland. The products—graceful stemware, chunky glassware, and a range of bowls and vases—are designed by

Frank Thrower (who has received a number of design awards) and produced by teams of roughly a dozen locally recruited workers, trained by Scandinavian master glassblowers. Tours run Monday through Friday, 9:00 A.M. to 3:00 P.M., all year; the shop (which also sells discounted seconds) is open Monday through Friday, 9:00 A.M. to 5:00 P.M. and Saturday 10:00 A.M. to 4:00 P.M.

CREATURE COMFORTS

Tomorrow's walk is centered on **Boscastle,** but there are half a dozen communities tucked into nooks and crannies in the coastal cliffs where a range of accommodations and meals can be found, according to your taste. None are more than a few minutes from our destination tomorrow and all are just a few miles west of the A39 along coastal lanes.

Daily Bed

There are plenty of places to choose from on the north Cornish coast, from small hotels and beamy old inns to farm and village B&Bs. **Crackington Haven,** nestled in a fold in the coast range, has a small hotel facing a rock-rimmed beach and some excellent farmhouse B&Bs (see Further Reading for addresses). **Boscastle** climbs steeply up from a picturesque dogleg harbor and has several small hotels, B&Bs, and restaurants. **Tintagel** (pronounced "tin-*tadge*-ul") wallows in phony Arthurian legend, has plenty of accommodations, but is incredibly commercial. Tourist Information Centres in Bude and Camelford can help find accommodations (seasonal). There are also youth hostels in both Boscastle and Tintagel.

In stark contrast to Tintagel, **Port Isaac,** a few miles farther south, is a resolutely genuine fishing village and has been for centuries. The streets—both of them—make little accommodation with the present: they are only one car wide and quite steep. Aptly named Squeezebelly Alley admits no cars at all. Parking is on the shingle beach at low tide or at the top of the hill. The cottages that cling to the cliff sides, as if glued to their tiny plots, are crisply whitewashed and trimmed with bright fishing-boat colors, the air has the unmistakable tang of the sea, and the surrounding cliffs echo with the raucous complaints of wheeling gulls. Stumbling onto Port Isaac in the evening, as a white fog creeps up from the beach and snakes around the fishing shacks, is pure magic.

Port Isaac and its neighbor **Port Gaverne** (pronounced "*gave*-en") both offer a choice of atmospheric accommodations.

Daily Bread

Good food (and plenty of fresh fish in season) is to be found at the main hotels in **Crackington Haven, Boscastle,** and **Port Gaverne,** at the small café on the cliff above **Port Isaac,** and in the friendly pubs in **Port Isaac, Crackington Haven,** and **Port Gaverne.** In addition, the seafood restaurant on the harbor in **Padstow,** roughly 30 minutes to the south, has an international reputation.

Tiny Port Isaac still takes fishing seriously.

♦ DAY SIX

A Day on the Cornwall Coast Path

BOSCASTLE ♦ CRACKINGTON HAVEN BOSCASTLE

- ♦ A day walk along the tortured Atlantic cliffs
- ♦ An afternoon tour of Tintagel Island

This Cornwall is very primeval: great, black, jutting cliffs and rocks, like the original darkness, and a pale sea breaking in, like dawn. It is like the beginning of the world....
—D. H. Lawrence, 1916

Isolation, both geographic and social, is palpable in Cornwall. Shielded from the outside world by the rugged ramparts of nearly 300 miles (over 450 kilometers) of coastal cliffs, all but severed from the rest of England by the Tamar River, there is something almost otherworldly about the southwest peninsula. Its landscape is littered with mysterious stone circles, quoits, and megaliths. Its history is steeped in legend. Its landmarks carry names unmistakably foreign, in a language that owes more to Celtic Ireland and Brittany than to Anglo-Saxon English. And its churches and villages are named after saints you've never heard of before—St. Just, St. Columb, St. Piran, and scores more. Secretive, wary Cornwall keeps to itself and has for millennia, avoiding, resisting, or simply ignoring Romans, Saxons, and Normans alike. It is on the way to nowhere.

This is a hard, harsh land. Gales scream in from the Atlantic, punishing the cliffs, stunting and twisting the trees, and ripping heavy slate shingles from thick-walled farmhouses. The soil is thin and farming is difficult. Still, Cornishmen have found ways to eke a living from the land. As many as 4,000 years ago they diverted streams to expose tin ore and sold the metal to Phoenician traders. Later they dug tin and copper mines, hundreds of feet deep and reaching far out beneath the ocean, until the industry collapsed in the nineteenth century (ruined stone towers that once housed steam engines, used to drain water from the mines, still haunt the cliffs). They also smuggled—brandy and tobacco and anything else of value—and scavenged wrecks, which were frequent (though stories that Cornishmen lured ships onto the rocks appear to be unfounded).

And they fished. They fished despite fearsome reefs, treacherous tides, unpredictable storms, and inadequate harbors. Later they traded in fish, especially in the pilchards that appeared in great silvery inshore shoals, watched for by cliff-top lookouts called "huers" (from whom we get the phrase "hue and cry"). Cleaned, pressed, salted, and packed in barrels, the tiny pilchard brought a long period of prosperity to the villages huddled here in the clefts on Cornwall's north coast. But the pilchard fishery collapsed in the mid-nineteenth century—cruelly, at the same time the market for tin collapsed.

Now tourism has come to Cornwall, in a big way in some places and not always attractively. But there is much of Cornwall that is still remote, still a bit wild and rough around the edges, and absolutely breathtakingly beautiful. Today's walk takes in a small part of the best of Cornwall.

🚶 ON THE EDGE: WALKING THE NORTH CORNWALL CLIFFS

Distance: 7.5 miles/12 kilometers one way, allow 3-4 hours; 12.5 miles/20 kilometers round trip, allow 5-6 hours
Difficulty: Moderate, with strenuous climb to High Cliff
Elevation Gain: 731 feet/223 meters at High Cliff
Gear: Walking shoes/boots (sneakers if it's dry), trousers or high socks (to protect against nettles, blackberry bramble), rain gear, sunblock, camera
Map: Ordnance Survey 1:50,000 Landranger or 1:25,000 Pathfinder series

How you structure today's walk depends in part on where you spent the night. You can begin at Boscastle, hike to Crackington Haven, and then hike or hitchhike back. Or, if you're already in Crackington Haven, start there, taking the second half of the itinerary first. To get to Boscastle from Port Isaac, take the coast road north through Port Gaverne and across the fields, then turn **left** onto the **B3314** and drive through **Delabole** (passing the largest quarry in Britain, 500 feet (150 meters) deep and 1.5 miles (2.5 kilometers) wide, from which the slate for roofs throughout Britain once was mined) until you reach the **B3266**. Here turn **left** and follow signs to Boscastle. As you enter the upper village, look for the **right** turn down **High Street** (which

116 ITINERARY: DAY SIX

changes its name as it plummets downhill to Fore Street, Dunn Street, and Old Road). At the bottom, turn **right** across the bridge over the Valency River and park in the lot on the right. If you stayed in **Crackington Haven** but still want to start from Boscastle, drive south up the steep hill from the beach, turn **right** onto the unclassified road signposted for High Cliff, continue just over 3 miles (about 5 kilometers), then turn **right** onto the **B3263** to Boscastle. The car park will be on your left near the bottom of the hill.

Boscastle has a split personality. The upper village, a wonderful collection of stone buildings with crazily tilted rooflines and big stone chimneys, grew around Bottreaux Castle, built in the twelfth century and now a grassy picnic area. (*Boscastle* is a corruption of *Bottreaux Castle.*) The lower village began to take shape in the mid-sixteenth century, when a quay was built to "improve" the narrow, crooked harbor, barely a crack in the cliffs but the only safe haven along some 40 miles (65 kilometers) of the north Cornwall coast. Even then it was no treat: the entry is so treacherous that sailing vessels were towed in by eight-man rowboats, aided by men with ropes on shore. By the 1800s the harbor was booming despite its limitations. Slate, china clay, and manganese ore were exported, and limestone (baked in a quayside kiln into fertilizer), timber, and general cargo were imported from Bristol. A shipbuilding yard, a malting house, a busy forge, and other workshops lined the harborside. Teams of horses for hauling goods up and down the steep valley were stabled in what now is the youth hostel. But the end was near; in 1893 the railroad reached nearby Camelford and the port began its inevitable decline. It's now used primarily by fishermen and pleasure boaters, and most of the harbor is owned by the National Trust.

Walk down along the right side of the harbor, past the National Trust shop (and the public lavatories), go up the lane toward a terrace of whitewashed cottages, and take the obvious path that climbs gently up the side of the slope toward Penally Point at the mouth of the harbor. Unless the day is very still indeed, you'll learn just how important this hard black slate headland is to Boscastle. Massive green swells, having traveled unbroken over thousands of miles of Atlantic, roll directly into the narrow harbor mouth, smashing into the opposite cliffs and shooting skyward from Eastern Blackapit, once a "blowhole" and now collapsed under the onslaught. Penally Point is Boscastle's natural jetty, a fantastic formation of wildly folded and buckled sedimentary rock that looks as if it had been squeezed by some giant fist while still warm. Later it was baked hard by the intrusion of igneous rock—the same volcanic activity that created the distinctive bands of white quartz in the cliff. The entire complex process, completed millions of years ago and revealed by the relentless ocean, is why Boscastle exists at all. Without Penally Point as a buffer, it would be only another ragged indentation in the coastline.

After exploring the headland, turn and climb north to the top of Penally Head (288 feet/88 meters), following the path to the fish-shaped wind vane. From here, follow the well-marked Coast Path along the cliff edge. The **Cornwall Coast Path** runs for 268 miles (429 kilometers) from North Devon, around Land's End, and back up to the South Devon Border. It is part of the **South West Peninsula Coast Path,** the longest of Britain's Long Distance Paths, running some 560 miles (900

118 ITINERARY: DAY SIX

Boscastle Harbor, the only "safe" haven along 40 miles of Cornwall's rugged coastline

kilometers) from Somerset to Dorset. With spectacular ocean views, soaring cliffs, rolling farmland, and a wealth of wildflowers, it may be the most beautiful walking country in Europe.

After perhaps 0.5 mile, the dark bulk of **Beeny Cliff** looms ahead across a deep, wave-wracked ravine. At its head is the delicate ribbon of **Pentargon Falls,** plunging from a suspended heather-clad valley to the black gravel beach 100 feet (30 meters) below. The path turns up the valley briefly to cross the stream by a small wooden footbridge, then turns left again, ascending the face of Beeny Cliff along a quartz-encrusted ledge (the best pictures of the waterfall are from here). Rounding the headland, the path skirts the steep drop to the ocean far below. Beeny Cliff projects farther out to sea and has steeper cliffs than many of the other headlands on this bit of the Cornish coast because it is made of *chert,* a flintlike rock harder (and blacker) than the slates that compose the rest of the coast. The views are terrific, both north to the **Beeny Sisters,** two rocky islets where gray seals sometimes bask, and south to **Meachard Rock,** just outside Boscastle Harbor.

At this point the path curves around to the north, turning slightly inland to avoid an area subject to landslides, then out to the cliff side again above **Gull Rock**. These slopes are an Impressionist painter's delight, splashed with brightly colored wildflowers—pink sea thrift and pale yellow primrose cling to rocky outcrops, bluebells shelter in the hollows early in the spring, blue violets and purple wild pansies contrast with yellow vetch and gorse and the tall magenta spikes of foxglove in midsummer, and acres of purple bell heather cloak the slopes in a color wash in late summer.

Farther along, the path turns inland again, climbing more and more steeply up the slope of **Rusey Cliff** toward the rocky outcrop at its summit. This is the hardest part of the walk—and a good opportunity to pause occasionally to enjoy the birds everywhere around you. Songbirds sing brightly from the brambles (which offer blackberries in the summer). Above the cliffs, buzzards prowl and gulls and kittiwakes float. Far below, black shags bob amid the ocean swells. From the top of Rusey Cliff, it's an easy traverse to **High Cliff,** just ahead.

At 731 feet (223 meters), High Cliff is the highest point on the Cornish coast. Looking up the coast, you can see much of northern Cornwall and a good bit of Devon as well. Inland, the dark bulk of Bodmin Moor rises above patchwork fields. Yet High Cliff is remarkable as much for its quiet as for its expansive views. The sea is there in all its terrible power, huge breakers foaming in to claw at the cliff face. But the thunder is lost to the wind; only songbirds break the aching quiet. It is as if the Atlantic were a silent movie projected on a vast blue screen.

Off to the north lies **the Strangles,** a wicked reach of reef that has claimed ships and lives for centuries. The beach below the long slope of landslides and ledges is a popular, but dangerous, swimming area—and a long walk back up. At the northern end of the beach is **Samphire Rock,** which takes its name from the plant whose fleshy gray leaves were once picked and pickled as a delicacy. Beyond Samphire is the reptilian head of **Cambeak** which, like Beeny Cliff, juts out to sea because it is harder than the surrounding rock. From High Cliff, the remaining 2 miles (3.2 kilometers) to **Crackington Haven** are a short, springy downhill stroll across close-cropped turf. Off to your right, across rolling meadows, is the handsome complex of **Trevigue Farm.** Tucked into a fold in the fields, its back to the wind, slate-roofed and stonewalled Trevigue has been altered relatively little since the sixteenth century. Today it is a dairy farm that operates a National Trust office and, in the summer, offers B&B and afternoon teas. (If you don't want to go as far as Crackington Haven this is a good place to rest and turn back to Boscastle, following country lanes.)

Assuming you began this walk at about 10:00 A.M., you should arrive at Crackington Haven at about 1:00 P.M.—with plenty of time for

Above Eastern Blackapit, a collapsed "blowhole" at the mouth of Boscastle Harbor

lunch at the beachside pub. In midsummer this is a busy, convivial place; in winter and early spring the little village, nestled in its valley, is virtually deserted. The hotels and many of the houses are shuttered against the storms, and sand blows across the road from the beach, gathering in lonely drifts in the pub's car park.

After lunch, you have a choice. If you're not up to walking back to Boscastle or the weather has taken a turn for the worse, simply stand opposite the pub car park and hitch a ride south. Folks are friendly here and you will be offered a lift quickly; Boscastle's only a five- or ten-minute ride away. (You may also be able to make arrangements for your B&B host to pick you up.) Then, consider visiting the ruins on Tintagel Island (see Diversions) this afternoon.

If there's still spring in your step (or the pub has revived it), walk south up the road out of Crackington Haven. Ignore the first right turn (signposted to High Cliff) and take the **second right** instead, up a lane to a farm. Continue **straight** ahead at the farm, ignoring turns to the left and right, go through the gate with the yellow marker, and follow the obvious path into the woods. A few hundred yards farther on, cross a small bridge and bear **right** in the direction signposted for "Woodgate." Cross a second bridge and turn **left** and continue south along the stream bank through the pretty, steep-sided valley. There are masses of primrose here in the early spring, along with bluebells. After perhaps 0.5 mile, ignore the second signpost to Woodgate (uphill right) and continue along the valley. Eventually you come to a four-way signpost (the right turn goes up to Trevigue Farm). Here again, continue **straight** ahead (bearing slightly to the right) in the direction of Pengold Farm. Cross a tributary stream, then bear **right** and climb the open hillside in the direction of the power lines. Stay to the right of the embankment and, when you reach the power-line poles, bear **right** and go up to the gate. Then go through the gate and turn **left** along a farm track. Go through the farmyard and down the lane (ignore the lane branching left), and eventually (after perhaps 0.5 mile) you'll reach the coast road.

Turn **left** and follow the coast road south through rolling fields. At the next farm you have another choice. If you follow the main road ahead and to the left, you'll quickly reach the B3263, where you can turn **right** and hitchhike the remaining 3.5 miles (5.6 kilometers) south to Boscastle. Alternatively, you can turn **right** into the lane opposite the farm and carry on (bearing **right** at the first intersection and **left** at the second) into the little hamlet of **Beeny**. Then just follow your nose around to the **left**, downhill and over the stream that becomes Pentargon Falls, then up again, past the campground, to the **B3263**. Here turn **right** and follow the road a further 1.5 miles (2.4 kilometers) down into Boscastle—having taken in both the breathtaking and the pastoral sides of the Cornish coast.

Tre, Pol, and Pen

An old Cornish rhyme says, *By Tre, Pol, and Pen, shall ye know most Cornishmen,* and the landscape is littered with these prefixes, as if there had been a shortage of alternatives. The language, though it sounds distinctly foreign, is the one native to these isles—a form of Celtic similar to Welsh, Breton, and Scots and Irish Gaelic. The prefix *tre* means "homestead" or "hamlet," *pol* means "pool," and *pen* means "chief," "hill," or "headland." Almost extinct a few years ago, Cornish is now being taught again in schools and universities, and if you are very lucky you may stumble into a Cornish-speaking evening at a pub.

DIVERSIONS
Tintagel

Tintagel. It has a magical, spine-tingling ring. Visions of the wizard Merlin and the great Arthur in his castle, his knights gathered at the Round Table, rise unbidden from the rocks, like a winter sea mist.

It's all fiction, of course. The castle here, in which Arthur is said to have been born, wasn't even built until seven centuries after he is said to have died. Still the legend remains, a product mostly of the last century—of Tennyson's *Idylls of the King* in particular—though fictitious "histories" involving Arthur go back as far as Geoffrey of Monmouth's twelfth-century *History of the Kings of England*. In the late 1800s, Victorian romantics flocked to the site and a huge "King Arthur's Castle Hotel" was built near the cliffs (prompting the National Trust to move quickly to make the coast north and south of Tintagel Island their first coastal property in England). It was at this point too that the little village of Trevena changed its name to Tintagel and threw itself enthusiastically into taking maximum economic advantage of its fortuitous location.

Still, Tintagel Island, far removed from the commercialism of the village itself, is wildly evocative and well worth a visit (open daily April through September 9:30 A.M. to 6:30 P.M.; October through March, Saturdays and Sundays 9:30 A.M. to 4:30 P.M.). Park at the western end of town and walk down the steep lane to the coast. The name Tintagel comes from the Cornish *tyn,* for "fort," and *tadgell,* or "constriction," and when you clear the cliff edge the reason is immediately

Gateway to legend: looking back at the Cornish coast from Tintagel Island

clear: the island is not an island at all, but a spectacular promontory connected to the mainland by a narrow, wave-worn neck of rock. The ruins of the twelfth-century castle cling to the cliffs while even more ancient ruins, dating from the fifth to eighth centuries and now thought to have been a trading settlement, are scattered across the summit and slopes of the promontory. Visit on a clear day and the views from the point are magnificent—a long stretch of wind-whipped, jagged coast, replete with caves and ledges, that looks as if it were torn asunder and heaved up out of the ocean only yesterday. Visit on a dreary day, with the cliffs veiled in mist and the vicious ocean only an ominous, invisible roar below, and the Arthurian legends seem palpably real.

CREATURE COMFORTS

See yesterday's suggestions.

"Cornish Cuisine"

It's said that the devil never came to Cornwall for fear of being put into a pie, and certainly pies of all kinds, especially fish pies, are an old staple in a county where the sea is never more than a few miles away and alternatives are few. There's mackerel pie, bream pie, conger (eel) pie, even "starry-gazy pie" made from pilchards (like sardines, and fished nearly to extinction) with their heads sticking up through the crust. But the "pie" most associated with Cornwall has nothing to do with the sea at all. The **Cornish pasty** (pronounced "*pass*-tee," to distinguish it from the scanty female garment of the same name) was the traditional lunch of Cornwall's tin miners. Cornish pasties are a short-crust pastry shell filled with chunks of steak (nowadays ground beef), potatoes, yellow turnip (called "Swedes" in England), onions, salt, and a lot of pepper. They are baked golden brown and originally sometimes even had fruit or jam at one end for "dessert." The best pasties come fresh from the local bakery, their crescent edges decoratively crimped (as distinct from the Devon pasty, which is folded in the center), and make a savory—and filling—lunch, best washed down with a pint of local ale.

◆DAY SEVEN

Exploring the Lizard
NORTH CORNWALL
LIZARD POINT/LAND'S END

- ◆ **A drive south to the cliffs of Bedruthan Steps**
- ◆ **A walk around Lizard Point**
- ◆ **An optional archaeological tour of the Land's End peninsula**

> *The wildest most impressive place I ever saw on the coasts of Britain . . . impressive in itself and as the notablest of British Capes.*
> —Thomas Carlyle, 1882

At the southern tip of England—the Land's End and Lizard peninsulas—sea, wind, and rock are locked in mortal combat. The rock is losing. There are sandy beaches—overdeveloped ones at Newquay and St. Ives and nearly deserted ones at Porthcurno—but for the most part this is a landscape of towering cliffs whipped by the wind, lashed by the sea, and finally yielding to the torture, leaving behind jagged pinnacles and fearsome reefs to snare passing ships. Above sheer cliffs of purple and green rock called *serpentine*, seabirds float on updrafts, wildflowers carpet the misty cliff edges, and what few trees survive hunch their gnarled shoulders, their branches twisted leeward like hair streaming in the wind.

Inland from the cliffs and the coastal farms, the southwest peninsula is empty. Once, millennia ago, this was all sea bottom and the heights of Bodmin Moor to the north were the shoreline. Then the sea retreated, leaving a barren expanse of gorse- and heather-cloaked moorland where today the Defence Ministry, a satellite tracking station, and the birds maintain an uneasy peace.

There is abundant evidence that people lived and farmed in these moors, thousands of years ago when the climate was more forgiving, and there are a few struggling inland communities once supported by tin mining. But most of the recent human settlement clings to the coastal perimeter, where cracks in the cliffs once gave shelter to fishermen and smugglers alike and now tourists come to enjoy the picturesque remains of another era, threatening to overwhelm what they seek to enjoy. Our challenge today is to trace a route that provides opportunities to experience the best and avoid the worst.

🚗 SOUTH TO THE LIZARD

Distance: About 95 miles/153 kilometers
Roads: Combination of minor and primary roads
Driving Time: 3-4 hours, including stops
Map: Michelin Map #403

From whichever north-coast community you spent the past two nights, drive east to the **A39**, then turn south. Below **Wadebridge**, at the head of the Camel River estuary, turn **right** onto the **A389**, through softly wooded vales, to **Padstow**. Padstow is a lovely old fishing and shipbuilding port, and the brightly painted shops around its sheltered boat basin are good places to buy the makings for a picnic lunch. Then follow signs for the **B3276** down the coast toward **Newquay**. About 15 minutes south of Padstow, watch for the National Trust sign on the right for **Bedruthan Steps**.

Bedruthan is a magnificent seascape. According to local legend, the "steps" were placed on the beach by the giant Bedruthan so he could cross the bay. In fact, the towering granite stacks are all that remains of what once were headlands. Sand and seawater under tremendous pressure ate into seams and layers of softer rock in the cliffs, first creating caves, then breaking through to form arches which ultimately collapsed, leaving the harder headland divorced from the mainland. Eventually the steps too will give way to the corrosive power of the sea, but today they act as buffers to a broad, sandy beach that offers safe (and remarkably warm) swimming in midsummer. Stairs cut into the stone in 1953 lead down to the beach and to a rock tunnel, which leads to yet another beach just to the south (accessible only at low tide).

From Bedruthan continue south on the A3276 for a few minutes to **Trenance**. Here the road forks; take the left fork to **St. Mawgan**, through the deep, wooded Vale of Mawgan, until you reach the A39 again (avoid Newquay, an overdeveloped coastal resort of little charm and dense traffic). Turn **right** onto the A39 and, after a few miles, follow signs for the **A30** to **Penzance**, some 40 miles (65 kilometers) to the south, much of it on high-speed divided highway.

At the roundabout east of Penzance you'll need to make a decision. The itinerary that follows takes you to the Lizard peninsula for an afternoon walk through three very different coastal landscapes, including the southernmost point of mainland England. The Diversions section, on the other hand, offers a tour of the archaeological wonders of the Penwith (Land's End) peninsula. For the former, read on; for the latter,

Exploring the Lizard **127**

turn to Diversions for directions.

For the main itinerary, turn **left** onto the **A394** away from Penzance (you may want to detour to take in the harborfront promenade or visit the Tourist Information Centre there), then drive east, past **St. Michael's Mount,** to **Helston.** Here, follow signs for the **A3083** to **Lizard.**

If you left North Cornwall at 9:00 A.M., it should now be about 1:00 P.M.—time to get settled and have lunch. See Creature Comforts below for the best places to stay, check in, grab a bite to eat, and then head off for an easy but varied afternoon walk.

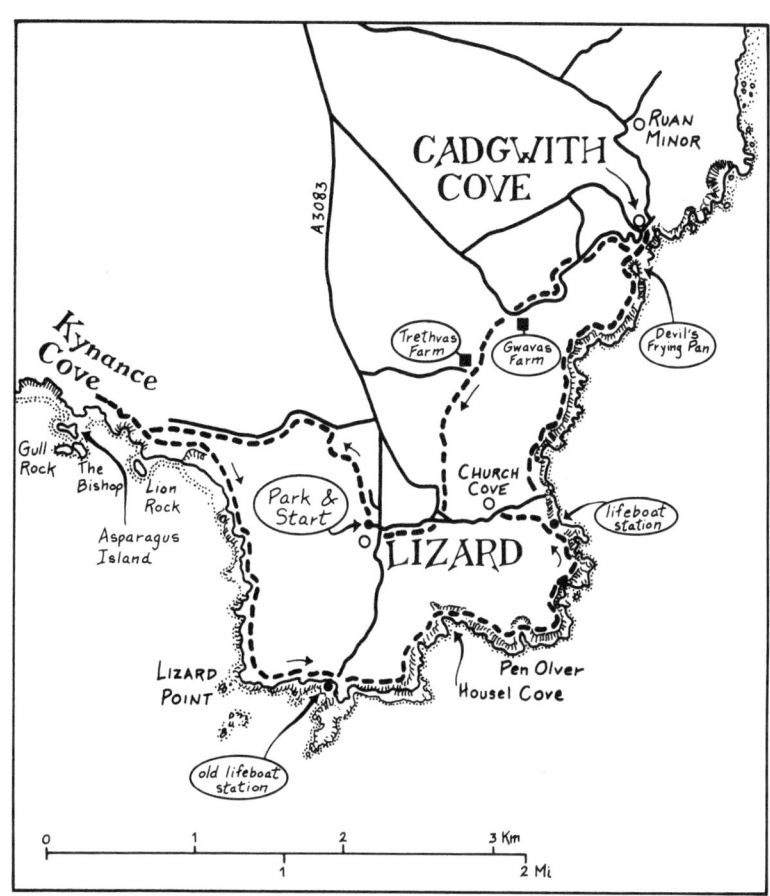

🚶 A WALK AROUND THE LIZARD

Distance: 6 miles/9.7 kilometers excluding Cadgwith, allow 2 hours;
   10 miles/16 kilometers extended to Cadgwith, allow 4 hours
Difficulty: Easy to moderate, with shortcuts possible
Total Elevation Gain: Negligible (short climb in Cadgwith)
Gear: Sneakers/walking shoes, rain gear, sunblock, camera
Map: Ordnance Survey Pathfinder Series #1372 (Sheet SW 61/71)

Unlike Land's End, where commercialization runs rampant, most of the Lizard peninsula is sufficiently off the beaten track to retain its charm. Yes, there's a café and gift shop at Lizard Point, but thanks to

The towering stone stacks at Kynance Cove, Lizard peninsula

the fast, arrow-straight A3083, the day-trippers come and go quickly. No matter where you start this afternoon's walk, the chances are you'll have the coast to yourself within five minutes of the car park.

This easy and scenic walk begins at the car park in the middle of **Lizard** village, but could just as easily begin at the National Trust car park at Kynance Cove or at Cadgwith Cove, should you decide to take the longer option. Your choice of whether to take the 2-hour or 4-hour walk should be influenced, in part, by the time of year. If it's summertime and you begin this walk at 2:00 P.M. you have plenty of daylight ahead of you to take the longer option. If it's anytime from late fall to early spring, however, you'll really have only enough light for the shorter walk.

From the middle of Lizard village, walk up the **A3083** in the direction of Helston for several yards and turn **left** into Chapel Lane. Keep to this unpaved track until it ends at the National Trust's paved road to **Kynance Cove.** Turn **left** and follow the road through the flat heathlands, rich with yellow gorse and magenta heather and pale lilac Cornish heath (which grows only on the Lizard) to the Kynance Cove car park. Walk to the northwest corner and out to the cliffs. Ahead is one of the finest seascapes in Britain.

Apart from sea, sky, and cliff, Kynance Cove looks nothing like the rest of Cornwall. There is none of the softness of the eroded sedimentary bluffs above the Strangles or even Bedruthan Steps. Here the cliffs are steep and hard, rising to 200 feet (60 meters) above a turquoise cove fringed by a magnificent white beach from which vicious towers of rock jut like prehistoric monuments. The shape and texture of the landscape here is defined by the unusual rock from which it is made: the igneous (volcanic) rock called *serpentine* because the pattern of its constituent minerals looks a bit like a reptile's skin. It is a durable and colorful rock, ranging from rusty purple to deep green, that is hard enough to stand up to the surf, yet soft enough to be carved and polished into jewelry and other decorative novelties by local craftsmen. (Ironically, the Lizard does not get its name from the serpentine of which it is made, but from the Cornish *lis,* for "palace," and *arth,* for "high" or "holy.") If you take the time to climb down to the beach you can see how weaknesses in the rock have been exploited by the sea, creating deep, mysterious caves, a blowhole called the Bellows, and weird pinnacle reefs—Lion Rock, Steeple Rock, the Bishop, Gull Rock, and Asparagus Island (where wild asparagus once grew). At low tide, it's a magical playground for children and a great place to swim.

From Kynance Cove, turn south along the well-marked coast path, skirting **Pentreath Beach,** dipping down into **Caerthillian Cove,** then back up to the cliff top again, following a generally level path along this most-exposed section of the peninsula. As you round **Old Lizard Head,** it becomes abundantly clear why there has been a lighthouse here at England's southern tip since 1619 (the first permanent light was built in 1752): the sea here is a mass of ragged reefs, laid in regular rows like shark's teeth and stretching out well over 0.5 mile (0.75 kilometer). Local residents apparently were not pleased by the first lighthouse; wreck scavenging was a regular and welcome source of income they were loath to lose. Today, the new lighthouse, just east of the tip, has a 5.5-million-candlepower light that can be seen 21 miles out to sea.

Reaching the point, the path wanders past a café and souvenir stand, then passes beneath the gaze of the brilliantly white lighthouse and uncomfortably close to the twin foghorns. Here the edge of the cliff is blanketed with the thick-stemmed Hottentot fig, called "ice plant" in California, and its fringed pink flowers dapple the slope. Next the path curves into **Housel Cove,** crosses a stream that plunges down to the small beach below, then climbs uphill along a deep ditch under an almost complete canopy of blackthorn that has clouds of white blossoms in the spring. On the other side of the cove is the headland of **Pen Olver,** from which the Spanish Armada was first seen in 1588.

Now the path turns northward, up the east coast of Cornwall, and the mood changes quickly. The first thing you notice is the quiet; birdsong seems more exuberant, if only because of the absence of wind, a constant companion for the last two days. The landscape is gentler and wildflowers are more varied too, sheltered here from the weather. In addition to the hardy gorse and heather of the north coast, there is flowering garlic early in the spring, along with pansies and dog violets, primrose, red campion, flag iris, and great yellow drifts of daffodils. After a few more minutes the lifeboat station appears below you on **Kilcobben Cove,** a reminder that even today scores of lives are saved each year by Britain's volunteer lifeboat crews. They are supported entirely by public contributions, so think of them the next time you see a lifeboat-shaped donation box at a pub.

Turn off the coast path at this point and walk up the paved lane from the lifeboat station. Below you on your right are the thatched and rose-covered cottages of Landewednack, more commonly called **Church Cove,** as simple and unspoiled as any Cornish hamlet can be in the twentieth century. In a small hut beside the stream that cuts the little valley, you can buy handmade serpentine jewelry for a fraction of the cost in the gift shops just a mile away in Lizard village.

If the day (or your energy) is waning, head up the road leading out of Church Cove, past the little Church of St. Winwalloe, made of serpentine and granite blocks, past more modern holiday bungalows, and straight into the center of Lizard village. If you want to continue, turn downhill toward the cove, and then **left** at the signpost to continue along the coast path. Following the path up out of the cove you pass another of Cornwall's scores of disused quarries, then reach the cliff top again, high above the English Channel. After perhaps a 1.5 miles (2.5

The lifeboat shed at Kilcobben Cove, Lizard peninsula.

kilometers) of gently following the cliff side, the path cuts sharply left and teeters along the vertiginous rim of a 200-foot (61-meter) chasm called the **Devil's Frying Pan**—actually a collapsed sea cavern. Then the path ducks through England's only stand of dwarf elms, emerges in back of a group of holiday cottages maintained by the National Trust, skirts around to their left, and drops down into beautiful **Cadgwith Cove**, a tumble of whitewashed and thatched stone cottages running down to a tiny shingle beach still used by fishermen catching crab, lobster, and mackerel.

After you've poked around this lovely village, backtrack uphill, behind a building called "the Long Barn" (which may have stored masts or sails), until you reach the switchback of a rutted lane. Instead of climbing up to the National Trust cottages again, however, turn **right** and follow the lane uphill as it zigzags past the blue-trimmed B&B overlooking the harbor, all the way to the holiday bungalows at the top of the hill. When a paved road joins from the right, continue **straight** ahead. The road takes a sharp turn to the **left**, then another to the **right**, and approaches Gwavas Farm, on the left beneath a grove of trees. Ignore the paved road as it turns right and continue **straight** ahead instead, down a short bit of farm track, over a gate stile, and then up to the top of a turf-clad stone wall—called a "hedge" in this vegetation-poor bit of England. Continue along the top of this wall, with neatly trimmed green pastures spread out left and right, until the path drops down stone steps set into the wall and follows a lane around the front of the farmhouse at Trethvas Farm. Then turn **left** down a short farm track and follow the marked footpath along the side of a wall, through several pastures, to the settlement of **Cross Common** dead ahead. When you reach the road, go **straight** ahead past the modern houses, turn **right** at the junction, and follow the road into **Lizard** village to your car.

DIVERSIONS
🚗 Touring Prehistoric Penwith

Distance: About 40 miles/65 kilometers (returning to Penzance)
Roads: Mostly minor "B" roads
Driving Time: About 4 hours, with stops
Maps: Ordnance Survey Landranger Series #203

If you are drawn irresistibly to places with names like **Land's End**, or if the weather doesn't look like cooperating with an afternoon walk around the Lizard, this car tour takes you down some of the least-traveled roads in the southwest tip of Cornwall and back into prehistory to visit a few of the Penwith peninsula's more than 800 archaeological sites.

Turn **right** at the roundabout outside of Penzance, drive west almost to the edge of town, and watch for signs for the **B3311**, a **right** turn off the A30. Take the B3311 to **Badger's Cross** and turn **left** onto a minor road (if you reach the intersection with the B3309 you've gone too far). About 1.5 miles (2.4 kilometers) farther, look for the signpost for **Chysauster**, an extraordinarily well-preserved Iron Age village. (From April through September, it's open 9:30 A.M. to 6:30 P.M. Monday through Saturday, and Sunday 2:00 P.M. to 4:00 P.M. From October through March, hours are 9:30 A.M. to 4:00 P.M. Monday through Wednesday and on Saturday, and Sunday 2:00 P.M. to 4:00 P.M.) From the small car park, walk uphill along a path through the trees to the main village complex, a group of eight circular houses—two rows of four on each side of a central "street"—made of carefully crafted thick stone walls that still stand as high as 3 feet (1 meter) in places (there are also several outlying buildings). The houses, excavated during the last century, all face away from the prevailing wind and are massive, averaging about 100 feet (30 meters) in diameter. The entries,

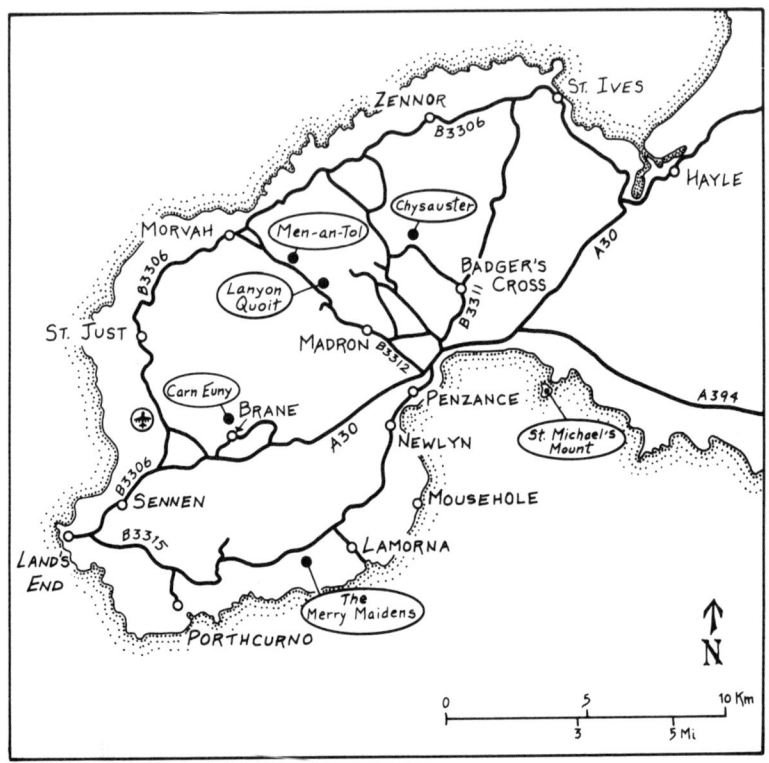

some with huge stone pillars on each side, lead to open internal courtyards for livestock and then to smaller round internal living quarters, each of which originally had a thatched roof supported by a central post. The eerie thing about Chysauster, given its excellent state of preservation, is how incredibly old it is. Archaeologists estimate it was first settled between 200 and 100 B.C. and was a busy settlement—guarded by a hill fort a mile away—for three or four centuries. Certainly the pastoral farmers who lived here had terrific views; you can see for miles across Mount's Bay and deep into the Penwith mainland from the main street.

From Chysauster, continue along the same road and turn **left** at the T-junction. Your objective is the town of **Madron** and you can get there either by zigzagging roughly southeast through minor lanes or by returning to Penzance and picking up the **B3312**. From Madron head northwest on the B3312, then follow the unclassified road toward **Morvah** on the opposite coast. Halfway across the peninsula you'll encounter massive **Lanyon Quoit** on the right. A *quoit* is a stone construction, like a giant picnic table, that once covered a *cromlech* or tomb, the whole complex having originally been covered with earth. There were Neolithic settlements here on the Penwith peninsula as long ago as 4000 B.C., and Lanyon Quoit, with its 18-foot (5.5-meter) capstone, is estimated to be some 5,000 years old. Its three upright supports were originally 8 feet (2.4 meters) high but were damaged in a storm in 1815 and had to be shortened when the structure was restored. It is still a marvel of primitive human engineering.

A mile or so farther on the same road, a small lane leads off to the right. Park opposite the art studio, walk perhaps 0.5 mile up the lane, and turn right at the signpost to **Men-an-Tol,** especially if you have back trouble. Men-an-Tol is a group of three standing stones, the central of which has a hole carved through it. According to tradition, if you crawl through the hole nine times your back problem will be cured. (On the other hand, if you can perform these maneuvers the problem couldn't have been too serious in the first place.) Men-an-Tol is but one of several ancient monuments within a few hundred yards of this spot. There is an engraved stone further up the lane, and a stone circle, called the **Nine Maidens,** off to the east. All are estimated to date from the period between 2000 and 1500 B.C.

Now return to your car, continue west to Morvah, and turn **left** onto the **B3306** coast road. Drive south through the former tin-mining center of **St. Just** and, just beyond the Land's End airport, bear **left** onto a minor road leading to the A30. Turn **left** at the T-junction, then **left** again almost immediately up a lane to the hamlet of **Brane.** At the fork in the center of the settlement bear **left** and follow the posted footpath up the rise to **Carn Euny,** another miraculously well-preserved Iron Age settlement with a bonus: a *fougou,* a 65-foot (20-meter) underground tunnel, roofed with granite slabs, leading to a corbeled chamber, the purpose of which is unknown—possibly a burial chamber, evolved from the earlier aboveground quoits, perhaps a temple.

From Brane, backtrack to the A30, turn **right,** and follow it south to **Land's End.** Until recently, this windswept bit of cliff top with the romantic name was little more than a tourist trap. Recently, however, an English developer bought the whole place—lock, stock, and souvenir shops. Preservationists were horrified at the thought of what he might do with it (he also bought the *other* end of the road, John O'Groats in far northern Scotland), but all he's really done is clean the place up. It's still commercial, just less tacky than before.

When you've had enough, drive back out the access road and turn **right** onto the **B3315,** following it through a gentler landscape of pastures and tiny port villages. **Porthcurno** is famous for its open-air Minnack Theatre, chiseled out of the cliffs high above the ocean. (The Minnack offers performances from Shakespeare to contemporary, from May through September.) The road now undulates from narrow bosky clefts to high, rolling hilltops. Just south of **Lamorna** watch for a sign

Chysauster, a 2,000-year-old village so well preserved you half expect the hearthstones still to be warm

identifying **the Merry Maidens,** a circle of nineteen standing stones (a *henge*) which, according to a legend that smacks more of recent puritanism than paganism, is allegedly a group of young ladies who were turned to stone for dancing on the sabbath. The two pipers who encouraged them are also frozen in stone, across and up the road a bit. The entire area around Lamorna is dotted with ancient monuments—standing stones, burial barrows, stone circles, and fougous—but no one really understands their significance. Clearly, however, Penwith was densely settled and much revered centuries, even millennia, before the birth of Christ.

CREATURE COMFORTS

Where you spend the night tonight will be determined by whether you decided to walk the Lizard or tour Penwith. You'll be heading north again tomorrow, so either location is fine. Options for lodging and meals in both areas are described below.

Daily Bed

The best places to stay on the Lizard are in **Mullion** and **Mullion Cove** halfway down the west coast, and **Cadgwith Cove** on the east coast just below Ruan Minor. Mullion is larger, has more places to stay and eat, but can be crowded in midsummer. Cadgwith Cove is a tiny thatched fishing village with only a few B&Bs and only one pub (which also has accommodations) but is completely unspoiled and is on this afternoon's walk route. Another good choice is **Helford,** an impossibly quaint hamlet tucked up a tidal creek on the Helford River at the northeast corner of the Lizard, and its nearby neighbors **Manaccan** and **St. Anthony.** This peaceful area of leafy valleys and sheltered inlets was a smuggler's paradise and is the locale of Daphne du Maurier's novel *Frenchman Creek.* After a day on the Cornish moors and cliffs, it might be just the right contrast. There are also farmhouse B&Bs scattered throughout the Lizard; check the books in Further Reading for addresses and phone numbers, or stop in at the Tourist Information Centre in Penzance en route for details.

On the Penwith peninsula, as on the Lizard, accommodations are scattered among a number of coastal villages, including **Zennor** (where D. H. Lawrence lived while writing *Women in Love*), **Sennen Cove, Lamorna,** and **Mousehole** (pronounced "mao-zul"). In addition, there will be lodgings galore in both **Penzance** and the resort town of **St. Ives.** For options that are a bit more off the beaten track, consult the listings in Further Reading or stop in at the Tourist Information Centre in Penzance. For advance reservations and assistance, write the Penzance TIC at Station Road, Penzance, Cornwall, TR18 2NF, or call (0736) 62207.

Daily Bread

Scenery, not food, is Cornwall's strength; beyond fish and chips (which can be fabulous here) and Cornish pasties, menus run to the predictable and quality is often mediocre. There are a few exceptions, however. There are good choices of restaurants and pubs in **St. Ives** and **Mullion,** and the pubs in both **Manaccan** and **Helford** have imaginative, well-executed menus and wonderful atmosphere. There are, of course, a lot of restaurants—both freestanding and in hotels—in **Penzance,** and there is one superb (and expensive and often booked-up) restaurant on the riverside at **Helford.** In addition, if you choose to stay in a farmhouse B&B in a more remote area, ask if evening meals are available, since you'll be able to check in very early.

♦ DAY EIGHT

The Secret Side of Cornwall

HELFORD ♦ THE FAL ESTUARY
FOWEY ♦ DARTMOOR

- ♦ A tour through smugglers' and pirates' lairs
- ♦ Ferry rides across languid estuaries
- ♦ A choice of sheltered landscape gardens
- ♦ Back into Devon and eerie Dartmoor

> ... there, suddenly before her... was the creek, still and soundless, shrouded by trees, hidden from the eyes of men.... her hands went clammy, her mouth felt dry and parched, and she felt, for the first time in her life, a funny strange spasm of fear. This was the Frenchman's hiding place—that was his ship.
>
> —Daphne du Maurier
> *Frenchman's Creek*, 1941

The south coast is Cornwall's soft underbelly, a gentle landscape where the crooked fingers of the sea reach deep into thickly wooded valleys, creating some of the finest deep-water moorings in Britain. It comes as a bit of a shock, after the towering cliffs and bleak, wind-blasted moors of the north coast, to stumble onto these tranquil vales. Yet this secretive side is just as central to Cornwall's mystique as the rugged north: it is guarded and devious, the lair of smugglers and pirates.

South Cornwall is a "drowned coast." Millions of years ago, Cornwall was a broad plateau, high above the sea. Streams draining the higher elevations gradually cut deep into the granite rocks on their way to the sea, creating deep valleys. Then the plateau began tilting, its northern edge lifting higher, creating dramatic cliffs, its southern edge dipping into the sea and creating miles of tidal creeks and deep estuar-

The Secret Side of Cornwall   **139**

Fowey: once thick with pirates, today it harbors wealthy yachtsmen.

ies. In the days when ships had shallower drafts, and before these inlets' upper reaches were silted in, villages far inland were active trading ports for tin, copper, timber, and other bulk commodities. Almost as important for the local economy, the secluded, tree-draped tidal creeks were ideal havens for the small, fast ships favored by pirates and smugglers: easily reached, well protected, and maddeningly difficult for pursuers to penetrate.

Today, most commercial activity—legal and illegal—has given way to pleasure boating. Thousands of sailboats bob at anchor in Cornwall's creeks, halyards slapping languidly against a forest of aluminum masts. Herons haunt the shoreline and curlews pick their way across muddy tidal flats. Out of the wind and blessed by warm sea currents that moderate the winters, formal gardens flourish along the south coast, and wildflowers—white sea campion, bindweed, and daisylike sea asters—grow along the beaches and marshes.

For most of the day today, you'll be meandering along this serrated coast, moving from one quiet village to another. Then, as the day draws to a close, you'll abandon the shoreline and head inland to the moody but magnificent wilderness of Dartmoor.

CREEKS AND CASTLES, FERRIES AND FISHING PORTS

Distance: About 110 miles/177 kilometers, Helston to Bovey Tracey
Roads: A combination of primary and secondary roads
Driving Time: Most of the day, with frequent stops
Map: Michelin Map #403

The brochure for a restaurant in **Helford** describes the village as "absurdly pretty" and it's not tourism hyperbole. In this tiny hamlet strung along the banks of an inlet of the Helford River, it is not difficult to imagine Cornwall as it was a century or two ago. The one-lane road (closed to cars in midsummer) slips down the hill to the village, squeezes past a clutch of simple cottages, whitewashed and thatched, fords the creek by means of a "splash" (a drier alternative is a few yards farther on), passes a general store, and dribbles to a dead end at a wonderfully atmospheric pub. A few small fishing boats rest on the mud at low tide. In season, a tiny ferry runs pedestrians across the river (to another pub). Frenchman's Creek, from the du Maurier book of the same name, is the next inlet upriver. If you have not already discovered Helford, perhaps at dinner last night, it's worth a detour this morning.

Then find your way to the **A394** running north from **Helston,** past ruins of the tin-mining industry, toward **Penryn.** Outside of Penryn follow signs for the **A39** toward **Truro,** but after about 5 miles (8 kilometers) watch for a sign to the **King Harry Ferry** off to your right (or simply continue to the **B3289** and turn right). The minor road plunges down into a leafy valley with trees arching overhead and glossy green ivy carpeting the slope, finally reaching **Trelissick Garden** just above the River Fal. Trelissick is a 376-acre woodland garden specializing in rhododendron, azalea, camellia, and more than 130 varieties of hydrangea—all lovers of the acidic soils common in Cornwall. The neo-Greek nineteenth-century mansion is not open to the public but the grounds, which offer lovely views of the Fal estuary, are managed by the National Trust (open March through October).

The King Harry Ferry (so named because Henry VIII allegedly swam his horse across the river here) winches itself slowly across the pastoral river, still so deep here that oceangoing vessels moor in the channel. From the ramp on the opposite shore follow the B3289 south to **St. Just in Roseland.** The entire peninsula is a garden spot, but the little thirteenth-century Church of St. Just, on the hillside above its own inlet, has its own miniature subtropical botanical garden. Farther south, on the **A3078,** is **St. Mawes Castle,** a squat bastion of three cloverleaf-shaped walls surmounted by a central crenelated tower. The castle, built between 1540 and 1543 by Henry VIII, is one of two designed to guard the entrance to Carrick Roads, the deepwater harbor at the

The Secret Side of Cornwall **141**

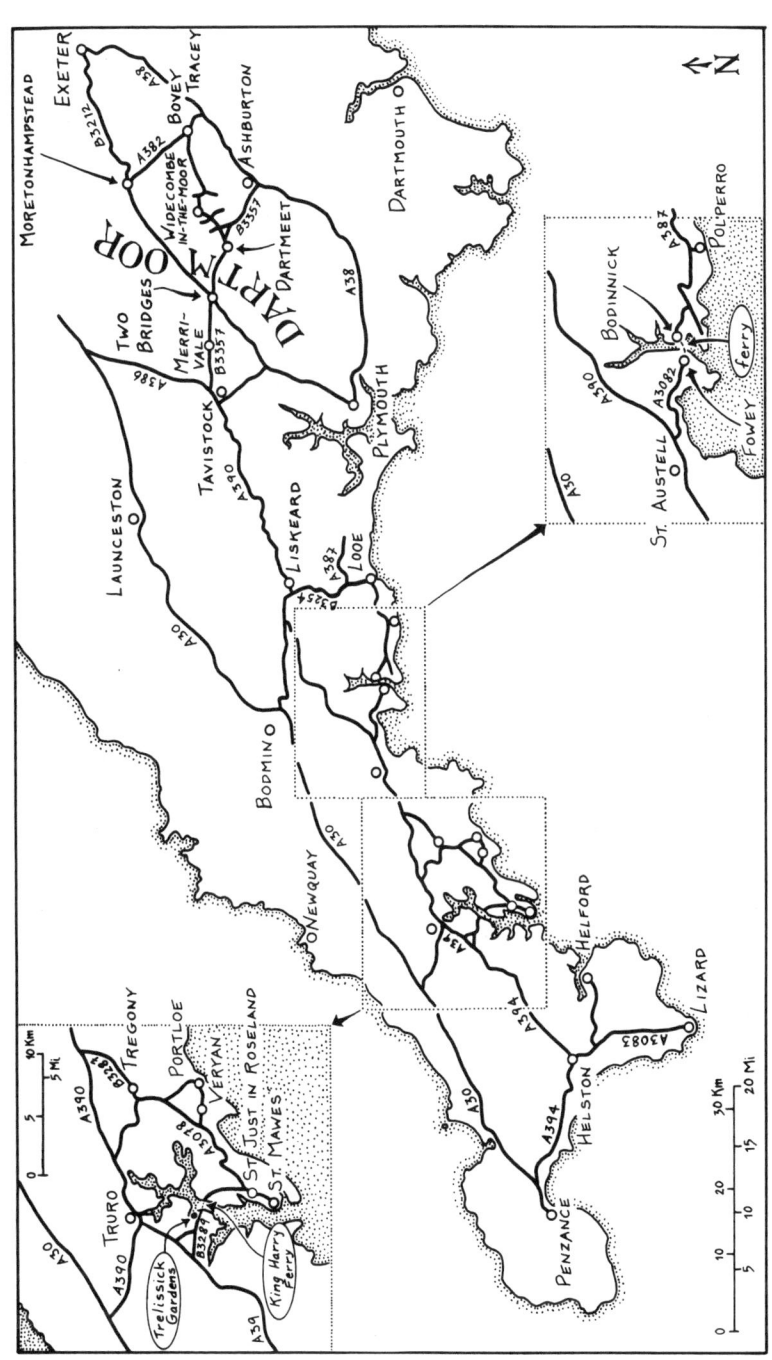

Henry the VIII's fortress on the Fal

mouth of the River Fal. (Ironically, it fell to a land attack by Cromwell's troops in 1646 without a shot being fired because all the guns are facing the sea.)

From St. Mawes, take the **A3078** north and, after about 6 miles (9.7 kilometers), turn **right** onto the minor road signposted for **Veryan.** You dip down into the Pendower Valley, then up again, and enter Veryan village, nestled in a little wooded swale—a lovely cluster of whitewashed cottages with splendid gardens. Five of the houses are round and topped with crosses, built by devout villagers in the nineteenth century who wanted to be sure there were no corners in which the devil could hide.

Follow the road to the coast signposted for **Portloe,** a classic Cornwall fishing village tucked away in a crack in the cliffs, then swing inland again and, when you reach the A3078, turn **right.** At the intersection with the **B3287** in **Tregony** turn **right** again and, a few miles later, turn **right** onto the **A390.** Ahead and to the left, the white peaks of the "Cornish Alps"—the spoil heaps of the china clay works—scar the landscape. China clay, originally used to make porcelain, today is used to make paper shiny, for cosmetics, and for some medicines. It is not "clay" in the common sense of the word; it is extracted from decomposed granite and feldspar, and represents only a little over one-tenth of the mined stone. The rest is waste, and while the mining companies have begun reclaiming it, they have a lot of catching up to do.

Continue through St. Austell on the A390, then follow signs to the **A3082** and **Fowey** (fans of the "Poldark" novels and television series may want to detour to Charleston, the tiny port just below St. Austell that figures in many scenes). The road skirts the dunes at **Par Sands,** then turns south. A minor road branches right to the former pilchard-fishing village of **Polkerris** and to **Menabilly Barton.** Menabilly House, the seventeenth-century manor house, was the home of novelist Daphne du Maurier and one of the models for "Manderley" in *Rebecca*.

Fowey (pronounced "foy") may be the most charming village on the entire south Cornwall coast. Elizabethan, Georgian, and Victorian houses cascade down narrow switchback streets to the harbor, which it shares with its neighbor **Polruan** across the mouth of the River Fowey. Fowey lacks the more modern bungalow development that mars many other coastal communities, largely because most of the usable land was built up centuries ago. Once the most important port on England's south coast, today it is a major yachting center (though freighters still ply the river beyond Bodinnick to take on china clay). In the fourteenth and fifteenth centuries this was the home port of the notorious "Fowey Gallants," pirates, privateers, and smugglers who repeatedly attacked ships in the channel and invaded French ports to gather what spoils they might contain, until the French finally retaliated in 1456 and burned most of the town. Later, Henry VIII built two small castles, one on each side of the harbor mouth, across which a chain was drawn to seal it off from invaders. Fowey is a terrific place to have a late lunch, at any of several comfortable pubs or the restaurant on the quay. Afterwards you may want to wander some of the back streets or take the tiny passenger ferry across the harbor to Polruan.

Then, drive upriver and take the car ferry across to Bodinnick. Drive up the hill past the inn and follow signs through the maze of minor lanes that crisscross the countryside to **Pencarrow Head** and **Polperro.** If you are traveling in the height of summer, your best bet is to avoid this picturesque artist's haven and **East** and **West Looe** as well. Off-season they are lovely, but in midsummer the trinket and ice cream stands blot out most of what is genuine about these villages. Follow the **A387** from Polperro to West Looe, cross the bridge to East Looe, and stay on the A387 as it runs up the east bank of the river. After a couple of miles, fork **left** onto the **B3254** for **Liskeard.** Here rejoin the **A390** and turn **right,** drop down into the steep-sided Tamar River Valley east of **Gunnislake,** cross into Devon, and zigzag back uphill to **Tavistock.**

UP INTO DARTMOOR

As you enter Tavistock, turn **right** at the sign for the town center, then **left** at the roundabout. A few blocks farther you run directly into the imposing Town Hall. Tavistock is the western gateway to **Dartmoor,** and during the summer season (Easter through October) there is a National Park and Tourist Information Centre in the Town Hall building. If you are unsure about where to stay tonight in Dartmoor, this is a good place to get local accommodation brochures and, if it's getting late, to book a bed ahead.

Then take the **B3357** (right as you face the Guildhall) east out of town, over the River Tavy, and sharp **left** up the slope above the river. Almost immediately, the landscape begins to change. The road climbs steadily out of town and, on the other side of a cattle grid, you leave pastoral Devon behind. The hedgerows disappear, the cattle give way to sheep, and cultivated land yields to boulder-strewn, close-cropped grazing land with scattered clumps of gorse, blackthorn, and bracken. Up ahead, a bizarre rocky outcrop looms above the rolling moorland—a classic Dartmoor tor (from the Celtic *twr,* or "tower").

A few hundred yards beyond the pub at the wryly named hamlet of **Merrivale,** you begin to see evidence that this bleak landscape was heavily settled thousands of years ago. On the moorland to the right of the road a row of parallel stones, a lone standing stone, and a stone circle lie within a few yards of each other. Farther ahead, there is evidence of primitive hut circles. The best way to appreciate the extraordinary richness of Neolithic, Bronze Age, and Iron Age sites scattered across Dartmoor is to take one of the National Park Authority's guided walks,

Dartmoor's characteristic tors are eerie, forbidding—and great fun to climb.

and that's the plan for tomorrow morning. This afternoon, therefore, the only remaining task is to get settled. The best places to find accommodation are **Widecombe-in-the-Moor** and the eastern fringe of the moor between **Bovey Tracey** and **Moretonhampstead**.

It's not easy finding your way around Dartmoor; signposts are inconsistent and tend to disappear altogether in the remotest places. Natives say this is a hangover from World War II, when signposts were stripped to confuse German spies parachuted in under cover of darkness. The truth is more prosaic: the National Park Authority wants to guide most of the traffic to the major roads, to protect the fragile countryside. Consequently, it helps to have an Ordnance Survey Map (Landranger Series #191)... or a great deal of patience. To get to Widecombe, continue on the B3357 through **Dartmeet**—little more than a pair of hotels and a bridge—and then take the first **left**. Follow this single-lane road straight ahead into the hamlet of **Ponsworthy**. In the center of the village, turn **left** through the "splash" and continue straight ahead, along a slope above the East Webburn River, into Widecombe, distinctive for the tall tower of its Church of St. Pancras. Late in the afternoon, after the day-trippers have departed, this is a lovely spot, an oasis of pastoral tranquility amidst the vast, barren moorland. If you're staying here tonight, you're home. If you are going on to Bovey Tracey, continue up the steep hill out of the village on the **B3387** and stay on this road for about 7 miles (11 kilometers). The National Park Headquarters is at **Parke,** on your left and well marked, and the Tourist Information Centre in Bovey Tracey is near the car park on Station Road, on the right beyond the roundabout.

DIVERSIONS

The Dartmoor National Park Authority offers evening talks and slide shows at four locations—Ashburton, Postbridge, Princetown, and Parke/Bovey Tracey—on a wide variety of subjects, including legends and folklore, archaeology, wildlife, and history, among others. If you have time this evening (and especially if tomorrow's weather report suggests that walks on the moors are unlikely) take in one of these talks, offered for a minor charge by experienced and enthusiastic park officials and local volunteers. A complete listing of talks (which generally begin at 8:00 P.M.) can be found in the park authority's newspaper, the *Dartmoor Visitor*. (**Note:** In midsummer, when the sun lingers until 9:00 P.M., evening guided walks are also offered; they too are listed in the park authority newspaper.)

CREATURE COMFORTS
Daily Bed

Farmhouse B&Bs are well organized in and around Dartmoor. Most are listed in *Stay on a Farm* (see Further Reading) and several also print their own brochures, available at Tourist Information Centres. Dartmoor is sparsely settled; with the exception of Widecombe-in-the-Moor, most accommodations—from B&Bs to guesthouses and hotels—are around its eastern and northern fringes, especially between Moretonhampstead and Newton Abbot. Given how much time you can spend wandering around the narrow lanes of Dartmoor, your best bet may be to use the Book-a-Bed-Ahead service at the information center at Tavistock, Town Hall Building, Bedford Square, Devon, telephone (0822) 2938. If you find yourself on Dartmoor's eastern fringe as evening falls, go to the Bovey Tracey Tourist Information Centre, Station Road, Devon, telephone (0626) 832047 and use their accommodation service. For advance bookings, the Dartmoor Tourist Association publishes an annual *Guide to Dartmoor* with details on accommodations; for a copy, write to the Tourism Development Officer, DNP Visitor Information Centre, The Duchy Hotel, Princetown, Devon, or telephone (0822 89) 567. The West Country Tourist Board, Southernhay East, Exeter, Devon EX1 1QS also has a variety of brochures. Ask for the color *Devon Farms* B&B brochure. There are also two youth hostels in Dartmoor, at Steps Bridge (northeast corner) and Bellever (near Postbridge).

Daily Bread

As in most remote areas, pubs and hotels are your best bets for dinner tonight, unless the place you are staying offers evening meals. The *Dartmoor Visitor* newspaper, published seasonally by the park authority, has detailed listings and is available (free) at any Park Information Centre. The choices will be better in larger villages, like **Bovey Tracey, Ashburton, Manaton, Chagford,** and **Okehampton.** See Further Reading for recommendations on the best pubs.

Fanciful fisherman's cottage, Fowey

◆ DAY NINE

A Day of Contrasts: Dartmoor and Dorset

DARTMOOR ◆ ABBOTSBURY

- **A guided walking tour of Dartmoor**
- **An alternative drive through Dartmoor's highlights**
- **A short drive into pastoral Dorset**

> *As you value your life or your reason keep away from the moor.*
>
> —Arthur Conan Doyle
> *The Hound of the Baskervilles,* 1902

Dartmoor, England's last great wilderness. Grim, forbidding, and elemental, its bleak, windswept moors and weird granite outcrops rise from the gentle soul of Devon like a nightmare. Shattered tors thrust up out of the sodden peat like the claws of some malevolent beast lurking just beneath the quivering surface.

Vast and silent under moody leaden skies, Dartmoor is what the earth must have looked like when the first rains came and only the most primitive forms of life could survive.

Ordnance Survey maps of Dartmoor are largely blank; roads, villages, farms, even footpaths hesitate around the edges, then seem to lose heart. Few penetrate inland. In their place the maps post stark warnings—DANGER AREA—dozens of them, printed in red amidst the crooked blue fingers of hundreds of tiny streams and bogs. It's said that only one escapee from Dartmoor's fearsome prison ever went uncaptured; he was swallowed up by Fox Tor Mire—the "Grimpen Mire" of the Baskerville mystery. The rest have all been found—hopelessly lost in

The barren prospect from Hound Tor

the trackless waste, paralyzed by fear of the gaping unknown or their own evil imaginings, or simply sick and wet.

So desolate and eerily menacing is Dartmoor that it comes as a shock to discover that this profoundly inhumane landscape was once densely populated. Some 3,000 to 5,000 years ago, more people lived in Dartmoor than do today. The evidence of their passing is everywhere; hut circles, standing stones, cairns, tombs, stone rows, and tumuli of every description cover the moors. Even if the climate were more forgiving than it is today, life on prehistoric Dartmoor must have been brutally harsh. Somehow the ancient remains only reinforce the otherworldliness of the place, the queer feeling that time and evolution are somehow suspended here. Sherlock Holmes's partner Dr. Watson said it best: "... if you were to see a skin-clad, hairy man crawl out from a low door, fitting a flint-tipped arrow on the string of his bow, you would feel that his presence there was more natural than your own."

Frost-shattered and eroded, Dartmoor's tors seem like live things clawing their way to the surface from deep within the earth.

🚗 NATIONAL PARK GUIDED WALKS

Distance: Varies; most last 2-3 hours
Difficulty: All but the 6-hour walks are easy
Total Elevation Gain: Generally negligible
Gear: Walking shoes/boots, preferably waterproof, rain gear, lunch for 6-hour walk
Map: Unnecessary, but Ordnance Survey Landranger Series #191 may make orientation and driving easier

The best way to unlock the secrets of Dartmoor is to take one of the hundreds of **guided walks** scheduled by the National Park Authority from April through October (a more limited schedule is offered off-season). In midsummer, as many as four guided walks may be offered each day, covering different parts of Dartmoor and a wide array of special subjects, from megaliths and other antiquities to industrial archaeology, wildlife, and farming, among others. The walks (for which there is a minor charge) are led by entertaining and informed volunteers and park officials, and range from 1½-hour strolls to 2-, 3-, and even 6-hour moorland walks.

A complete listing of departure times, topics, and locations of guided walks is printed in the park authority's newspaper the *Dartmoor Visitor,* along with a map to help locate the starting points around the park. For the independent-minded, the park authority also publishes a series of walking guides and brochures, available at any Park Information Centre.

Devon Cream Tea

All those signs you see outside tea shops, bakeries, and even remote farmhouses for "cream teas" have very little to do with tea at all. The signs are code for Devon's most famous delicacy, *clotted cream,* an incredibly rich form of heavy cream created by steaming milk from Jersey cows on a double boiler until the cream, which rises to the top, forms a thick, buttery crust. Tea, in fact, is just an excuse to consume clotted cream, with jam-covered scones as the "carrier." The correct form to follow in this English version of the tea ceremony is to split a scone crosswise, slather it with strawberry jam, and top it with as large a dollop of clotted cream as you can get away with. Tea—with milk and without sugar—is used to wash it down and cleanse the palate for a fresh attack. You may wish to practice this methodology several dozen times to be sure you've got it right.

🚗 A DRIVING/WALKING TOUR
🚶 OF DARTMOOR

Distance: About 30 miles/48 kilometers
Roads: Minor and one-lane roads; watch for sheep!
Driving Time: 5-6 hours, including stops and walks
Map: Dartmoor National Park Map or Ordnance Survey Landranger #191

Dartmoor is a 365-square-mile (950-square-kilometer) relic, the deteriorated remains of a huge dome of rock that, some 350 million years ago, may have reached Alpine heights. The dome was created when molten rock welled up beneath the sedimentary layers that covered the land's surface, pushing the whole mass skyward. Over the eons, rain-fed streams, wind, and frost cut through the softer surface rocks, exposing the harder granite below. The ragged tors that puncture Dartmoor's horizon are the fractured remains of the once-molten mass. Their bizarre shapes, and the rubble and boulders (called *clitter*) that cover their slopes, are evidence that the destruction continues today—wind and water eating away at the weak planes in the granite structure, frost wedging them apart.

In between the tors is a deep, soggy blanket bog—vast acreages of peat created when rain falls too fast to drain off. Outsiders tend to think of moors as low-lying swamps, but the truth is quite the opposite: Dartmoor, rising to over 2,000 feet (610 meters), is the highest spot in southern England. As moisture-laden air sweeps in off the Atlantic, it rises and cools as it struggles to clear the tors, dropping an average of 60 inches (152 centimeters) of rain annually—and as much as 100 inches (254 centimeters) at the moor's western edge. Even on a sunny Devon day, dense, disorienting mists can descend on Dartmoor in minutes.

Under these sodden conditions, vegetation has no opportunity to decay. The result is a gigantic mossy sponge, terrific for flood control but too acidic for all but a few plants. The plants that survive are obvious throughout Dartmoor: bilberry, spiky yellow-flowered gorse, and a variety of sedges and grasses, all of which have thin, hard leaves and stems that resist transpiration and minimize the amount of acid water the plant must take up. The heather that adds such color to this otherwise bleak landscape in August has an additional advantage: a fungus that penetrates the entire plant and is able to use the acid in the water. Wherever drainage is better, bracken quickly colonizes the area.

Ambitious eighteenth-century agricultural developers tried to convert the moorland to farms, but the land rebuffed them; today stone walls enclose tracts of stubbornly wild moor, mute testimony to their failure. On the lower slopes, tough Blackface and Cheviot sheep, hardy

A Day of Contrasts: Dartmoor and Dorset

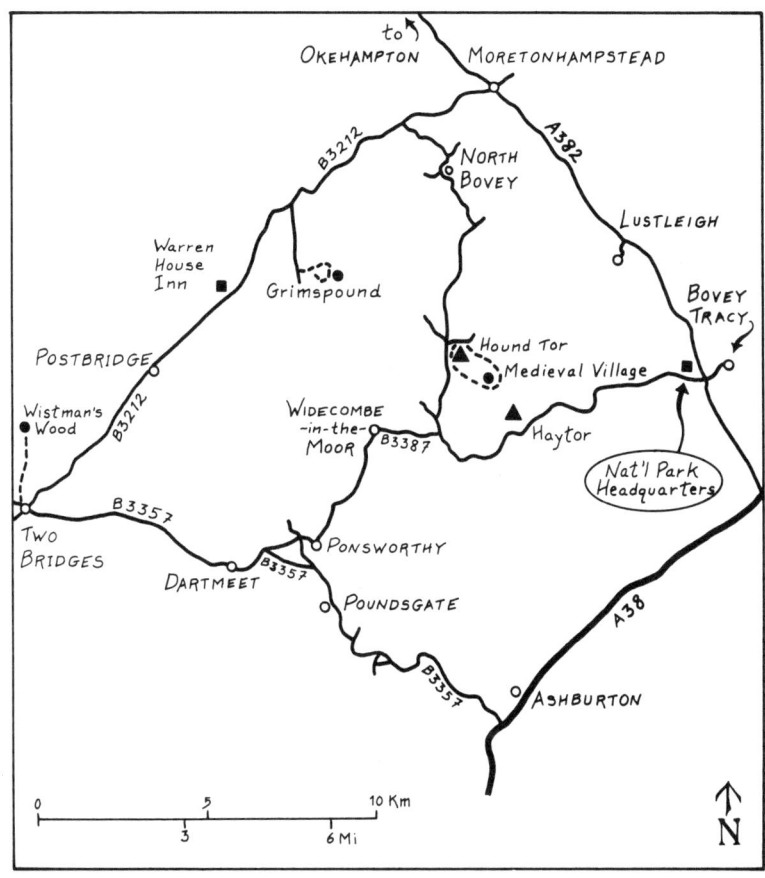

long-haired Galloway cattle, and wild (and dangerous) Dartmoor ponies compete with the bracken for grazing space. The bracken always wins, however, and must be burned off regularly.

Still, scientists think the climate must have been more hospitable here thousands of years ago, when Neolithic and Bronze Age man came to Dartmoor. How else to explain the amazing density of their settlements and monuments? Today's driving tour—which includes a few short walks as well—explores some of the most intriguing parts of this wet wilderness, including the largest Bronze Age settlement in the moor.

Begin at the turnoff from the **B3387** to **Hound Tor,** roughly halfway between **Widecombe-in-the-Moor** and **Haytor Vale.** It's the second left if you start by climbing up out of Widecombe, and the first right after Hay Tor if you come from Bovey Tracey. The one-lane road runs north along the top of the grimly named Bonehill Down

Dartmoor's wild ponies are picturesque but dangerous, especially in foaling season.

(bear **right** at the first fork) and, up ahead on the right, **Hound Tor** dominates the skyline. Bear **right** at the next intersection and park opposite the tor. Don your waterproofs and begin the morning's first exploration.

Hound Tor has its Baskervillian name because its eroded rocks are said to look like a pack of running hounds. It's an arguable notion. There is a longstanding legend that the black hounds of hell roam these hills, but a more likely explanation comes from the fact that the wind howls through the clefts in the tor during severe storms. If the morning is misty (most mornings in Dartmoor are) Hound Tor can be magically evocative. If you are blessed with sun, the summit of Hound Tor offers spectacular views of the surrounding moorland, including the massive hump of Hay Tor to the southeast.

After you've had a look around, climb down from the tor and, with your back to the car park, walk a few hundred yards downhill to the remains of a settlement sheltering in the lee of Greator Rocks. These stone walls are the best-preserved remains of what are estimated to have been over 100 medieval farming villages in the moors. Excavations here suggest that this site was occupied by farmers between the tenth and fourteenth centuries. It was probably abandoned during the

Black Death, which killed more than a third of Devon's population. Standing amidst the ruins you cannot help being overcome by how brutally primitive life must have been here only 600 years ago.

Return to the car park by walking around the left side of Hound Tor. At the top of the ridge, near the edge of a rectangular patch of gorse, there is a circular *cist,* a small prehistoric tomb. Then return to the car park.

Now take the road in the center of the three-branched fork, heading due north (as if you had continued straight ahead earlier instead of stopping at Hound Tor). After 1.5 miles (2.4 kilometers), turn **left** at the T-junction, then **right** almost immediately thereafter, and finally **left** again down the narrow road signposted for **North Bovey.** You enter this lovely little village on the edge of the moor over a narrow bridge across the River Bovey, pass its church, on a knoll on the left, and come upon its central green, surrounded by thatched-roof stone cottages. Continue past the hotel, then bear **left** at the fork and drive out to the **B3212,** which runs between Moretonhampstead and Two Bridges. Turn **left** toward Two Bridges and drive south a little over a mile (over 1.5 kilometers), then turn **left** and drive another 1.5 miles or so (around 2.5 kilometers) to the signpost for **Grimspound** on the left. Park off the road and walk up the clear path between Hookney and Hameldown Tors. After a hundred yards or so, you enter what you gradually realize is a huge stone circle, or *pound,* enclosing an entire village of round stone huts.

There is some evidence that Mesolithic man had begun clearing the forests of Dartmoor as early as 8000 B.C., but the first real population boom came in the Bronze Age, beginning roughly in 2500 B.C. This was Dartmoor's busiest period; Bronze Age farmers cleared most of the remaining forest, established formal field systems divided by parallel stone walls called *reaves,* and lived in groups of circular stone huts with turf or heather thatch roofs. Grimspound, with its huge protective wall, is one of the largest and best preserved of these settlements in Dartmoor.

Next, return to the B3212, turn **left** and continue southwest across the barren, windswept moors, past the isolated Warren House Inn (whose fire is alleged not to have gone out in over 100 years), through **Postbridge,** with its medieval "clapper" bridge made of huge flat granite slabs, to **Two Bridges** on the West Dart River. Here, park in the lot opposite the Two Bridges Hotel, and after fortifying yourself with lunch at the pub, walk the 2 miles (3.2 kilometers) up the marked footpath to **Wistman's Wood** for a view of what Dartmoor may have looked like before the coming of man.

Wistman's Wood, an 8-acre remnant of the original forests that covered this bleak plateau, is a strange, almost sinister place—entering it is a bit like walking into an Arthur Rackham illustration for one of the

Hundreds of prehistoric remains, like this burial pit, suggest Dartmoor was once a more hospitable landscape than it is today.

brothers Grimm's fairy tales. Gnarled and twisted dwarf oak trees, their branches cloaked in emerald green moss, huddle against the elements amidst a field of lichen-encrusted granite boulders. There is no real evidence to support the local legend that Druids once worshiped here, but it is the kind of thing you can easily imagine in this mystical environment.

🚶 EAST INTO HARDY'S "WESSEX"

Distance: About 80 miles/130 kilometers
Roads: Primary and motorway, except for last few miles
Driving Time: 2 hours
Map: Michelin Map #403

After exploring the wood, return to the car park and turn east on the **B3357** toward **Ashburton** to leave Dartmoor behind and cross into **Dorset.** As you enter Ashburton, follow signs for the **A38** north toward **Exeter.**

The A38 is a high-speed divided highway. After the exit for Bovey Tracey, it climbs steeply out of the valley of the River Teign and into deep pine forest. Just south of Exeter, follow signs straight ahead for the **M5** north. Leave the M5 at Exit 29, following signs for the **A30** to **Honiton,** about 12 miles (19 kilometers) to the east. As you approach Honiton—on the bed of an old Roman road, in fact—a steep, razor-sharp ridge rises on your right, the southernmost extension of a deeply etched plateau called the Blackdown Hills. The A38 bypasses Honiton center; watch for clear signs for the **A35** and **Dorchester,** 37 miles (60 kilometers) to the east in Dorset.

The A35 immediately zigzags up over the crest of the ridge, with sweeping views back to the Vale of Exeter behind, then enters a lovely landscape of rolling hills, rich sheep meadows, and plowed fields of deep red soil, many of which are planted to produce daffodils as a cash crop. The small villages along the way east are composed of slate- or

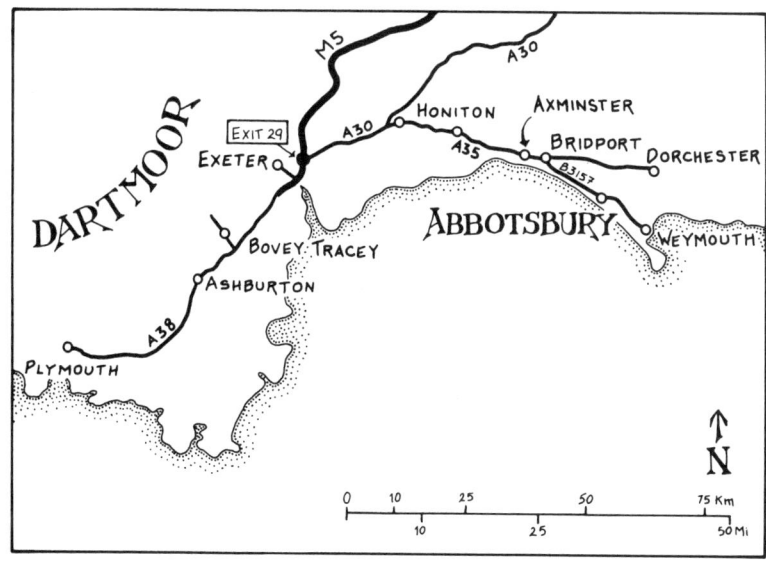

thatch-roofed red sandstone cottages, many of which have been harled (stuccoed) and painted the color of Devon clotted cream.

The road descends from the Blackdown Hills into the valley of the River Axe, continues through the carpet-producing town of **Axminster,** and heads southeast toward the gently curving shingle beaches of Lyme Bay and the Regency resort town of Lyme Regis, the backdrop of novels by both Jane Austen and John Fowles. At the charming little village of **Chideock,** it becomes evident that you have left Devon behind and entered Dorset; the red sandstone cottages are gone, replaced by warm yellow Dorset limestone—the same vast bed of limestone, in fact, that reaches north all the way to the Cotswolds and beyond.

At **Bridport,** a handsome Georgian town with wide streets built that way to facilitate drying and braiding the rope that was once its principal product, you may wish to stop at the Tourist Information Centre (seasonal; telephone (0308) 24901) in South Street. If you are unsure about accommodations tonight, they offer the Book-a-Bed-Ahead service, and you may wish to pick up a packet of the Dorset Trust for Nature Conservation's self-guided walks.

At Bridport, take the **B3157,** signposted for **Weymouth.** This is a particularly lovely stretch of road, with alternating views of honey-hued villages and long, sweeping vistas of coastal meadows, cliffs, and beaches, with Lyme Bay and the English Channel sparkling in the distance. As the road climbs up to the top of the coastal ridge there are equally expansive views inland, across rolling meadows and downland, outlined by well-maintained hedgerows and punctuated by hilltop beechwood copses.

Your first glimpse of this afternoon's destination, ancient **Abbotsbury,** is the glittering beaches of Chesil Bank, stretching off to the **Isle of Portland** far away in the haze to the southeast; the reedy, brackish lagoon, called the Fleet, speckled white by hundreds of mute swans; and the lonely tower of St. Catherine's Chapel, high on its curiously terraced hill. Then the road plunges off the edge of the ridge and down into the village itself, a dense little cluster of limestone houses built right up to the edge of the narrow, curving main street.

CREATURE COMFORTS
Daily Bed

Largely because almost the entire village is owned by a single family, places to stay in Abbotsbury for the next two nights are relatively limited, though pleasant. B&B accommodations are offered at a farm on the eastern edge of the village (which also offers pony trekking), in one house on Rodden Row, at a house down the road to the Swannery overlooking the ruins of the eleventh-century Benedictine abbey, and at the two inns. A mile or two farther east, the village of Portesham has

Some of the Swannery's swans at Abbotsbury

additional B&B accommodation. Beyond Abbotsbury, there are additional B&Bs, guesthouses, and hotels listed in the guidebooks cited in Further Reading, and a year-round Tourist Information Centre at **Dorchester**. For assistance or advance reservations, write Tourist Information Centre, 4 Acland Road, Dorchester, Dorset DT1 1EF, or phone (0305) 679920.

Daily Bread

The inns in the center of Abbotsbury and in the village of West Bexington, a few miles to the west, offer extensive bar menus and ambitious restaurant menus and are quite luxurious as pubs go. Simpler bar meals are also available at pubs on the eastern edge of Abbotsbury and in Portesham. A wider selection of restaurants can be found in Dorchester and Weymouth, each less than 10 miles (16 kilometers) away.

♦ DAY TEN

Exploring Hardy's Dorset

ABBOTSBURY AND ITS ENVIRONS

- ♦ A walk on the channel coast and Dorset downs
- ♦ A visit to a medieval swannery
- ♦ An alternative drive through Hardy's "Wessex"

Either the change in the quality of the air from heavy to light, or the sense of being amid new scenes . . . sent up her spirits wonderfully. Her hopes mingled with the sunshine in an ideal photosphere which surrounded her as she bounded along against the soft south wind. She heard a pleasant voice in every breeze, and in every bird's note seemed to lurk a joy.
—Thomas Hardy
Tess of the D'Urbervilles, 1891

There is about Dorset—the heart of Hardy's "Wessex"—a kind of drowsiness, like the ennui that overcomes you on a warm summer afternoon. A soft haze drifts in off the azure Channel and penetrates deep into the golden valleys. Lazy rivers trace aimless ribbons through verdant water meadows. Narrow lanes, frothy with blooming cow parsley, lead to sleepy thatched villages where no one stirs. Black-and-white Fresian cows recline amid meadows bright with buttercups, like lounging voluptuaries. A tractor creeps slowly across an age-softened hillside, trailing a cloud of white chalk dust, but so far away that it makes no sound, as in a dream.

In Dorset, the pace of life is slow. Time accumulates like dust, imperceptibly but continuously, cloaking everything with the patina of antiquity. History hides beneath the landscape's gentle contours: a velvety smooth slope suddenly ripples, betraying medieval farm terraces; a hilltop unexpectedly planes flat, revealing an Iron Age hill fort; a ridgetop footpath becomes unaccountably lumpy, as it traverses Neolithic burial mounds. The economic boom that has transformed so much of

Abbotsbury's vast medieval tithe barn, today only half its original length

southern England in the last decade has missed Dorset almost entirely, as the Industrial Revolution did before. There are no major industrial centers in the county. There are no motorways; they hurry around the edges on the way to somewhere else. So Dorset dozes on, absorbing the present into its gentle rhythms as it absorbed the past.

Abbotsbury itself is a kind of relic—occupied at least since 3000 B.C., its hill fortress was overthrown by the Romans soon after they landed in Britain in A.D. 43. Historians believe a monastery of some kind may have existed here as early as A.D. 500. It passed into the acquisitive hands of the abbots of Glastonbury in the ninth century A.D. when King Alfred's son Athelstan was consolidating the great Saxon Kingdom of Wessex. When the Viking King Canute finally overcame the Saxons in 1016, he gave the land to his Chamberlain Orc who, in turn, invited the Benedictines of Cerne Abbey to build a new abbey in what became Abbotsbury. The new Abbey of St. Peter prospered, building the longest tithe barn in Britain (270 feet/82 meters) and becoming by the fifteenth century quite appallingly corrupt. In 1541, during the Dissolution of the monasteries, Henry VIII sold Abbotsbury to Sir Giles Strangways, one of his Dissolution Commissioners, ordering him to tear the abbey down (he turned it into a mansion and kept most of the barn instead). The family has owned the village, its farms, and surrounding land ever since; virtually everyone in Abbotsbury is a tenant of the Fox-Strangways family.

ITINERARY: DAY TEN

Feudal as this may seem, one result is that Abbotsbury is thoroughly unspoiled, despite its magnificent site overlooking the Channel and Chesil Bank. Today's main event is a magnificently scenic walk around Abbotsbury and its environs—a walk that touches upon nearly every period in its long history.

🚶 A BEACH AND RIDGE WALK AROUND ABBOTSBURY

Distance: 14 miles/22.5 kilometers; allow 6.5 hours. Shorter option: 7 miles/11.3 kilometers.
Difficulty: Easy, except for steep climb to ridge top
Total Elevation Gain: 590 feet/180 meters
Gear: Walking shoes/sneakers, sunblock, rain gear, camera
Map: Ordnance Survey Landranger #194

Today's walk begins at the gateway to the ruined twelfth-century abbey from which Abbotsbury takes its name. It's located on the lane

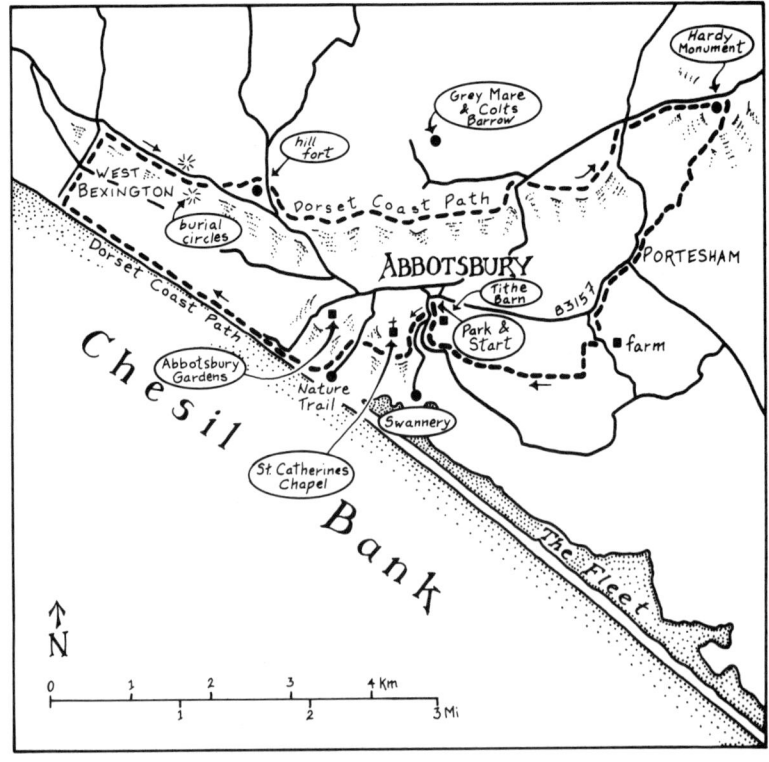

that departs from the main road at a sharp bend, and runs downhill to the Swannery from the center of the village. South of the current parish church is the only other remnant of the once-great abbey, a haunting bit of crumbling end wall. The folks who run the Abbey House B&B next door (which, like most of the town, was probably built from pieces of the abbey) have excavated the abbey's water mill, which they discovered beneath their side lawn. Downhill and across the pretty duck pond is the abbey's tithe barn. Even though only half of it is intact, the barn is huge. Currently used to store locally grown thatching reed, it was the model for a shearing barn in Hardy's *Far from the Madding Crowd*: "The vast porches at the sides, lofty enough to admit a waggon laden to its highest with corn in the sheaf, were spanned by heavy-pointed arches of stone, broadly and boldly cut. . . ."

From the barn, continue down the curving lane toward the Swannery, past the steeply sloping pasture on the left, bright with pink and white bindweed and yellow nipplewort in midsummer. Beyond the car park, turn right down the paved walk paralleling a stream toward the entrance to the Swannery.

Abbotsbury's Swannery

The Swannery was established by the Benedictine monks of St. Peter's Abbey as a source of fresh winter meat, and dates from the fourteenth century at the latest, but probably much earlier. Managed swanneries were not uncommon in those days, but this is the only one still in existence in Europe. The brackish water and eelgrass in the Fleet, sheltered behind Chesil Bank, provide an ideal habitat not just for the mute swans that live here year round, but also for wintering eider duck, brent geese, whooping swans, mergansers, shovelers, grebes, scaups, teals, and many other wildfowl. The reeds ringing the Fleet are cut in the winter and the breeding pairs of mute swans (a small minority of the total) nest among the new growth in April. They incubate their eggs in May, staking out "territories," which they defend fiercely. A variety of butterflies also haunt the reed beds—the silver-washed fritillary, peacock, red admiral, tortoiseshell, and painted lady, among others. The swans themselves, hundreds of them, are a stunning sight, brilliant white in the sun, sailing serenely across the Fleet ahead of a fleet of gray cygnets, or napping in the reedy shallows, each with a head tucked under a lifted wing. (Open daily, 9:30 A.M. to 4:30 P.M., May through September.)

About halfway between the car park and the Swannery, a footpath signposted for St. Catherine's Chapel plunges through a dense thicket of ancient pollarded willows (their spring shoots are split and used to bind reed bundles), then crosses a stile and runs up a steep meadow. At the stone marker turn **left** (signposted THE GARDENS), following a path around the southern base of the hill. The fourteenth-century chapel on the hill above you, built entirely of stone, should have been destroyed after the Dissolution, but apparently survived because it served as a beacon for sailors skirting the hazards of Chesil Bank on their way to Weymouth. The hillside on which you are walking, like the slopes on neighboring hills, has soft terraces—called *strip lynchets*—that here are prehistoric in origin, but were resurrected during the twelfth and thirteenth centuries when rapid population growth pressed every available acre into food production.

Here, only a few hundred yards away from the Swannery, you are completely alone, even in the high season. Below you, the English Channel shimmers in the midmorning sun and Chesil Bank slashes away to the southeast like a giant scythe, cutting the Isle of Portland off from the Dorset mainland. Ahead and to the right, softly rounded hills rise to the high coastal ridge. It is incredibly quiet—the only sounds are the drowsy buzzing of bumblebees in the blackberry bramble bushes and the ripping and chomping of the cows grazing the grassy slope. Occasionally the raucous call of a pheasant echoes across the valley from the woods on the opposite slope.

On the other side of the hill, climb over a stile, cross a sloping meadow, climb another stile, and then turn **left** down a farm track clearly signposted COAST PATH TO WEST BEXINGTON, with the diamond waymarker for the coast path painted on the post. The lane is lined with bramble decorated with daisies, Queen Anne's lace, lovely yellow flowers with the unlovely name of *ragwort*, and, closer to the beach, clumps of yellow poppies (there is a self-guided nature walk through the scrub brush behind the beach). Chesil Bank itself is a natural wonder. At 18 miles (29 kilometers) it is the longest pebble beach in Europe. And in a phenomenon scientists still cannot fully explain, the sea manages to sort and distribute the pebbles of the beach precisely by size, with the smallest pea-sized pebbles to the west, near Bridport, and fist-sized boulders to the east at the base of the limestone cliffs of Portland. It's said that smugglers and fishermen landing under cover of fog could tell where they were simply by the size of the pebbles.

Tempting as it may seem to walk along the beach accompanied by the rattle and hiss of the pebbles in the surf, a few yards of trudging through ankle-deep slippery round stones will have you crunching back

Ancient St. Catherine's Chapel, high above Abbotsbury, overlooks more secular pursuits.

over the crest of the bank to the lane in no time. The sandy edge of the lane is studded with patches of pink sea thrift, white sea campion, bluish green sea kale, purple, prickly sea holly, and other wildflowers.

After about 0.5 mile (0.8 kilometer), the road from the village and Abbotsbury Gardens comes down from the right. There is a car park with the inevitable ice cream van (don't be tempted; English ice cream is dreadful) and a clutch of sunbathers and surf-casting fishermen during the summer. Technically, the road ends at the car park, but in fact it continues behind the beach—indeed, T. E. Lawrence (of Arabia fame) used to race his Brough Superior motorcycle along this stretch of dirt road... until he was killed in a motorcycle accident. Follow this unpaved road, past a cottage that grows masses of fragrant dianthus and carnations for the cut-flower market, all the way to West Bexington, the little steep-sloped village you can see a little over 2 miles (3.2 kilometers) ahead.

West Bexington, where you turn **right** and begin the climb to the coastal ridge, is a relatively young village built on the ruins of a medieval settlement called Bexington, which was sacked by French raiders in 1440. The footings of its church were discovered only a few years ago when builders were expanding the car park for the hotel halfway up the hill on the right. The little hotel offers excellent pub lunches, which you can enjoy in the pretty garden overlooking the channel while taking a breather.

After lunch, continue up the hill and, where the road turns sharply left, continue **straight** up the hedge-lined farm track. Near the top of this track, a clear path veers diagonally to the **right.** Follow this path through a bramble and hawthorn thicket until it reaches a meadow running parallel to the **B3157** along the ridge. Continue along this meadow back in the direction of Abbotsbury, high above the beaches and sheep meadows. After a few hundred yards a signpost points ahead for the inland portion of the coast path, toward the Hardy Monument. You pass the ruins of an ancient limekiln (owned by the National Trust) and three round Bronze Age burial barrows. After a little over a mile (over 1.5 kilometers) of walking parallel to the road, pass the first signpost (to Litton Cheney), continue along the fence line, then take the second footpath to the **left,** crossing the road. Climb over another stile, then turn **right** toward the peculiarly shaped hilltop that dominates the landscape ahead.

The hilltop is what's left of **Abbotsbury Castle,** a 5-acre Iron Age earthen hill fort, built by the Durotriges tribes who lived in Wessex for perhaps a thousand years before being overcome by the Romans in A.D. 44. The flat, roughly square hilltop is fortified by two deep ditches and high banks below a steep final slope. Archaeologists have found large quantities of sling stones here, used in a battle, pitifully unsuccessful, to resist the Romans. The view is a 360-degree panorama: to the south the broad sweep of Lyme Bay edges by the bank to the east and

Along the Dorset Coast Path, above Chesil Bank and the Fleet

the steep cliffs of Golden Cap to the west; to the north, the soft contours of the chalk downs undulate inland, separated by neat hedges, oak and beech woods, and the occasional coniferous windbreak. Occasionally, you can spot a kestrel patroling the summit, hanging on the wind sweeping up from the channel—hovering, sideslipping, adjusting, hovering again—then plummeting on folded wings to the heather- and gorse-covered slope below after a field mouse or vole.

From the summit, descend, cross a lane and another stile, then simply follow the ridge top. The path is less a path than a 100-yard-wide (90-meter-wide) avenue, which, except for the occasional Neolithic burial mound, is as green and flat as a billiard table, curving gently eastward. In the spring, the lee side of the ridge is carpeted with drifts of millions of bluebells, a magical sight. Away across the inland downs the landscape is a vast quilted counterpane, punctuated here and there by the spires of invisible churches in the center of invisible villages nestled in the folds. After the climb to the top of the ridge, this is a luxuriously easy stroll with spectacular views in every direction. When you have passed through the second iron gate, you'll see a signposted path that leads down a fold in the ridge to Abbotsbury, making a handy shortcut if you find yourself tiring or the weather is threatening. The main path, clearly marked with an acorn waymarker, continues eastward across wide, sloping meadows. A half-mile or so (about 0.75 kilometer) farther on, another shortcut to Abbotsbury leads off to the right and a signpost pointing roughly **left** along a fence line indicates the way to the **Hardy Monument**. A bit beyond this signpost you go through a steel gate, turn **left** up a narrow road (a right will return you to Abbotsbury), round a bend, then turn **right** at the signpost for the coast path once again. You may have noticed that this is the *third* signpost that has promised the monument to be only 2 miles (3.2 kilometers) away; this may be an example of dry Dorset humor.

(**Note:** If you're more interested in prehistoric remains than scenic views, stay on the road, turn left onto the next farm lane, and, where that road forks, continue straight ahead on the footpath to "The Grey Mare and Her Colts," a Neolithic long barrow tomb perhaps 6,000 years old, sited—as are most long barrows—prominently on the ridge line ahead.)

The path to the Hardy Monument—memorializing not Thomas Hardy the novelist, but *Sir* Thomas Hardy, flag captain of the H.M.S. *Victory* at the Battle of Trafalgar—teeters along the edge of a steep embankment, following a cow path, then splits. Bear **left** here, heading uphill, over a ladder stile, and follow the hedgerow along the left-hand side of a field with yet more wide views of the coast. On the other side of the field, go through a steel gate and, just a bit farther on, over a stile at another steel gate. A very primitive **stone circle,** probably constructed between 1800 and 1200 B.C. on a spectacular site, is just ahead on the right. Continue along the farm track, with the monument straight ahead on the next hilltop, climb over two more stiles, and cross the farmyard and walk down the driveway to the road. Turn **left** (right takes you to Portesham) and walk up the road to the intersection. Turn **right** here and walk up the gentle grade about 0.75 mile (a little over a kilometer) to the top of Black Down. It's a good thing the monument wasn't meant for Hardy the novelist; it's an aesthetic nightmare, little better than an octagonal factory chimney. But the view far across Dorset is magnificent on a clear day (if it isn't clear, skip this leg). Directly below the monument, along the ridge line to the east, is one of the most extraordinary Neolithic burial sites in Britain: a string of more than sixty "bowl barrows" running almost to the outskirts of Weymouth. The barrows, 4,000 years old, date from the heyday of the "Wessex Culture," an especially prosperous period during the Bronze Age when an apparently wealthy aristocracy was able to afford—or command—monumental burial sites.

To return to Abbotsbury, take the footpath around the east side of the monument, downhill through the wood at its base, and out across a meadow studded with more Neolithic tumuli and a long barrow. This path enters Portesham at the top of the village. Here turn **left** onto the road, walk through the village, then turn **right** onto the **B3157**. The most direct way to return to Abbotsbury is to continue along this road for a bit less than 2 miles (3.2 kilometers). For a more scenic return to the village, turn **left** onto the first side road you come to, walk up to the group of farm buildings ahead, turn **right** and then **left** to the end of a farm track, then turn **right** onto the Dorset Coast Path and follow it to the Swannery road.

DIVERSIONS
"Casterbridge" to Corfe Castle: The Dorset of Thomas Hardy

Few writers have exploited a landscape as thoroughly and successfully as Thomas Hardy did with Dorset, the heart of his fictional "Wessex." Hardly a town or village in the county is without its thinly disguised fictional twin. Yet even if you've never read a Hardy novel, this rolling rural countryside is full of attractions, from the largest Iron Age hill fort in Britain to a wildly romantic ruined castle, from high-hedged winding country lanes and romantic water meadows to dramatic sea-carved coastal cliffscapes. If today's walk around Abbotsbury suits neither whim nor weather, this meandering car tour provides an attractive alternative.

Begin by driving east out of Abbotsbury on the **B3157** and turn **left** at the King's Arms in **Portesham.** Drive through the little flower-trimmed village with the stream running along the left side of the road, continue up the steep hill, and turn **right** at the junction at the top, toward the Hardy Monument. After taking in the sweeping views from the monument, continue down the other side of the hill to **Martinstown,** also know as Winterbourne St. Martin, after the River Winterbourne—a stream that flows reliably only in the winter in these fast-draining chalk hills. Turn **right** at the T-junction and drive east on the **B3159,** following the banks of the pretty Winterbourne, edged with daffodils in the spring. After about 1.5 miles (2.4 kilometers), turn **left** onto a minor road that runs around the southern base of **Maiden Castle,** just ahead.

Maiden Castle, its massive earthen ramparts looming high above the Frome River valley, dominates the landscape for miles around. It is a superb example not just of the hill-fort technology of the Iron Age, but also of the "creative reuse" of strategic sites by successive ages of man. Excavations indicate that this hilltop was the site of a long barrow constructed perhaps 6,000 years ago. Some 5,000 years ago one of Wessex's forty causewayed enclosures—an oval compound surrounded by a ditch and bank and bridged by several causeways—was erected on the same site, possibly as a marketplace or place of ritual celebration. The hilltop was abandoned about 1800 B.C., but was returned to use in the fourth or fifth century B.C., when an earthen rampart was con-

170 ITINERARY: DAY TEN

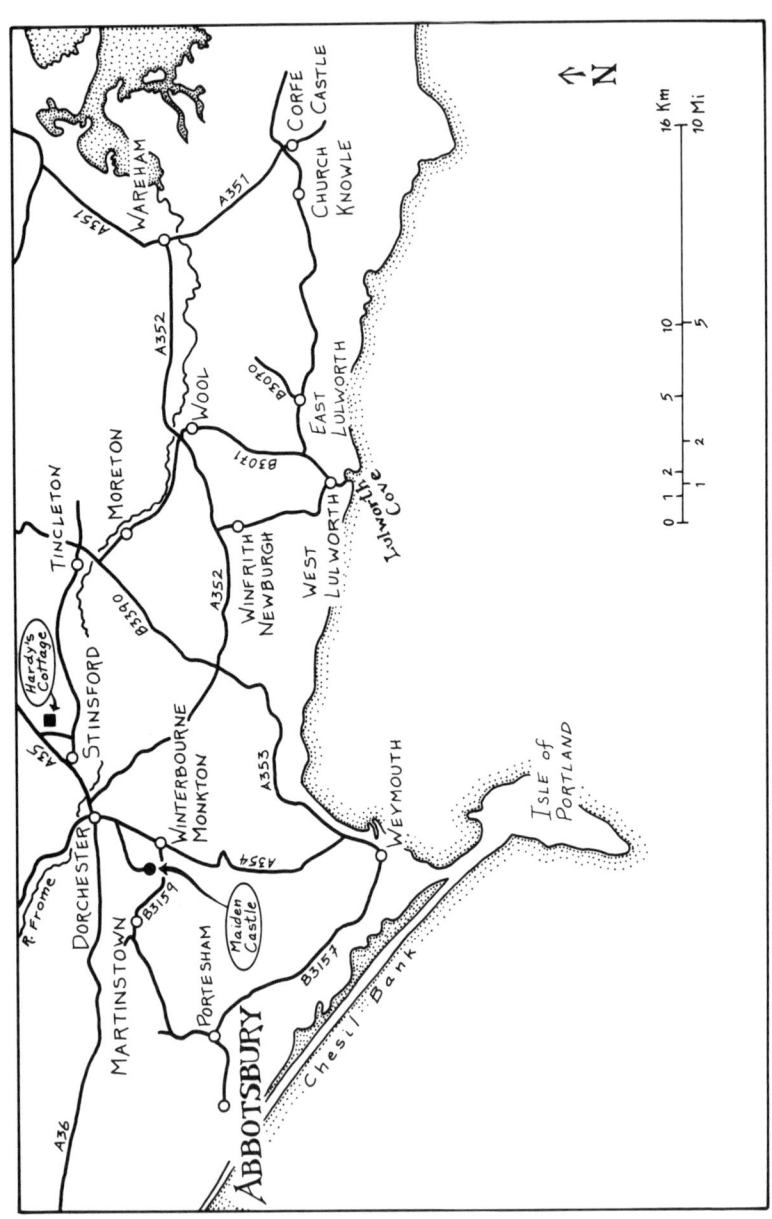

structed on a knoll at the eastern end of the existing site, possibly as a place to store and protect the grain that was every Iron Age community's most valuable asset. Gradually, over several centuries, this enclosure was expanded to the western edge of the hill, then surrounded by three huge ditch-and-bank rings, 2 miles (3.2 kilometers) around and 60 to 90 feet (18 to 27 meters) high, surmounted by wooden palisades. Labyrinthine passageways on the east and west, interrupted by as many as seven ditches and banks, were designed to bewilder would-be attackers and expose them to defensive attack. The system appears to have been successful; there is evidence that as many as 5,000 members of the Durotriges tribe lived within the hill's ramparts for perhaps two centuries. Then, in A.D. 44, Roman troops under General Vespasian descended on the settlement, crushing the defenders. Some 50,000 sling stones carried to the hill from Chesil Bank were never even used. The Romans set up their own settlement in what is now Dorchester. Three hundred years later, when the Romano-Britons who stayed after the Romans departed wanted to build a temple, they chose Maiden Castle hill as their site.

From Maiden Castle, continue east on the same minor road through **Winterbourne Monkton** to the **A354**. Turn **left** and drive along this arrow-straight and obviously Roman road into the center of **Dorchester.** Dorchester is a classic English market town, a jumble of rooflines and building façades of every imaginable period. Worth a special stop is the **Dorset County Museum** on High West Street, with an excellent collection of archaeological finds and rural crafts and a reconstruction of Hardy's study (open Monday through Saturday, 10:00 A.M. to 5:00 P.M.). The museum's main hall is itself an attraction: a three-story Victorian "galleria" complete with intricate ironwork.

Leave Dorchester by the **A35** heading northeast, cross the broad valley of the River Frome, and take the first **right** on an unclassified road, passing **Stinsford** (the "Mellstock" of *Under the Greenwood Tree*), where Hardy's heart is buried. Just after the village, take the first **left** to **Higher Bockhampton.** The thatched cottage where Hardy was born and in which he later wrote *Far from the Madding Crowd* and *Under the Greenwood Tree* is open only by appointment (telephone (0305) 84363), but the grounds are open to visitors (daily April through October, 10:00 A.M. to 6:00 P.M., except Tuesday mornings.)

Then backtrack to the intersection and turn **left,** following the verdant meadows of the River Frome downstream through the hamlet of **Tincleton** until you reach the **B3990**. Turn **right,** cross the river, and as you pass through a tunnel of trees watch for a **left** turn into **Moreton.** Now continue down the right bank of the river to **Wool** (the "Wellbridge" where Tess and Angel Clare honeymooned in *Tess of the D'Urbervilles*). Here turn **left** onto the **A352** toward **Wareham** (Hardy's "Angelbury") and, as you approach the town, follow signs for the

A351 toward **Swanage.** The road dips down into a broad swale, then begins rising up the huge chunk of limestone known as the **Isle of Purbeck.** Dominating the landscape ahead is the most romantic ruin in Dorset: the shattered hulk of **Corfe Castle,** with its little gray limestone village gathered at its feet. Begun shortly after the Norman Conquest, the castle was substantially refortified by King John in 1285. During the Civil War, the lady of the manor, Lady Bankes, managed to defend the castle through two years of siege. It fell in 1646 only after a traitor let Cromwell's troops in. They subsequently blew it up—creating overnight an exceptional quarry for local builders (castle open daily, March through October; weekend afternoons in winter).

Backtrack a few hundred yards and turn **left** onto a minor road toward **Church Knowle** and **Lulworth.** This road crosses an army tank range and is occasionally closed, but when it is, the diversion route is well marked. At **East Lulworth,** turn left onto the **B3070** and follow signs for **West Lulworth** and **Lulworth Cove.** Here, within a few minutes' walk, are several spectacular coastal formations: Lulworth Cove itself, a huge oval bay created when the sea broke through the uptilted coastal limestone ridge and ate away at the layers of softer clays behind; Stair Hole, a remnant of the ridge in which several new holes are being created and a new cove is being born; and Durdle Door, a splendid natural arch at the end of a wildly folded and tortured formation of limestone and sedimentary beds, a little over a mile (1.6 kilometers) west of the car park up the obvious pathway (you can return by way of the fossil-strewn beach, climbing back up to the ridge near the holiday bungalows).

Below: *The graceful arch of Durdle Door, west of Lulworth Cove.* Opposite page: *The village of Corfe Castle and its shattered ruin.*

Exploring Hardy's Dorset **173**

From Lulworth Cove, take the B3071 north again, but turn **left** at the first opportunity and follow this minor road around to the tiny village of **Winfrith Newburgh** and the **A352.** Turn **left** and follow the A352 all the way into Weymouth (Hardy's "Budmouth"). Then watch for signs for the B3157 west to Abbotsbury.

CREATURE COMFORTS
Daily Bed
See yesterday's listings.

Daily Bread
Dorset seems to be in competition with Devon for "cream teas," but if your taste runs more to the savory, look for **Dorset blue vinny** cheese. Like a Stilton, blue vinny takes its name from the blue veins that run through the skimmed milk cheese. It's best eaten with **Dorset knobs,** dense rolls with a crisp brown crust. Together they make a terrific picnic base or ploughman's lunch.

A "Wessex" scene

◆ DAY ELEVEN

Into the Land of Enigma

ABBOTSBURY ◆ CERNE ABBAS
SALISBURY ◆ OLD SARUM ◆ AVEBURY

- ◆ A visit to the valley of the obscene green giant
- ◆ The "piddles" and "puddles" of North Dorset
- ◆ The soaring spire and hushed grandeur of Salisbury Cathedral
- ◆ Clambering over the crumbling walls of Old Sarum
- ◆ A distant glimpse of Stonehenge
- ◆ A night amid the stones of Avebury

[Avebury] as much surpasses Stonehenge as a cathedral doth a parish church.
—John Aubrey, 1663

You come upon it suddenly, spectacularly. Racing across the crest of the billowing Marlborough Downs, with vast unbroken expanses of blue-green barley and lemon yellow rapeseed stretching off to the horizon, you slow and then turn sharply down a narrow lane through a farmyard. As you approach a rise, a rough-hewn stone looms to greet you. You top the rise and see another... and another... and then dozens of them—huge stones standing at attention in parallel rows reaching all the way to the next hilltop, like sentinels guarding the gates to prehistory.

And then another surprise, even more astonishing: just beyond the next hill a stone circle so vast that you cannot take it in all in one sweep, so huge that a village is enveloped in its ancient, enigmatic embrace.

It is Avebury, the largest Neolithic monument in Europe and the center of an area of prehistoric sites so dense and dumbfounding that generations of archaeologists have yet to grasp its meaning. Yet the magic here is palpable. And deeply primitive. It dwarfs the impact of its younger, more famous southern sibling, Stonehenge, and makes it look contrived, overdone. What's more, there are no fences here; you are free to drift among the mute monoliths, run your hand over cool stone smoothed by the millennia, climb to the top of the huge earthen bank, sit, and ponder the imponderable.

You should see Avebury at that magical hour, late on a summer afternoon, when the slanting rays of the sun burnish the ancient stones gold and their long, dark shadows stretch away into the haze of history. Or very early in the morning, when they are shrouded in mist like the dawn of the first day and the rising sun refracts and crowns each stone with a shimmering halo.

Avebury is a bit off the beaten track, tucked away in a lonely corner of Wiltshire, just north of Dorset. Tour buses roar through the county by the hundreds, stop briefly at Stonehenge, then roar off again, ignoring the more magnificent monuments to the north and missing entirely the gentle beauty of Wiltshire's quiet villages and lush river valleys. Taking all this in—plus Britain's most beautiful cathedral—is today's agenda. Along the way, you'll see Britain's smallest pub and largest... ummm... fertility symbol.

🚗 IN SEARCH OF SACRED STRUCTURES

Distance: About 95 miles/153 kilometers
Roads: Mostly primary roads
Driving Time: All day, with several stops
Map: Michelin Map #404

Take the **B3157** east from Abbotsbury to Portesham, turn **left** at the King's Arms, and drive up the hill through the village. Turn **right** at the top, pass the Hardy Monument, descend into Martinstown (Winterbourne St. Martin), and turn **right** onto the **B3159**. At the eastern end of the pretty thatched village, bear **left** at the fork in the direction of **Dorchester**. At the new roundabout at the top of the hill, follow signs for the **A37** to **Yeovil**. You follow this new bypass to the next roundabout and turn **left** onto the A37 toward Yeovil and **Charminster**. After passing an estate with a round medieval tower, turn **right** onto the **A352** through Charminster and north toward **Cerne Abbas**, 6 miles (9.7 kilometers) ahead.

The road runs north along the pretty River Cerne, shortly reaching **Godmanstone**. On the right is the aged, thatched Smith's Arms, England's smallest pub. Three centuries ago, when this was still a blacksmith's shop, King Charles II stopped in to have his horse shod. While he waited, he demanded a drink. When the smith replied that he had no license, the king granted him one on the spot. No doubt a pub, even a very small one, was more profitable than a smithy, so pub it became and remains today.

Into the Land of Enigma 177

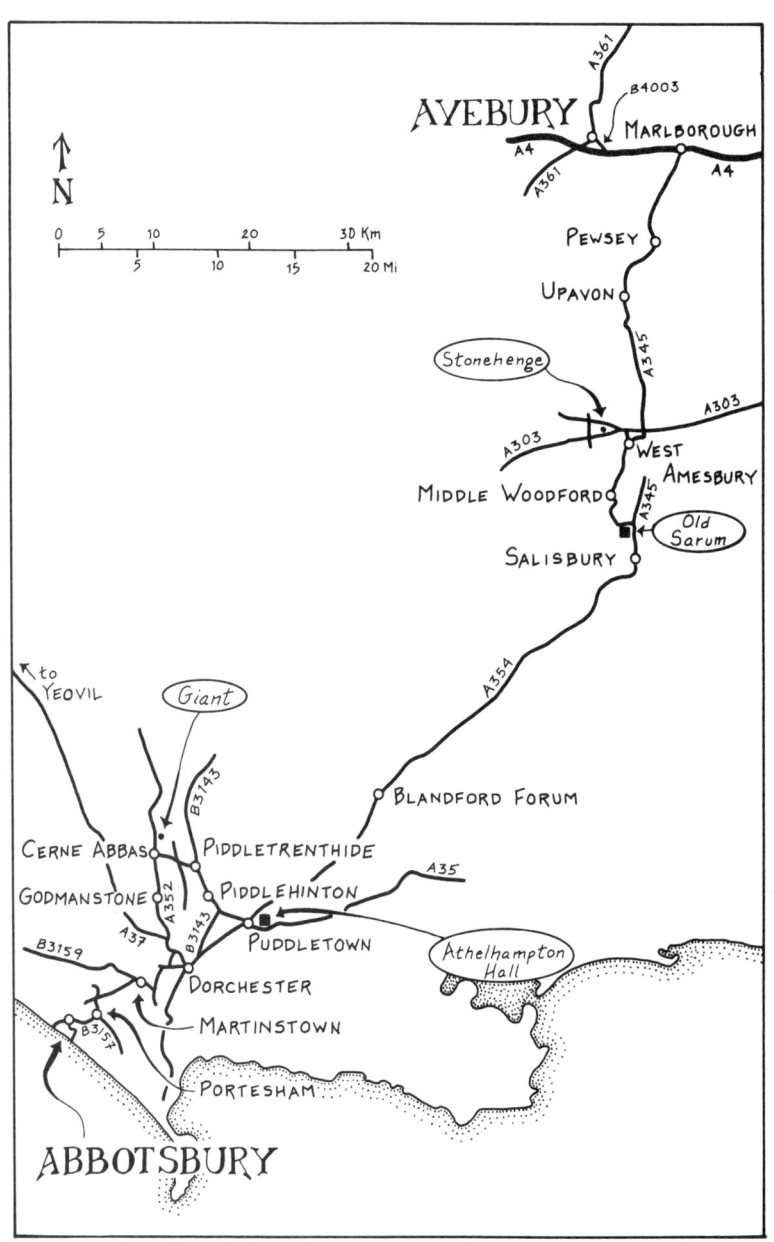

The Cerne Giant: the only X-rated postcard forwarded by Her Majesty's Royal Mail

Continue north for a few miles and ignore the turn to the right signposted for Cerne Abbas, continuing on the A352 another couple of hundred yards (or meters) instead. Turn right into the car park, directly opposite the infamous **Cerne Giant.** If you're traveling with small children, you may have a bit of explaining to do: the giant, outlined in chalk in the sloping green hillside, is a 180-foot (55-meter) full frontal nude of rather insistent masculinity, brandishing a club. The giant's origins are a mystery. Because he resembles traditional representations of the god Hercules, archaeologists think he may have been cut by Roman-British tribes about 1,500 years ago. For obvious reasons, it has been a fertility symbol for centuries.

Perhaps for equally obvious reasons, the Benedictines founded an abbey here in A.D. 987 to convert the heathen (the giant remains but the abbey is gone; score one mark for the heathen). The village that grew around it, however, is delightful. Drive down the minor lane from the car park and turn **left** into the main street at the handsome stone New Inn (which is obviously not new at all). The village is composed of a lovely combination of whitewashed stone houses with thatched roofs, half-timber houses with overhanging second stories, houses faced with attractive patterns of brick and knapped flint, and more formal Georgian townhouses with intricately carved doorways. There are three excellent pubs and you may wish to take an early lunch here if that time has rolled around already.

Then continue in the same direction through town and turn **right** into the delightfully named Piddle Lane toward **Piddletrenthide**. This lane climbs steeply up to the top of a ridge high above the rolling chalk downs with wide views across neatly hedgerowed fields of wheat, barley, and rapeseed. At the intersection at the top of the hill, continue **straight** ahead, dropping down again into the valley of the River Piddle. Turn **right** onto the **B3143** and follow the little river—which takes its name from the Old German *pedel*, for "marsh"—through Piddletrenthide and **Piddlehinton**. Then turn **left** onto the **B3142** to **Puddletown** (there are even more "puddles" downstream). When you reach the T-junction with the **A354**, turn **left** toward **Blandford Forum** and **Salisbury**. (**Note:** Lovers of stately homes may want to visit **Athelhampton Hall**, a splendid fifteenth-century manor built on the legendary site of the palace of King Athelstan of Wessex. House and gardens open mid-April through mid-October, 2:00 P.M. to 6:00 P.M. Wednesday, Thursday, Sunday, and bank holidays, and Monday and Tuesday in August.)

The A354 rolls northeast across Dorset through a landscape dotted with villages that sound like the attendance roll of some insufferably aristocratic private school: Melcombe Bingham ("Here, sir!"), Milborne St. Andrew ("Here!"), Okeford Fitzpaine ("Present!"), Charlton Marshall ("Here!"), and so on. Blandford Forum gets its name from a Latin-smitten abbot who thought "forum" sounded more upscale than "market," which was what Blandford was. After a fire in the 1700s, Blandford was rebuilt (by two brothers with the unfortunate last name of Bastard) in Georgian splendor. Since then, a few Victorian flourishes have been added around the edges, but it remains an exceptionally harmonious whole. From Blandford, simply continue on the A354 all the way to **Salisbury**.

Even though its center is laid out in an orderly grid, the traffic patterns in Salisbury are fiendishly confusing. One quick look at a map will tell you why: Salisbury is the principal road intersection in southern England. Your objective is the cathedral, whose spire is so tantalizingly

close. Here is the simplest route: at the first and second roundabouts through which you pass as you enter the city on the A354, follow signs for **City Centre**. At the next roundabout, take the second **left** and enter the city's one-way traffic pattern. Then take the first **left** *after* the King's Arms Hotel (on the right). The very next **left** will take you under the medieval arch leading directly to the Cathedral Close. The car park here is small, expensive, and nearly always full. For free parking don't turn in through the arch but carry on **straight** ahead instead, over the little bridge, to an area of open parkland with free street parking on the left and a large "pay and display" car park, also on the left. One additional benefit of parking here is you have the view of the cathedral that so bewitched Constable: broad green meadows, grazing cows, the meandering Salisbury Avon river, and the cathedral spire soaring above the treetops. To reach the cathedral, backtrack and turn right under the archway into the close.

The most stunning thing about Salisbury Cathedral—apart from its 404-foot (123-meter) spire—is its serenity. Most cathedrals, hemmed in by the jumble of streets and buildings that characterize medieval cities, seem to struggle for room to breathe. Salisbury Cathedral, on the other hand, floats in the center of a broad green sea of grass, distanced from the secular hustle and bustle. When you pass through the archway in the old city wall, you enter another realm—a quiet, contemplative, open compound framed with elegant Georgian and medieval mansions trimmed in wisteria, rambler roses, and clematis. Students and visitors recline in the shade, reading books. Artists sketch. Cherubic clerics hurry by, their long black cassocks rustling across the manicured lawn.

The cathedral itself can be moody: cold and austere on a cloudy day, warm and glowing in the sun. It has a sumptuous unity of design that comes from having been built all at once, at the height of the Early English Gothic period. Construction began in 1220, when Bishop Richard Poore abandoned Old Sarum (see below) and founded New Sarum on the banks of the Wiltshire Avon. It was completed only thirty-eight years later. The long, gracefully proportioned nave, supported by rows of delicate buttresses, is decorated sparely, a nice foil for the intricately carved west front and central tower. The famous spire was an afterthought, added a century later. The 6,500 tons of additional weight, however, threatened to bring down the entire tower, so huge but remarkably delicate-looking piers of Purbeck marble were added inside (the spire still leans more than two feet from perpendicular). The interior is less heavily decorated than later cathedrals and has a simple dignity as a result. Decoration is in the details—the superb stone pulpit, the carved choir, the embroidered cushions. If you are very lucky, you may

The scene that captivated Constable: Salisbury Cathedral soaring above the watermeadows

catch the ethereal voices of the boy's choir echoing among the pillars, and the sudden explosion of childish energy—arms and legs flying, green surplices and white Elizabethan collars flying, all giggles and shouts—when they are dismissed.

Leaving Salisbury is somewhat easier than arriving. Go back out through the archway opposite the North Transept, turn **left** and go over the little bridge again, retrieve your car, and simply continue in the same direction until the road bends around to the right and passes behind the railroad station. At the T-junction, turn **left** under the railway bridge, go three-quarters of the way around the roundabout (ignoring the sign to Stonehenge), and exit the roundabout where the sign points to the **A36** east, with the **A345** in parentheses. At the next roundabout, get into the left lane and take the first **left** onto the A345 toward **Amesbury.** Go through two more small roundabouts but continue **straight** ahead, climbing a long hill. As you pass the athletic fields on the left, you can see the ramparts of an obviously fortified hill straight ahead. Slow down as you approach the top of the rise and turn sharply left at the signpost for **Old Sarum.** The driveway climbs steeply, twisting through a gap in the outer ramparts, then enters an inner field with the car park on the right (inner compound open daily April through September, 10:00 A.M. to 6:00 P.M.; October through March, Tuesday to Sunday, 10:00 A.M. to 4:00 P.M.).

Old Sarum—the original Salisbury—is one of those places tourists never seem to discover. Typically deserted even in high season, it is one of the most romantic and evocative ruins in Britain. You enter the old settlement, sheltering behind massive flint and chalk walls, by a steep wooden bridge over a deep dry moat. Immediately, you are in the realm of ghosts. So much remains—narrow streets now covered with springy green turf, the high walls of houses complete with their hearths, the central bishop's palace, the defensive walkway around the perimeter—that you can almost sense the busy comings and goings of the long-dead inhabitants. As you stand upon the outer rampart, you see immediately why this site had been occupied continuously by Iron Age tribes, Romans, Saxons, Danes, and Normans: you can see for miles in every direction, far out across the windy Salisbury Plain, down across the Avon valley to modern Salisbury, and beyond. It was a spectacular strategic stronghold. Ironically, Old Sarum fell not in battle, but in peace. After the Norman Conquest (William the Conqueror reviewed his troops here in 1070), life became more settled. A cathedral was built just below the hilltop, was destroyed by lightning days after being consecrated, and was rebuilt (the foundations can still be seen, just northwest of the fortress). The community became crowded and religious and secular leaders quarreled. The breaking point, however, was more mundane: the name "Salisbury" comes from the Saxon *searobyrg,* or "dry town." Here in the chalk hills, water is extremely scarce. Bishop Poore ordered the creation of the new town and cathedral in the valley below because the old site could no longer support its population.

After exploring Old Sarum, drive back down to the entrance and turn **left** onto the A345. At the bottom of the hill, turn **left** onto a minor road signposted for **Stratford Castle** and **Wilton**. You drive around the base of Sarum hill, then turn **right** over the bridge and **right** again on the other side, signposted for **Woodford** and **Stonehenge**. This quiet country road wanders upstream along the pretty River Avon, with blossoming fruit trees along the banks in spring and swans and ducks patrolling the sluggish river. The villages along the way—**Lower, Middle,** and **Upper Woodford**—are composed of cottages built of a combination of knapped flint and brick within a framework of oak, typically capped by a thick thatch roof. Eventually you reach the pretty village of **West Amesbury**. The road ends and you turn **left** toward Stonehenge, quickly merging with the **A303**.

Almost immediately after you join this road, you reach the crest of a hill and there below you, just to the right of the highway, is Stonehenge, outlined against the sky. This is the most moving view you will have of this most popular of ancient monuments. From here on, it's all downhill, literally and figuratively. Once you could roam among the giant stones; today they are trapped behind a chain-link fence erected for their protection. Hordes of visitors arrive in waves, take pictures, then recede again like the tide. The stones stand silent, aloof, and, one imagines, faintly embarrassed by it all.

Stonehenge is a complex structure, begun in 3100 B.C. as a simple circular ditch and bank and then abandoned. Some 1,000 years later it was renovated, with a formal entrance and a ring of standing stones brought from Wales. Then that project was suspended and the huge lintel-capped stone horseshoe and trilithons were erected, each stone tapered for perspective and locked together with sophisticated mortise and tenon joints. Later still another circle of smaller stones was added. The surrounding plain is studded with burial mounds rich with relics. Yet despite centuries of study, no one has a clue why any of it was created.

If you want to join the crowds visiting the museum and monument, turn **right** at the intersection ahead and into the car park (monument open daily until 4:00 P.M.). But if you want to preserve the magic, regard Stonehenge from afar, here on the hillside. Then go down to the intersection, make a **U-turn**, and head **east** on the A303. At the next roundabout, turn **left** onto the A345 again, heading north toward **Marlborough**. The road continues along the eastern slopes of the Salisbury Plain, with its vast, unfenced fields of grain, descends through several lovely villages along the Avon River (watch for TANK CROSSING signs near Fifield), then plunges down into the **Vale of Pewsey**. Hemmed in by the chalk walls of the Salisbury Plain on the south and the softer but taller hills of the Marlborough Downs on the north, the vale, 12 miles (19 kilometers) long, is one of the richest farming areas in

Stonehenge as it once was, unencumbered by protective chain-link fence

England, a pastoral mix of dairy and sheep farms, grainfields, and fruit orchards.

Just outside of the village of Pewsey the A345 crosses the **Kennet and Avon Canal,** which once connected Bristol with London. A few miles south of Marlborough, just north of the tiny village of **Clench Common** the road crosses the **Wansdyke,** a mysterious earthen bank with a ditch on its north side that runs from here all the way to the Bay of Bristol. Archaeologists think it may have been built in the fifth century to defend the Romano-Briton tribes from the invading Saxons, but as with so many Wessex monuments, no one is really sure.

When you reach the **A4,** you'll want to turn **left,** but drive through handsome Marlborough first. A fine market town with a square lined with Georgian homes, a colonnade, and delightful bow-fronted Regency shops, it is also home to one of Britain's finest private (mysteriously called "public") schools. The school is at the west end of town and in its precincts is a Neolithic mound called *Maerl's Barrow,* alleged to be Merlin's tomb, and from which the town takes its name. At the western end of the market square is a former church now used as a Tourist Information Centre.

Then continue west on the A4 past **Fyfield** and **West Overton** and, at the first opportunity after the roadside café on the right side of the road, turn **right** down a narrow lane, the **B4003,** and enter the realm of mystery. After you crest a small hill, the **West Kennet Avenue**—stone sentinels ranked in two parallel rows along the roadside to your left—leads you on to the next rise. There, curving out left and right before you, are the massive uncut megaliths of the **Avebury Stone Circle.** In the middle of the circle, like some kind of crack in the time-space continuum, is the modern village of **Avebury,** complete with pub, village store, and cozy cottages, carrying on as if it were no place special instead of the heart of the densest and most inexplicable array of Neolithic monuments in Europe.

If, by some miracle, you arrive early, stop in at the information center in the barn opposite the National Trust shop and buy the booklet *Footprints Through Avebury,* the definitive guidebook. Then get settled (see Creature Comforts below) and spend the golden hours of early evening wandering amid the massive stones, using the walking guide in tomorrow morning's itinerary. If it's late, get settled, have dinner, and prepare for a night in one of the strangest places in England.

CREATURE COMFORTS
Daily Bed

There are three well-marked B&B establishments scattered along Avebury's little main street. If you find them booked, stop in at the Tourist Information Centre in the barn opposite the National Trust shop and ask them to help. There are a number of farmhouse B&Bs scattered around the landscape and in nearby Winterbourne Monkton. If all else fails, there are a lot of places to stay in Marlborough, only fifteen minutes or so away.

Should you wish to book a room in advance, write directly to Tourist Information Centre, The Great Barn, Avebury, Wiltshire SN8 1RF, or phone (06723) 425. In Marlborough, write Tourist Information Centre, St. Peter's Church, High Street, Marlborough, Wiltshire SN8 1HQ, or phone (0672) 53989. Both are open seasonally.

Daily Bread

Avebury is a very small village and has no restaurants per se. The pub serves only light meals in the evening. An atmospheric old pub at the intersection of the A4 and A361, just southwest of the village, was once a carriage and freight-wagon station, where man and beast were both refreshed, and has an imaginative menu. There is a wide variety of other pubs, hotel restaurants, and freestanding restaurants in Marlborough, a town so handsome that it is well worth the detour to wander its market square and "yards" (alleys).

♦ DAY TWELVE

Time-traveling through Southern England

ANCIENT AVEBURY ♦ MODERN ENGLAND MEDIEVAL SUSSEX

- ♦ A morning walk around Avebury's prehistoric sites
- ♦ A drive east skirting England's "golden corridor"
- ♦ An afternoon visit to the Weald and Downland Museum

Avebury is a haunting place to see at all times and in all weathers, but most impressive of all on a still moonlit night, when the old church and cottages of the village seem quite new and insignificant...
—Sir John Betjeman, 1950

Circles within circles, "avenues" of standing stones, tombs, temples, causewayed enclosures, earthen banks snaking over the horizon: the landscape around tiny Avebury is a giant enigma, its meaning mysterious and impenetrable.

In private moments, elderly locals will confess they believe the various pieces of the mysterious landscape, taken together, are the representation of a goddess, a kind of Earth Mother, but even the most romantic imagination has trouble making that leap. For one thing, centuries separate the various parts.

One thing *is* known: the rolling hills of the Marlborough Downs and Salisbury Plain were the most densely populated region of Stone Age Britain, and Avebury was its ceremonial heart. The sheer human effort expended to create these monuments, involving millions of man-hours and an extraordinary administrative organization, suggest a driving force close to the very core of Neolithic English civilization. But despite extensive research, the nature of that force remains shrouded in mystery.

The mystery was troubling enough to superstitious medieval farmers that they buried several dozen of the great stones before one fell and killed a digger, frightening them from the task. Then greed, not superstition, drove seventeenth- and eighteenth-century farmers to break up the megaliths for building stone. Luckily the stones, nearly 100 percent silica, were uncooperative and the destruction was slow. Still, it was not until the mid-1800s that the monuments around Avebury began to be protected, by which time scores had been destroyed. In the 1920s, Alexander Keiller, heir to the Dundee Marmalade fortune and an amateur archaeologist, bought the town and much of the surrounding land and spent more than a decade demolishing encroaching farm buildings, excavating the sites, and reerecting the surviving stones. Later he sold the sites to the National Trust.

Today, the stones are being exploited in a more subtle but no less controversial manner: a developer has moved into Avebury Manor and turned the house into a "Tourist Attraction" complete with garish sign, torture chamber, and wax figures. Mercifully, the manor stands apart from the circle and village, so the project is not especially intrusive.

Meanwhile, the stones look on impassively, quietly asserting their immutability, as if to say: "We were here before all this, we will be here long after."

The ruggedly primitive Avebury Ring—so large it encircles the village

🚶 A MORNING AMONG THE ANCIENTS

Distance: 3.5 miles/5.6 kilometers; allow 2 hours
Difficulty: Very easy
Total Elevation Gain: Minor, perhaps 100 feet/34 meters
Map: Local walking guide *Footprints Through Avebury,* available at National Trust shop

If you're lucky, you will awake this morning to an Avebury cloaked in chilly morning fog. Be up and out early so you can wander among the stones of the **Avebury Ring** at their most mysterious, with the rising sun slanting through the mist and the vague, steaming shapes of grazing cows and skittish sheep your only companions. From the little car park opposite the craft shop in the village, turn **right** up the lane a few steps, then **left** through the kissing gate to the quadrant of the circle in which the majority of stones still stand.

The sandstone giants, raw and brutish, curve away along the edge of a deep ditch, their shapes alternately long and thin or roughly diamond or triangular. Keiller proposed that these might be male and fe-

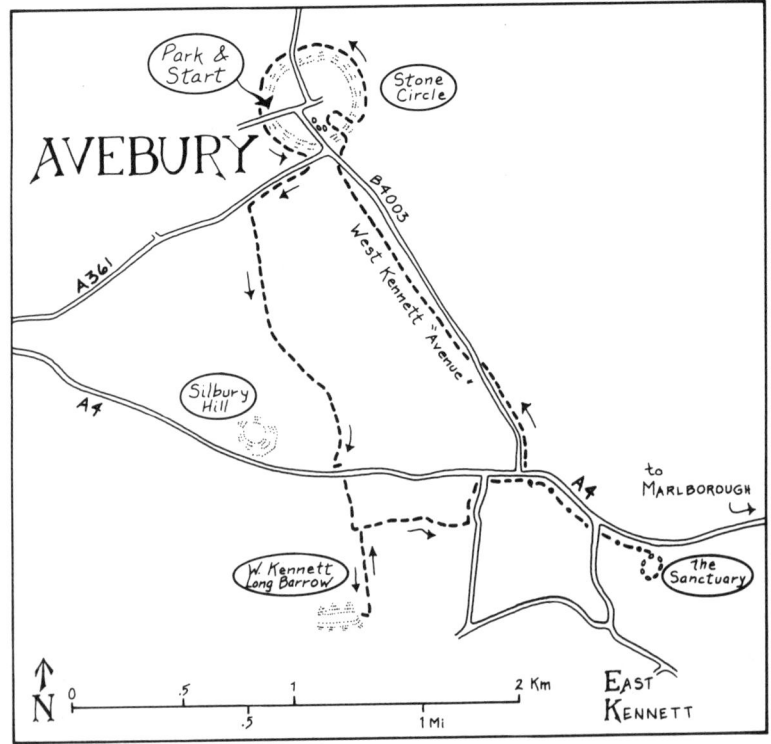

male symbols, respectively, but it's anybody's guess. The stones, ranging from 10 to 13 feet (3 to 4 meters) tall and weighing as much as 35 tons, are unhewn—more primitive and somehow more moving than Stonehenge. They were dragged here, perhaps on wooden sledges, some 30 miles (48 kilometers) from the Marlborough Downs, where such stones—called *sarsens*—once were plentiful. Even the name given these stones conveys the fear they invoked in the generations that followed: it comes from *saracen,* a word from the Crusades meaning anything fearful and ungodly. Originally, there were ninety-eight standing stones, spaced regularly around the circle, but only twenty-seven survive. The sites of missing stones are marked with concrete posts.

The stones and the encircling ditch and bank seem all of a piece, but are not. In fact, the stone circle is a relative newcomer to the Avebury complex. The oldest site is **Windmill Hill,** the eroded remnant of a causewayed enclosure just northwest of the present village and dating from about 2900 B.C., nearly 5,000 years ago. Defended by ditches almost invisible today, a primitive community existed here for nearly 1,000 years and then was abandoned. Later, between 1700 and 1400 B.C., the site was used for Bronze Age burial barrows, but by then a much more complex array of sites had been constructed. This morning's walk takes in most of them.

Walk past the standing stones in the first quadrant of the Avebury Ring, down the well-worn path into the ditch, and back up to the top of the bank, overlooking the intersection of the B4003 and the A361. Go through the gate and turn **right,** walking along the A361 to just beyond the other car park. Cross the road carefully and go over the stile, following the path south along the left bank of the River Winterbourne (this path can be muddy).

Ahead and on your right is cone-shaped **Silbury Hill,** perhaps the oddest edifice in Wessex. Some 130 feet (40 meters) high, Silbury Hill was begun in 2750 B.C., several centuries after Windmill Hill was established. Constructed of blocks of compressed chalk excavated from the surrounding ditch, it is the highest man-made prehistoric monument in Europe. Near the top you can make out one of what originally were six "steps" that were subsequently smoothed over with more chalk. Archaeologists estimate it would have taken 700 men, working only with deer antler picks, shoulder-blade scoops, and baskets, at least ten years to construct Silbury Hill. No one knows why they did it; several tunnel excavations into the hill have revealed nothing. Its top is flat and large enough to hold Stonehenge and it may indeed have been a kind of platform for a stone or timber temple, but there is no evidence to confirm this theory.

After you pass the hill (climbing Silbury is prohibited), turn **left** onto the A4 and walk downhill toward the cottages on the right. Cross the busy highway carefully and pass through the gate on the other side.

A clear path crosses the infant River Kennet, then turns **left**. Go through another gate, then follow the fenced path uphill. At the top of the ridge, facing the rising sun and with sweeping views across the downs, is the **West Kennet Long Barrow,** 340 feet (104 meters) long, a mausoleum built at the same time the Windmill Hill settlement was established, nearly 5,000 years ago. Only a sixth of the barrow has been excavated, a corridor lined and roofed with sarsen slabs from which branch five chambers. From the scattered remains of some fifty human beings discovered here, archaeologists conclude the builders of the barrow practiced "excarnation"—that is, their dead were left to the elements, after which the bleached bones were gathered and entombed. Then, from time to time, the tombs were picked over for bones that might make useful tools. Crude, but practical.

After being used for about 1,000 years, the barrow was suddenly filled with chalk rubble and sealed with massive stone slabs. Again, no one knows why. But this was clearly a turning point in the culture of the people who lived here. It was at this point that the truly massive building projects around Avebury—the Ring, Silbury Hill, and the Avenues—were begun. Vast and labor-intensive, these projects suggest a new, sophisticated, and highly organized social system—one which could command and cover the cost of hundreds of relatively specialized laborers who did nothing else but build ceremonial monuments.

From the West Kennet barrow entrance, walk back down the hill, but turn **right** instead of left this time, go over the stile, and walk east along the flint-studded field. When you reach the paved lane that runs between East and West Kennet, turn **left** and walk back to the A4. Here, turn **right** and then **left,** up the B4003 to the **West Kennet Avenue.** (**Note:** A short detour up the A4 to a point roughly opposite the café will take you to "the Sanctuary," a complex of stone and wooden post circles that once anchored the West Kennet Avenue, but was almost completely obliterated by eighteenth-century farmers.)

The West Kennet Avenue consists of the remains of what once were some 100 pairs of parallel stones running 1.5 miles (2.4 kilometers) between the Avebury Ring and the Sanctuary. A second avenue ran from the Ring westward toward Beckhampton. Again, the meaning of these constructions is obscure, but the general layout is quite similar to a younger arrangement at Stonehenge, so some kind of basic design "template" seems to have existed. Walk up the hill through the curving avenue (a number of ritual burials have been discovered at the base of these stones) to the gate in the fence at the northern end of the field. Cross the minor road, go through another gate, and climb through the trees to the top of the bank, once again overlooking the Avebury Ring.

You can tell immediately that the earthworks here were ceremonial

The West Kennet Avenue, one of two "avenues" of parallel monoliths that once led to the Avebury Ring

Where the ancient stones of the Avebury Ring have been destroyed, archeologists have replaced them with cement pillars—locals approve.

because the ditch is on the *inside* of the bank, and therefore was not defensive. Originally, the ditch was an astonishing three stories (9 meters) deep, twice as deep as it is today. It would have taken an estimated 1 million man-hours to remove the 200,000 tons of chalk that were dug from the ditch. The ditch and bank circle, nearly a mile (1.6 kilometers) in circumference, was probably begun around 2500 B.C., the stone circle a few centuries later. In the apex of this quadrant are the remains of one of two inner circles (the other is in the quadrant on the other side of the farm buildings ahead). This circle had an obelisk in its center that Keiller estimated was more than 6 feet (2 meters) taller than any of the other stones. The other inner circle had a group of four standing stones, weighing as much as 60 tons each, at its center.

After circumnavigating the rest of the Ring, you may want to visit the **Wiltshire Folk Life Museum** in the big thatched barn across from the National Trust shop (open daily April through October, 10:00 A.M. to 5:30 P.M.; Saturdays and Sundays, November through March, 1:30 P.M. to 5:00 P.M.), and the **Alexander Keiller Museum,** which houses some of his archaeological finds (open daily April through September, 10:00 A.M. to 6:00 P.M.; October through March, 10:00 A.M. to 4:00 P.M.).

Then it's off for a drive across south-central England to Sussex.

🚗 SKIRTING THE SILICON AND STOCKBROKER BELTS TO SUSSEX

Distance: About 130 miles/210 kilometers
Roads: Primary roads; some divided highway
Driving Time: The balance of the day
Map: Michelin Map #404

> *The southern boundary of this area is formed by the remarkable A272 road, which passes not a single objectionable or ugly place on its cross-country route.*
> —*The Illustrated Guide to Britain*

Five or six hundred years ago, when the English aristocracy began to find London altogether too crowded, sooty, and disease-ridden to be tolerated, they looked south to Kent, Sussex, and Surrey to build their "country houses." So strong was the attraction of the rolling hills, winding lanes, and lush forests south of London that the trend continued well into the nineteenth century. Today the landscape is littered with cavernous mansions attesting to the obvious wealth (if not always the taste) of their builders. The coming of the railroads in the 1800s brought many of these villages within commuting distance of the city and by the early 1900s broad swaths of Surrey became known as "the stockbroker belt" for its sprawling developments of mock-Tudor homes. Today, the area is once again following the lead of the transportation system; the M4, M3, and M23 corridors and the international airports to which they are linked have spawned rapid development of electronics-related industrial parks and associated housing and shopping developments, driving the cost of land and housing in southeast England through the ceiling (and making it difficult for traditional rural residents and businesses to survive).

This afternoon, we skirt the southern edge of this developed area and drive through some lovely English scenery to the area of south-

ITINERARY: DAY TWELVE

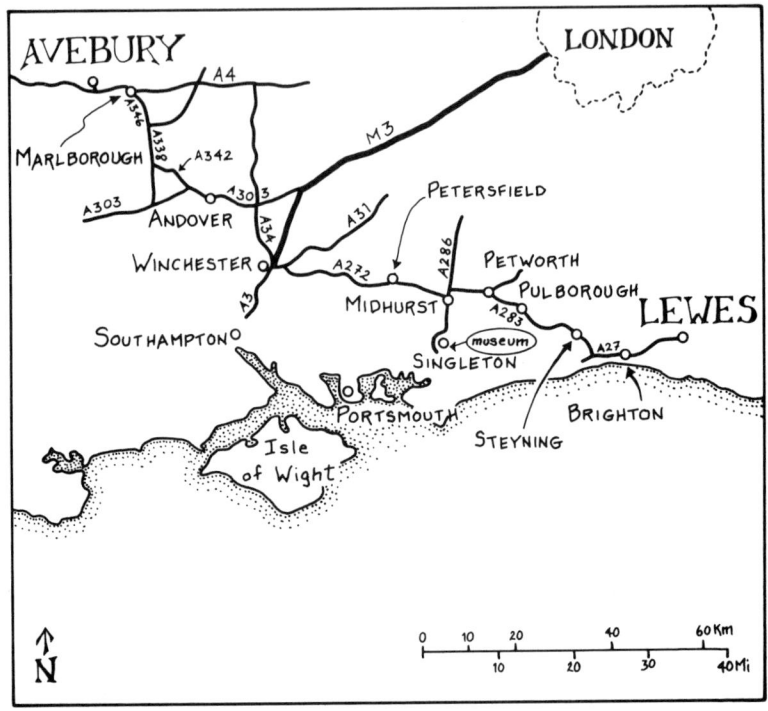

east England as yet relatively untouched by development: the **South Downs** of Sussex and the **Weald** of Kent. You'll spend much of the time on the remarkable **A272**—the only road that runs east and west through the countryside, rather than up to London.

From Avebury, take the A4 east to Marlborough, then turn southeast on the **A346** along the edge of the **Savernake Forest,** a Saxon royal hunting forest that went to seed and was relandscaped in the eighteenth century by—who else?—the ever-busy "Capability" Brown. You once again cross the pretty Kennet and Avon Canal, then merge with the **A338** at **Burbage** and continue south. When the A346 branches **left** follow it to join first the **A342** and then the **A303** heading east into **Hampshire.** The A303 skirts the southern edge of **Andover** and, after perhaps 5 more miles (8 kilometers), intersects with the **A34.** Take the A34 south in the direction of **Winchester,** a major Roman settlement, the capital of Saxon England, and the home of the longest cathedral in Europe. Just north of the city you enter a huge roundabout where the A34 intersects with the **M3.** Here follow signs for the **A31** toward **Alton**—and if you happen to be traveling in early spring you'll find the landscape here blanketed with acres of blooming daffodils, grown as a cash crop. At the next roundabout, turn **left,** again following signs for the A31 to Alton, and drive along the base of a ridge.

The **A272** toward **Petersfield** isn't accessible from this direction; so you have to drive a bit farther on, go completely around a roundabout, then double back the same distance, finally turning **left** onto the A272, heading east.

As soon as you do, you leave behind the fast-paced boomlands of the M3 corridor and enter a land of wide arable fields, lovely beech tree-lined roads, hawthorn hedgerows, and sheep meadows—the England of "gentleman farmers." Petersfield, an old wool-market town full of buildings combining the knapped flints of the chalk Downs and the bricks and tiles of the clay lowlands of the Vale of Sussex, sits in a deep valley through which the main London-Portsmouth rail line and the A3 run. At the roundabout just west of Petersfield continue to follow signs for the A272 straight into the village. On the other side of the town, you turn north briefly on the **A3** then turn **right** onto the A272 again, driving through the leafy valley of the River Rother toward **Midhurst.**

Midhurst is an especially handsome market town, full of half-timber buildings and ancient pubs (the Spread Eagle dates from the fifteenth century). A short detour south on the **A286** to the lovely village of **Singleton,** nestled in a fold of the chalk downs, will take you to one of the most intriguing museums in Britain: an "open air" museum of vernacular architecture—remarkable country buildings rescued from certain destruction and rebuilt in one place (see sidebar on page 196).

Heading east on the A272 from Midhurst, you know you are approaching **Petworth** long before you reach the village; an imposing wall runs along the left side of the road for miles, protecting something quite effectively from prying eyes. The "something" on the other side of the 13-mile (21-kilometer) wall is **Petworth House,** a massive Georgian "country house" built in 1688 by the sixth duke of Somerset and set in a 13-acre deer park landscaped by... well, you can probably guess who. Petworth House, famous for its furniture, frescoes, intricate carving, and paintings by Turner, Van Dyck, Rembrandt, and Holbein, among others, is today a National Trust property (park open daily year round, 9:00 A.M. to sunset; house open April through October, Tuesday through Thursday and weekends, as well as Good Friday and Bank Holidays, 1:00 P.M. to 5:00 P.M.).

At Petworth you leave the A272. Turn **right** at the roundabout in the village and follow signs (through two more turns) toward the **A283** and **Pulborough.** The A283 is yet another pretty drive, undulating through hills and valleys and charming villages like **Fittleworth** before finally descending into the valley of the River Arun. Drive through Pulborough and continue southeast on the A283, passing **Parham House**—a handsome Elizabethan mansion with a lovely garden *not*

The Weald and Downland Open Air Museum

In a way, it's a shame to call this award-winning 40-acre monument to architectural conservation a "museum." A nonprofit institution begun more than twenty years ago to acquire, dismantle, restore, and reerect humble countryside buildings threatened with destruction by new development, it has become a lively and fascinating place to see the evolution of architectural forms we take for granted today. There is a medieval farmhouse, complete with furniture and simple front garden, magnificent medieval barns housing rare farm animal breeds, a late-medieval water-lifting wheel that was probably powered by a small boy on a treadmill, handsome seventeenth- and eighteenth-century half-timber cottages with overhanging second stories, a fifteenth- or sixteenth-century market hall and seventeenth-century granary made of timber and brick, a working water-powered mill, a seventeenth-century tollhouse, a nineteenth-century schoolhouse, and many more. The buildings, grouped around a village square or scattered across the hillside just as they might have been before being moved, house a wide array of living craft exhibits: blacksmithing, farming (including huge Shire horses), fence making, timber management and lumber cutting, brickmaking, flour grinding, charcoal making, and more. Plan on spending at least two hours. The museum is open daily April through October, 11:00 A.M. to 6:00 P.M.; November through March, Wednesday, Sunday, and bank holidays, 11:00 A.M. to 4:00 P.M. To return to the itinerary, drive north again to Midhurst.

designed by "Capability" Brown—and continuing along the base of the South Downs escarpment to **Steyning**. Finally, the A283 breaks through a gap in the Downs cut by the River Arun and you turn left at a roundabout onto the main coastal route, the **A27,** heading toward **Brighton**.

This is the least pleasant part of the drive today. The towns of Shoreham, Southwick, Hove, and Brighton are a nearly continuous urbanization, through which the A27 slices at fairly high speed. There are attractions in these towns, especially the Regency resort facilities and oriental Royal Pavilion in Brighton, but they are overwhelmed by over-development and, on balance, are best forgone. Instead, hurry on over the Downs to **Lewes,** this afternoon's final destination.

CREATURE COMFORTS
Daily Bed

Lewes and the countryside around it offer an almost perfect base for the next two nights. Lewes itself is a charming jumble of Tudor, Elizabethan, Georgian, Regency, and Victorian buildings faced with wood clapboards, flint, brick, clay tiles, or limestone (sometimes several in one) and situated on a steep hill overlooking the River Ouse. It has the remains of an eleventh-century castle, bits of an ancient abbey, steep cobbled streets and alleys lined with antique and rare book shops, several good hotels and inns, and an excellent year-round Tourist Information Centre. In addition, the surrounding countryside is dotted with lovely little villages, many of which have B&B establishments, hotels, and good pubs. **Rodmell,** just south of Lewes, is a good example, and it also is home to Monk's House, where novelist Virginia Woolf lived. **Alfriston,** nearby and on tomorrow's itinerary, has ancient inns, guesthouses, and a highly commended freestanding restaurant. For specific suggestions, consult the guides in Further Reading. For advice in advance, contact the Tourist Information Centre, Lewes House, 32 High Street, Lewes, East Sussex BN7 2LX, or phone (0273) 471600.

Daily Bread

Southern England is wealthier than some of the more remote places you've visited on this itinerary and, as a consequence, it can support excellent town and country restaurants, as well as pubs that go beyond the usual for evening meals. As always, your best bet is to ask for recommendations where you spend the night. If you are willing to drive a half-hour or so, the range of choice, and price ranges, is wide indeed. Again, for specific suggestions consult the guidebooks recommended in Further Reading or ask for advice at the Tourist Information Centre.

♦ DAY THIRTEEN

In the Realm of Sea and Sky: A Day in the South Downs

SUSSEX COAST ♦ EASTBOURNE ♦ HASTINGS
HERSTMONCEUX ♦ ALFRISTON

- ♦ Exploring the white cliffs, grassy hills, and wooded valleys of the South Downs Way
- ♦ An alternative drive through the rural villages and Regency resorts of East Sussex

---

> *The glory of these glorious Downs is the breeze. It is the air without admixture. If it comes from the south, the waves refine it; if inland the wheat and flowers and grass distil it. The great headland... is windswept and washed with air; the billows of the atmosphere roll over it.*
> —Richard Jefferies
> nineteenth-century writer and naturalist

For one brief, giddy moment you think you might actually go over the edge. You're striding easily along the springy turf of a narrow emerald valley under a crisp blue sky, when suddenly, without warning —no sign, no fence, nothing—the earth simply drops away before you. For a split second you wrestle furiously with the sense of your own forward momentum before drawing back from the brink. Beneath you, and for miles left and right, a chalk cliff—so emphatically vertical it looks cut with a scalpel, so brilliantly, blindingly white it shimmers in the sun like a mirage—plunges down, down to the bottle green English Channel far below.

Along the South Downs Way

In the Realm of Sea and Sky

Nothing you read, no picture in a book, can prepare you for the sheer whiteness of the "Seven Sisters," the towering chalk precipice over which the South Downs, having traversed the breadth of Sussex, finally fling themselves into the sea. It is so white that it takes several minutes of squinting for your eyes to adjust, as if you had emerged from a darkened room. You squint so long the muscles in your face ache. Still, as you walk west up and over each of the "sisters," you keep returning to the windy cliff face, squinting and marveling at the towering whiteness.

The primitive scratchings on chalk slopes you have encountered elsewhere on this itinerary—the Uffington White Horse in Wiltshire, the Cerne Giant in Dorset—suddenly seem puny and superficial when you are confronted by the enormous depth of the chalk Downs exposed here at the Seven Sisters. From the air, the South Downs look like some giant velvety green earthen rampart erected along the entire south coast to defend England from invaders. It is an apt analogy; from the Stone Age hunter-gatherers who crossed the land bridge from the European mainland, to the later Roman, Saxon, and Norman invaders, the southeast coast has always been a landing stage. Mighty as this rampart seems, however, it is actually a mere shadow of its former self.

The story begins hundreds of millions of years ago, when much of the land here was covered by a shallow sea. Rain and wind eroded the surrounding mountains and, over the eons, mud, silt, and sand accumulated in layers on the sea floor. Then 100 million years ago, the climate turned dry and erosion ceased. In the clear shallow sea, tiny plankton flourished and, as they died, precipitated pure calcium carbonate from the seawater. Gradually, at the rate of about a foot every 30,000 years, a chalk bed accumulated, eventually reaching a depth of over 1,000 feet (300 meters). At the same time, the skeletons of marine creatures were sifting through the sediment, agglomerating in layers and clumps, later to become flint.

Then, some 40 million years later, in one of history's biggest fender benders, the section of the earth's crust geologists call the African Plate collided with the European Plate, ramming the peninsula of Italy northward and pushing up the Alps. In a kind of ripple effect, the layered seabed was thrust above the surface in a huge dome. The chalk at the summit cracked under the pressure and subsequent millennia of rain and frost eventually eroded the soft center, leaving behind a vast, shallow bowl encompassing southeast England and northwest France. Then the bowl cracked and the English Channel was formed. Where the shattered rim of chalk (the North and South Downs) met the Channel, England's famous white cliffs were formed. The land in the center, a mix of clays and sands, became the Weald. Later still, torrents of meltwater from retreating glaciers cut deep valleys through the chalk, lowering the water table and leaving behind dry valleys in the folds of the softly rounded hills.

The names early settlers gave to the landscape of Sussex and Kent tells us a good deal about how they used it. The word *downs* (which are, after all, *up*) comes from an ancient word for "grazed hilltop." *Weald,* in contrast, is Old Saxon for "forest" (we get *wood* and *wald* from the same root). As elsewhere in southern England, early man cleared the highlands, using them for grazing and as transportation routes, and left the lowlands for forest and hunting grounds, clearing them only later when tools improved and the demand for land increased. Grazing, especially sheep grazing, became the Downs' specialty. As recently as the last century, these hills were bare and featureless, nibbled relentlessly by roaming herds of South Downs sheep and by rabbits, which still pock the turf with their holes. Sheep still graze here today, but far fewer than in earlier centuries. Common Market grain subsidies and intensive farming techniques have turned many of the meadows into vast fields of wheat, barley, and rapeseed. In the spring, when the fields are freshly plowed, the idiocy of these subsidies is apparent: the fields, which look snowy at a distance, are little more than huge expanses of chalk and flint rubble, which have no business being tilled.

Up on the softly undulating tops of the Downs, however, lush green meadows survive and you have a marvelous sense of being on top of the world, with only the wind and the songs of skylarks as your companions.

🏃 A SOUTH DOWNS CHALK WALK

Distance: 12 miles/19 kilometers; allow 5-6 hours
Difficulty: Moderately strenuous along coast, then generally easy with a few moderate hills
Total Elevation Gain: A few hundred feet/meters
Gear: Comfortable walking shoes/sneakers, rain gear, sunblock, camera and film
Map: Ordnance Survey Pathfinder #1324

Today's walk, a remarkable combination of coastal, riverine, forest, and downland scenery interspersed with charming villages, begins just north of **Eastbourne,** roughly a half-hour drive from Lewes. Take the minor road south from Lewes through **Rodmell, Southease,** and **Piddinghoe** to **Newhaven** and turn **left** onto the **A259,** following signs for Eastbourne. Just east of **Seaford** the road climbs over a hill—called the "High and Over" locally—drops down into the valley, crosses the meandering River Cuckmere, then climbs another hill, with the Friston Forest on your left. At the top of this hill is the tiny village of **Friston.**

ITINERARY: DAY THIRTEEN

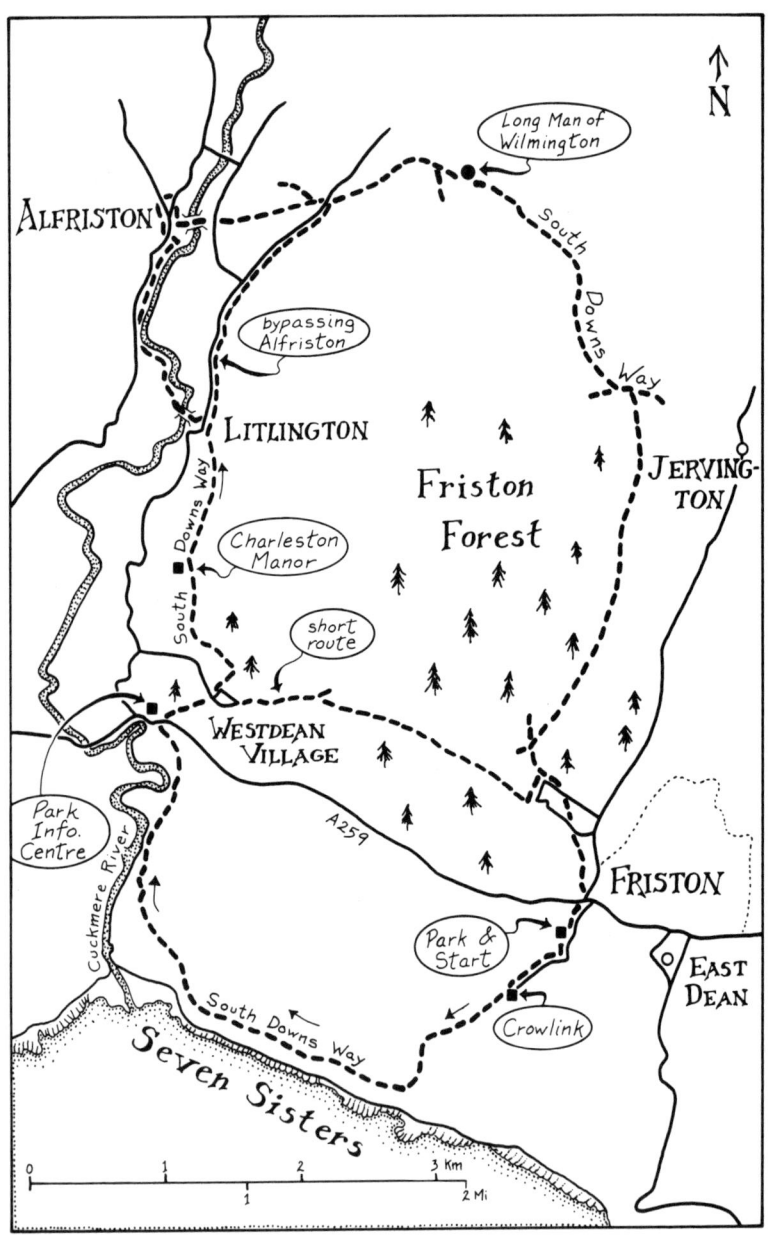

Turn **right** at the church, drive a few hundred yards (or meters) up a poorly paved road signposted for **Crowlink,** and park in the gravel car park a few yards ahead.

From the National Trust information sign, follow the paved lane downhill to the right, rather than crossing the green hilltop straight ahead. Around the bend, in a lovely dry valley tucked between the swelling hills, is the tiny settlement of Crowlink, a stunning cluster of cottages, barns, and manor house, complete with leaded windows, climbing roses, and snoozing cats. The paved road becomes a farm track, goes through a gate, then becomes a footpath, marked by a blue arrow waymarker. Ahead, the valley narrows to a broad green gap carpeted in close-cropped grass scattered with low-growing wildflowers—vetches, creeping thyme, daisies, and buttercups.

Then, suddenly, the sea. The meadow simply ends in a dizzying drop hundreds of feet to the English Channel. Ahead, sea and sky merge and boats that look like toys steam toward the French coast, invisible in the hazy distance. Below are the extraordinary chalk cliffs of the **Seven Sisters,** their dazzling white faces marked here and there by thin ribbons of flint, like beauty spots on geishas. You turn right here and begin the steep rollercoaster ascent and descent of four of the Sisters. This is the toughest part of the entire walk and you soon are giving thanks that you will make the acquaintance of only four of these ladies—Brass Point, Rough Brow, Short Brow, and Haven Brow.

At the last stile on top of Haven Brow, the Sisters end abruptly at a wonderful windblown bluff. Far below is the broad delta of the Cuckmere River, the only river mouth in southern England that isn't developed as a port, and a notorious haunt of smugglers in the eighteenth century. The South Downs Way continues straight ahead, downhill toward the beach, then curves around to the right to follow the river—its lazy meanders long since cut off by a straight channel. Instead of following the Way, turn right at the stile and walk diagonally across the slope, over another stile, and then gradually downhill along an obvious footpath, with the clumps of yellow flowering gorse on your left and the brow of the hill on your right. This higher route provides much better views of the river valley as you head upstream (though bird watchers may wish to get closer to the marshy oxbows of the old river bed). In a few minutes you reach the floor of the valley and pick up a white chalk lane, part of the Seven Sisters Country Park, and follow it to the car park next to the A259 at **Exceat.**

Cross the road and turn **right,** pausing to visit the excellent Park Interpretive Centre, located in a lovely group of flint-faced barns roofed in clay tiles (there also is a "Living World Natural History Museum"). Then, just above these buildings, turn **left** up a short driveway by a wooden NO PARKING sign and pick up the public footpath marked with a blue acorn waymarker. You climb up a steep meadow to the trees

The classic flint-faced country church at Westdean

ahead, go through a gate in a beautifully constructed flint wall (with superb views backward to the river mouth and sea beyond), and then enter the **Friston Forest**, heading down a path that is actually a series of wooden steps, marked for **Westdean**. The forest is dark and cool and carpeted in ivy.

At the bottom of the hill you pass the iris-edged duck pond in the pretty, isolated, and ancient little hamlet of Westdean, thought to have been the site of a palace built by Alfred the Great. (**Note:** For a shortcut back to your car, turn right at the duck pond and walk up the lane through the village. Where the road turns sharply left toward the church, continue straight ahead, up the hill and into the forest, following an unpaved track. At the fork turn right and carry on straight through the forest, where you can pick up the end of the main itinerary.) For the main walk, continue **straight** ahead past the duck pond and up the opposite hill, following signs for **Litlington.** Halfway up the hill, turn left at another signposted path and continue along high above the village, still following signs to Litlington. The broad green path soon picks up the right of way for a power line and leads through the forest. Eventually the path dead-ends and you go over a stile straight ahead and down another steep, stepped path through a thicket of blackthorn and wild cherry. Then follow the path as it curves along a line of beech trees edging Charleston Manor, a lovely complex of house and barn dating from the Norman Conquest (grounds open weekdays, May through September). Just opposite the barn the path turns **right** over a stile marked for the South Downs Way.

Here you break out into open fields again, climbing steadily to the ridge top. After several more stiles, you duck under a low-growing tree and proceed across the field past a lovely Georgian house, making for Litlington straight ahead. At the other side of this sloping meadow, turn **left** down a lane and **right** into the village. There's a good pub in the village with an extensive lunch menu.

(**Note:** If you want to avoid looping across the river through Alfriston, just head north on the road through Litlington and, where the main road turns sharply left, go straight up the hill instead, picking up the itinerary at the top.)

Behind the pub, a footbridge crosses the Cuckmere River. On the other side, turn **right** and walk upstream toward the spire of St. Andrew's Church, near the riverbank in **Alfriston.** St. Andrew's is both typical of Sussex churches—squat and vaguely Germanic, with a four-sided spire remarkably like a witch's peaked hat—and superior to many. It is built in the shape of a cross and faced in beautifully worked square knapped flints, as are the walls enclosing the green onto which it faces. Next door is the Clergy House, a superb example of medieval Sussex vernacular architecture and the first building ever purchased by the National Trust—in 1896 for £10. From the green turn **left** into the village itself and head north along its winding main street, lined with Tudor half-timbered shops and inns, some faced with flint, others draped in clay tiles. The most famous inn is the fifteenth-century Star, with its pretty trio of oriels and grotesquely carved red lion (the figurehead from a wrecked ship). The Star played a key role during the seventeenth and eighteenth centuries in Alfriston's principal industry—smuggling; it is said there was a 10-mile (16-kilometer) passage leading from one of its rooms to the sea.

Beyond the Star, the village ends in a little square shaded by a huge spreading chestnut tree and marked by a worn old market cross. From here, backtrack a bit and return to the river, crossing at the delicate white pedestrian bridge opposite the church. On the other side continue **straight** ahead, across the road and up the lane opposite, bearing **left** at the signpost toward the South Downs Way again. At the top of a meadow, cross a minor road and pick up a well-marked track continuing uphill along the spine of a ridge. Where the track veers around to the right continue **straight** ahead instead, following the fence line along the edge of a steep slope to the top of Windover Hill.

Directly below the crest of the hill is the ancient **Long Man of Wilmington,** a 227-foot (69-meter) giant cut into the north-facing chalk escarpment of the Downs. Like a demure version of the Cerne Giant, it is of undetermined purpose and age. Standing upright and holding a staff in each hand, it bears some resemblance to a figure on a Roman coin, but may be earlier or later. It may even be the representation of a medieval pilgrim, since it faces the ruins of the Benedictine priory at Wilmington.

Cresting the last of the "Seven Sisters" high above the Cuckmere River estuary

In truth, the Long Man is not the real reason for climbing this hill (he's better seen from below anyway); it is the magnificent view from the crest. From high on Windover Hill you can see far down the Cuckmere Valley and west along the whaleback ridges of the Downs to Firle Beacon and beyond. Northward, with the wind full in your face and the air full of birdsong, the great farmland and forestland of the Vale of Sussex is spread before your feet. Farther north, the rumpled clay hills of the Weald rise gently in the afternoon haze.

When you can tear yourself away from the view, continue uphill along the fence, go over the stile, then bear **right,** crossing the field diagonally to a gate on the other side and rejoining the lane as it comes around the hill from the right. Here bear **left** and follow the farm track a few hundred yards (or meters) to a point just beyond the apex of a deep, uninhabited combe on your right. Then veer **left,** following a series of concrete posts that mark the northern loop of the South Downs Way.

This is the Downs as they must have been a century or more ago: a high, wide, gently rounded ridge cloaked in springy green grass, well clipped by grazing sheep. The air is brisk and clear, the views spectacular. If you get down on all fours and look closely you find the turf is full of specially adapted flowers and herbs. They grow in flat rosettes or spreading mats, taking care to flower at ground level, rather than on tall—and edible—stalks. Yellow worts, pink vetches, magenta thyme, tiny white daisies, miniature buttercups, and creamy yellow primroses in spring—all have adapted to the threat of grazing sheep by lying low.

The plateau continues to curve ever so gently around to the east and south, eventually drawing even with the village of Jervington, in the dry valley below. After passing a bit of scrub woods on the left you come to a clear intersection. The South Downs Way turns left here and descends to the village. Instead, however, continue **straight** ahead, ducking through another bit of scrub woods before emerging once again at the edge of the same curving ridge, heading south.

After perhaps 1.5 miles (2.4 kilometers) of easy walking, keeping the boundary of the Friston Forest on your right, you come to a group of horse jumps. A path emerges from the forest on the right and crosses into a small wood on the left, fringed with flowering wild cherry in the spring. Turn **left** here and follow this path downhill, through the wood, across the intersection with another path, and **straight** ahead, following the signpost to Friston. Soon you emerge and follow a paved lane partway up a gentle hill until you reach a post pointing **right** to Friston and East Dean. Go up a few steps, through a gate in a beautiful flint wall, and across a field to another wall and gate. Here you descend into a lovely paved private lane lined with beech trees and hundreds of daffodils and narcissus in the spring. Cross to another gate in the wall on the other side, and climb diagonally uphill toward a bit of woods and a stile. On the other side, a series of wooden steps carries the path up through the wood and past a group of private homes, before turning **left** and emerging at the A259 opposite the church at Friston. Cross carefully and go up the lane, returning finally to the Crowlink car park.

DIVERSIONS
🚶 Cliffs, Marshes, Weald, and Downs: A Tour of East Sussex

Distance: About 75 miles/120 kilometers
Roads: Mostly primary roads, some minor roads
Driving Time: Most of the day, depending on stops
Map: Michelin Map #404

If today's walk is "not on," as they say here, a leisurely car tour, taking in many of the best natural and man-made features of East Sussex, is an intriguing alternative. Begin as if you were driving to the start of today's walk, by heading south on the unclassified road from Lewes through Rodmell, then turning **left** onto the **A259**. Beyond **Seaford** the road climbs up onto the Downs, descends into the Cuckmere River valley, then climbs up again along the edge of the Friston Forest. After passing Friston's little daffodil-trimmed church, the road tips over the edge of a steep hill. Before you reach the bottom, turn **right** into the postcard-pretty village of **East Dean.** Follow the road **left** past the village store, then turn **right** at the bottom, heading south along the floor of Birling Gap. Just as it seems about to reach the beach, the road bends around to the left and runs up along the back of the coastal ridge, climbing steadily to the top of **Beachy Head,** the towering chalk bluff that, at 534 feet (163 meters), is the highest point on the south coast. (A short walk here offers terrific views west to the Seven Sisters and east to Eastbourne.) From Beachy Head the road curves away from the sea; at the T-junction, turn sharply **right** and stay right, descending by the winding **B2103** into **Eastbourne.**

Eastbourne is what Brighton wishes it still were: a genteel Regency-era seaside resort. The beach, 3 miles (4.8 kilometers) long, is edged with a three-tiered promenade supported by classical columns and trimmed with wildly colorful formal gardens that change with the seasons. There is an elegant little waterfront bandstand surrounded by hundreds of cheerful blue and white deck chairs. And the entire shoreline is fronted with soaring Regency and Victorian hotels, brilliant white architectural confections unmarred by a single shop or "amusement" center. The centerpiece, however, is the resort's requisite pier, a graceful pleasure dome full of the vaguely oriental flourishes typical of the period, once again painted a blinding white, trimmed in blue, and

In the Realm of Sea and Sky **209**

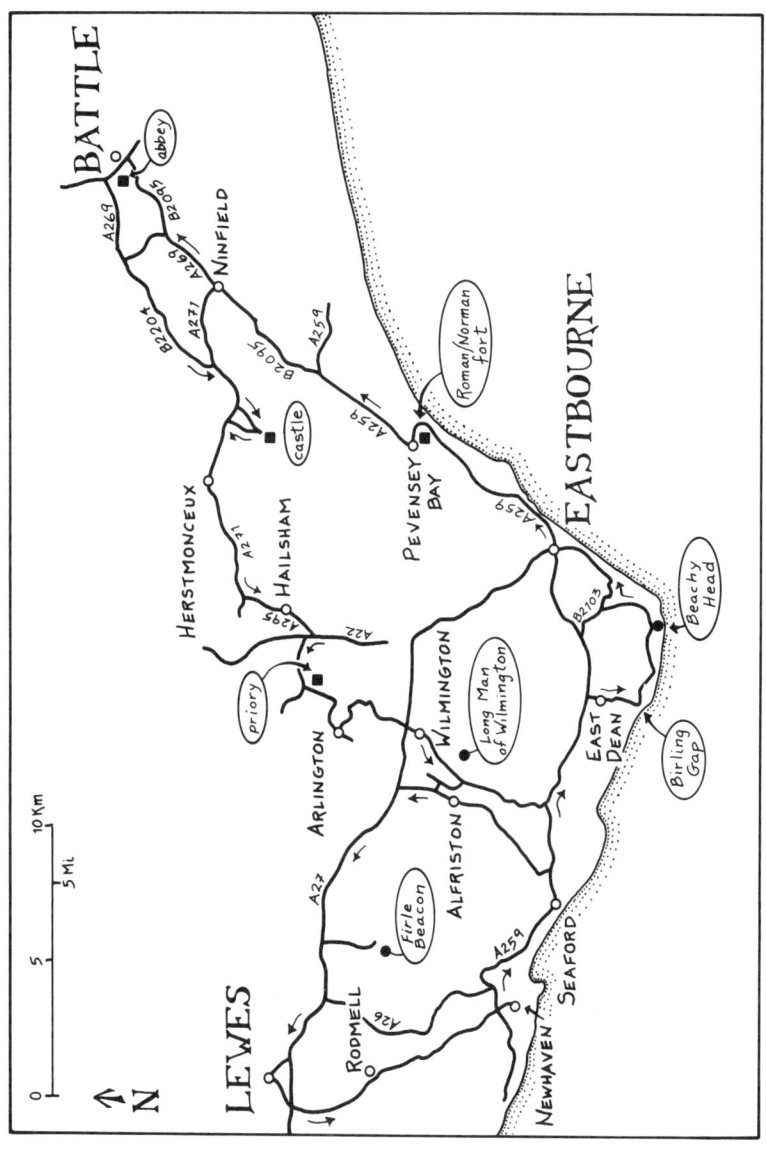

fitted out with marvelous Victorian cast-iron railings and lamps. If you squint slightly, you can almost see Eastbourne as it was a century ago, elegant carriages drawn up before the stately hotels and the promenades thronged with women in billowy white dresses and parasols and men in blazers and straw boaters.

After you've had a chance to explore, continue east along the seafront, past the Martello Tower (one of over a hundred gun turrets built along the coast in the early 1800s to defend against an invasion by Napoleon that never materialized) and through two roundabouts, finally picking up the A259 again toward **Pevensey Bay.** At the edge of this village, where the A259 turns right, turn **left** onto the **A27** instead to see the well-preserved remains of a fortress the Romans built here in the fourth century to rebuff the invading Saxons (open daily). Knowing a strategic site when he saw one (Pevensey was a port before the sea retreated), William the Conqueror's half-brother built a new castle inside the walls of the old Roman fort, and it remained a garrisoned stronghold for four centuries (open daily, summer only). It seems an oddity here among the vacation bungalows, but if you screen out the holiday development in your mind's eye, the fortress appears very different indeed: a squat, malevolent presence lurking in the reedy marshland, ready to pounce on the unwary invader.

Then return to the A259, heading east across the lush Pevensey Levels toward **Bexhill** and **Hastings.** After perhaps 3 miles (5 kilometers), bear left onto the **B2095** in the direction of **Ninfield** and **Battle.** At the T-junction in Battle, turn **left** and follow signs for **Battle Abbey.** It was here in 1066, not in Hastings, that perhaps the pivotal event in England's long history occurred: the defeat of the Saxon King Harold by the Norman William—forever since, "the Conqueror." In thanks for his victory the new King William I built an abbey on the battlefield, its high altar above the site where Harold fell. The village of Battle, now a busy market town with a lovely mix of architectural styles, grew around the abbey, which, like so many others, was dissolved and largely destroyed by Henry VIII. The battle grounds, laid out so you can follow the ebb and flow of the struggle, are managed by English Heritage (open daily Good Friday through September, 10:00 A.M. to 6:00 P.M.; October through Maundy Thursday, 10:00 A.M. to 4:00 P.M.).

From the abbey car park, turn **right** to the High Street and then **left** and up to the roundabout at the top of the village. Here turn **left** again, onto the **A269.** Then, where this road turns sharply left, go **straight** ahead instead, on the **B2204,** through lovely rolling Wealden farmlands, to the **A271.** Turn **right** and carry on along a ridge toward **Herstmonceux** (pronounced "hurstmonsoo"). Just west of the village of **Boreham Street,** watch for a minor road **left** to **Herstmonceux**

Caught in a Victorian time warp: the pier at Eastbourne

Sussex "Trugs"

For centuries, woodworkers in Herstmonceux have been making simple but beautiful oval-shaped wooden baskets called "trugs" (from the Saxon word *trog* for a boat-shaped vessel). Genuine Sussex trugs are made in only two places, both of them in this village (there are plywood imitations). They consist of a split, steamed, and bent sweet chestnut handle and rim, with the bark intact, and a gently curved basket made of lapped, tapered staves of split and shaved willow, nailed to the chestnut frame. Used by farmers' wives for produce and egg gathering and as market baskets, trugs were "discovered" by Queen Victoria at the Great Exhibition in 1851 and have been coveted by gardeners ever since. Craftsmen continue the tradition today both in the center of the village and just to the west on the A271.

Castle, a superb moated manor house built in the fifteenth century and one of the earliest brick buildings in Britain. Restored in 1910, it today is the home of the Royal Greenwich Observatory, which maintains a small astronomy exhibit here (open daily Good Friday through September). Then backtrack up the winding lane to the A271 again and turn **left** into the village, famous for its "trug" shops.

Continue west on the A271 for a few miles, then turn **left** onto the **A295** and drive through the busy market town of **Hailsham,** following signs for the **A22**. At the A22, turn **right,** then immediately **left** onto a minor road signposted for **Upper Dicker** and **Arlington**. After a few minutes you'll reach the beautiful remains of **Michelham Priory,** founded by the Augustinians in 1229. The priory complex was constructed on a 6-acre island created when the monks diverted the River Cuckmere through a long moat. The church was destroyed during the Dissolution, but the splendid gatehouse, mill, rectory, medicinal garden, and several workshops remain. The grounds are blissfully peaceful, the quiet broken only by the splashing water at the mill and quacking ducks in the moat.

From the priory driveway, turn **left** into Arlington and **left** again in the middle of the village, toward **Wilmington**. Cross the A27 and continue south into the sleepy village. Wilmington is a classic example of the medieval strip village: houses lined up cheek by jowl along the roadside, running up from a small green to the church at the other end of town; long, thin plots of land running out their back doors; and the whole complex surrounded by larger enclosed grazing and arable fields. As you pass the church, the **Long Man of Wilmington,** etched in the chalk of the northern escarpment of the South Downs, confronts you directly ahead (see earlier description).

Continue along this road, circling around the base of Windover Hill, then dropping down to the Cuckmere Valley at **Lullington**. Turn **right** here, heading north along the river, then turn **left** over the bridge and **left** again into **Alfriston**. After you've explored the village, one of the nicest in East Sussex, head north again, passing the bridge over which you crossed earlier. In **Drusillas** there is an English Wine Centre where you can sample the products of the rapidly growing English wine industry. Afterwards, turn **left** onto the **A27** and, after perhaps 4 miles (6.4 kilometers), turn left onto a minor road signposted for **Firle Beacon,** at 713 feet (217 meters) the highest point in the eastern Downs, with magnificent views south to the channel and north across the Weald. Then return to the A27 and turn **left,** and you'll quickly be back in Lewes.

CREATURE COMFORTS

See yesterday's listings.

♦ DAY FOURTEEN

Among the Gardens of the Garden of England

RYE ♦ BODIAM CASTLE ♦ KENT'S GARDENS
LONDON

- ♦ A visit to a landlocked seaport
- ♦ A walk around England's most romantic castle
- ♦ A drive through the Kentish countryside
- ♦ Visits to three of England's finest gardens
- ♦ Returning to London

> *On, on! through meadows managed like a garden, a paradise of hops and high production...*
> —Lord Byron
> *Don Juan*, 1819-1824

Imagine it is a chill autumn night in the late eighteenth century: a dense white fog rolls in off the sea and coils its way up the steep streets and alleys of the ancient town of Rye, mixing the tang of the sea with the sharp smell of coal fires burning in unseen grates. The little shops, their tiled and weatherboarded walls leaning this way and that, their roofs tilting crazily downhill, huddle together in the shadows, silent and dark. The leaded windows of the buildings overhanging the streets cast dim pools of light on the glistening cobbled pavements below, the interconnecting smugglers' passages in their attics invisible behind dripping façades. The muffled sounds seeping from the ancient black and white half-timbered Mermaid Inn suddenly swell to an angry roar, then recede again, as a drunken seaman lurches out the door and off into the damp darkness.

That's when you may hear him... tap, tap, tapping up the hill... his cane preceding him, his arm outstretched to avoid collision, his sightless eyes peering through the swirling mist—Old Blind Pew, messenger of death, come to deliver someone the "black spot," the pirates' code for impending execution.

When the twentieth century sun rises and burns through the eighteenth century mist, however, Rye shakes off its piratical past and becomes, once again, what it is today: a charming anomaly, a medieval seafaring town abandoned by the sea. Looking for all the world like a beached frigate with flags still flying, Rye is marooned high and dry on its hill above the grassy green sea of Romney Marsh. The wheeling, screeching gulls are still here, the whiff of salt is still in the air, the crooked streets and crooked buildings are unmistakably maritime, but the sea has long since retreated some 5 miles (8 kilometers) to the south.

With the downs, marshes, and sands of Sussex stretching out beyond the bridge to the south and the rolling, fertile hills of the Kentish Weald rising beyond the north gate, the medieval portals of Rye make the perfect transition between these two very different English counties. Today's itinerary, the last in the open countryside, turns away from the sea and cuts a wide arc through the interior of Kent, the "Garden of England," before returning to London.

The Mermaid Inn, Rye

🚗 ROMANTIC CASTLES AND RAVISHING GARDENS: A TOUR THROUGH KENT

Distance: 100 miles/161 kilometers (to the M25 London orbital)
Roads: Mostly well-marked primary and secondary roads
Driving Time: All day, with frequent stops
Map: Michelin Map #404

Begin this morning by driving east from the Lewes area on the A27 toward **Hastings**. Beyond Pevensey Bay, where the A27 becomes the A259, the road curves inland across the flat expanse of the Levels. Then it turns back to the sea again, running along behind the shingle beaches between **Bexhill** and Hastings.

Hastings was already a busy port when William the Conqueror landed here in 1066. Today, it's a typically characterless coastal urbanization, but there is a pearl hidden within this rather unattractive shell: as you enter the city, follow signs for "Town Center" and then "Old Town." After you have passed most of the city, a massive sandstone cliff looms ahead above a tightly packed cluster of medieval houses a few hundred yards from the water. Brightly painted fishing boats are winched up on the shingle beach and narrow, three-story black net-drying shacks stand singly and in groups among the boats, like penguins on a beach. After you've wandered around the fishing boats a bit, take the A259 Folkstone Road uphill for several blocks, and turn **right** at a small park onto Harold Road, and then **right** again onto All Saints Street. Suddenly, it's the Middle Ages again, when Hastings—with Dover, Hythe, New Romney, and Sandwich—was a *Cinque* (French for five, but pronounced "sink") *Port,* with a royal charter requiring they provide ships and men to protect the coast from French invaders and granting tax exemptions and a blind eye to piracy in return. All Saints Street preserves that era, with wonderfully crooked little weatherboarded and half-timbered houses, shops, and pubs all crammed together on the steep hill, overhanging the street so closely that hardly any light reaches the pavement. In this setting it wouldn't surprise you at all to see a swarthy peglegged seaman clumping up the hill, with a parrot perched on his shoulder.

Complete this detour by turning **right** down by the boats and then **right** again onto the A259 out of town toward **Winchelsea** and **Rye**. The ancient towns of Rye and Winchelsea had equal status with the Cinque Ports, but were treated very differently by Mother Nature. Where the sea left Rye high and dry, its sister Winchelsea—whose name means "shingle island on the levels"—was engulfed in a storm in 1287. Today, old Rye and "new" Winchelsea could hardly be more different.

Among the Gardens of the Garden of England **217**

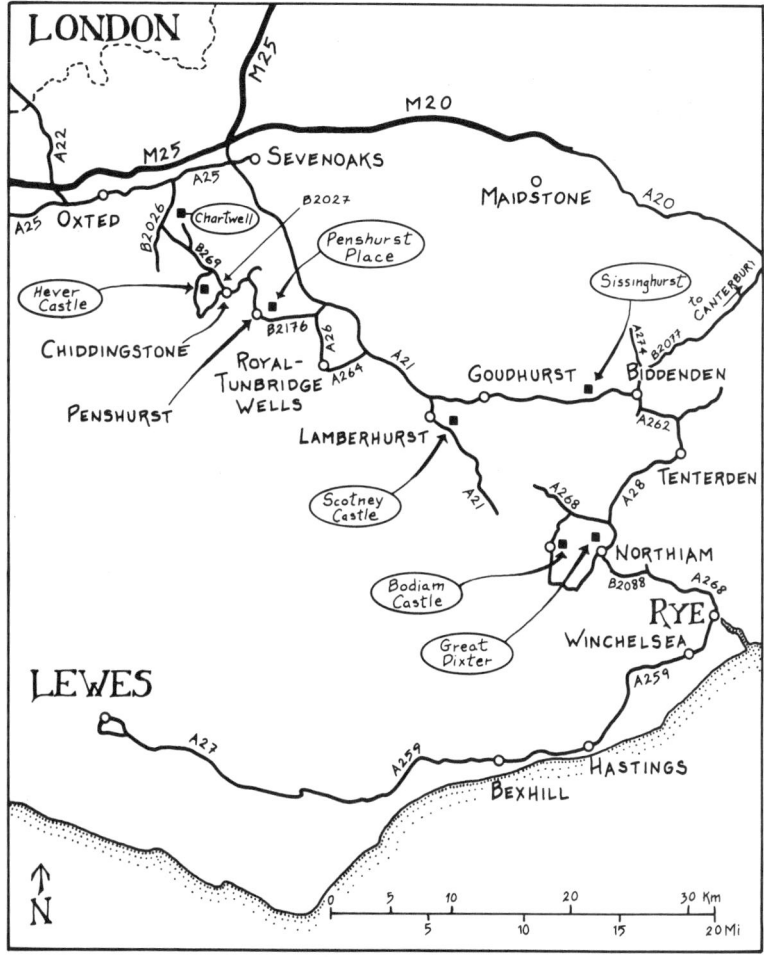

The new town, built by Edward I on a hill overlooking the sea, was England's first planned village. Enter it by turning right onto a minor road just before the A259 takes a sharp left around the hill. Passing through New Gate, you discover a little village of neat, flower-bedecked cottages and shops, tile-hung, weatherboarded, and whitewashed, laid out in an orderly grid with the church at the center. Since Winchelsea was repeatedly attacked by the French after it was built, neither the church nor the village ever really regained their former glory and the entire charming place has an air of sleepy incompletion about it.

Leave Winchelsea by the Strand Gate and rejoin the A259 as it crosses the drained marshland separating it from Rye, straight ahead on

Moated, gated, crenellated: romantic Bodiam Castle

the opposite hill and rising to a point at the spire of the Church of St. Mary the Virgin. As you approach the town, follow signs for "Town Centre" (not Rye Harbor), curving around the left side of the hill, then turning through the two barreled towers of the fourteenth-century Land Gate and up the hill. Ahead, running along just below the top of the hill, is Rye's handsome High Street, lined with shops, restaurants, banks, and a gracious old hotel. Even though the sea retreated—or, to be more accurate, was rebuffed by the buildup of silt from the three rivers at its feet—Rye managed to stay in the seafaring business until tourism came along to rescue it. And while its narrow and picturesque cobbled streets and the ancient Mermaid Inn—*rebuilt* in 1420—are a magnet for visitors, Rye somehow keeps its calm.

It may be this literal and figurative "above it all" tranquility that accounts for Rye's powerful attraction for writers. American expatriate Henry James lived here for sixteen years before his death in 1912, writing both *The Golden Bowl* and *The Ambassadors* at Lamb House, just off Mermaid Street (open Wednesday and Saturday afternoons, April through October). E. F. Benson, whose "Mapp and Lucia" stories are set in Rye ("Tilling" in the books), moved in shortly after James's death. Conrad Aiken, Stephen Crane, H. G. Wells, Joseph Conrad, Ford Madox Ford, and many others lived here or nearby.

After you've wandered about Rye's charming back streets, head down the other side of the High Street hill, turn **right** at the bottom, and at the roundabout turn **right** again, retracing your earlier steps. Then follow signs for the **A268** in the direction of **London** and **Hawkhurst**.

The road traverses the meadows of the wandering River Rother, passing through pretty weatherboarded villages. At **Four Oaks,** turn **left** onto the **B2088** through **Beckley**, then **right** onto the **A28** at **Northiam**. In the center of the village, turn **left** at a signpost for **Bodiam Castle.** At the next intersection you have a choice: straight ahead, perhaps a half-mile (under a kilometer) down a leafy lane, is **Great Dixter,** a fifteenth-century half-timber manor house restored by Sir Edward Lutyens, the famed garden designer, in 1911 and today the home of contemporary garden authority Christopher Lloyd. The house, set in a broad lawn dotted with daffodils, is backed by a magnificent array of perennial border gardens edged with yew hedges and topiary (open daily except Mondays, April through mid-October, 2:00 P.M. to 5:00 P.M.).

If you choose not to visit Great Dixter, turn **left** at the same intersection (or right if returning from Great Dixter), onto an unclassified road, following signs 4.5 miles (7.3 kilometers) for Bodiam. The route takes you through beautiful countryside, first down a lane overarched by trees, then across fields of grain and grazing sheep, through the village of **Ewhurst Green,** with a group of conical oast-houses converted to homes.

From Ewhurst Green, continue following signs for Bodiam, eventually descending into a pastoral valley with the castle entrance on the right. **Bodiam Castle** is a fairy-tale castle at its simplest and most romantic. Built in 1386 and restored in 1916, it is a four-square, crenellated mass of creamy gray stone anchored at its corners by huge barrel towers. Surrounded by a wide, lily-pad-dotted moat, it is connected to the outside world by means of a causeway and drawbridge. It sits serene and quiet in its own green valley, and is best appreciated from its grounds, so you may want to skip going inside (open daily, April through October, 10:00 A.M. to 6:00 P.M.; Monday through Saturday, November through March, 10:00 A.M. to sunset).

The Oast-Houses of Kent

Cone-shaped oast-houses, looking a bit like windmills without wings, are fixtures of the Kentish landscape. *Oast* is an old word for "kiln" and oast-houses are used to dry hops, a vine imported from Europe in the sixteenth century the female blossoms of which give English ale its characteristic nutty flavor. The oast-house has three parts: the ground level, housing the heating unit; the second story, the drying floor where 2 to 3 feet (1 meter) of hops would be spread; and the cone, which carries off the smoke and heat. The ventilation is controlled by the revolving white cowling at the peak. The hop vine grows as much as 6 inches (14 centimeters) per day, its tendrils twining clockwise around a network of wires strung from 20-foot (6.1-meter) poles by vine stringers ... who work on stilts!

Leaving the castle, turn right toward **Sandhurst,** then **right** again onto the **A268.** You have crossed into Kent now—the "Garden of England." Where once great oak forests were felled to frame frigates and fire iron forges, the Kentish Weald has turned to more peaceful pursuits: more than 40,000 acres are planted in apple orchards and thousands more produce pears, plums, cherries, strawberries, raspberries, currants, and hops. In springtime, with the orchards abloom, it is perhaps the prettiest place in England. Its architecture is distinctive, too; you'll see much more wood here than anywhere else, a legacy of the great oak forests of the High Weald. In fact, Kent's white weatherboard houses often look more like New England than Olde England. It's yet another example of how dramatically the countryside of England can change over very short distances.

Beyond Sandhurst, at the intersection with the A28, turn **left** and drive north to **Tenterden,** entering this elegant market town along a broad avenue of ancient sycamore trees. If lunchtime has already arrived, this is a good place to stop, with a number of excellent pubs.

From the center of the town, stay on the A28 for perhaps 2 miles (3.2 kilometers), then turn **left** onto the **A262,** picking up the **High Weald Country Tour** route, a scenic drive established by the Kent Tourist Board.

As you enter **Biddenden,** at the sign of the Siamese twins who, born here in 1100, lived to adulthood and established a charity for the poor, turn **left,** again following the A262 and High Weald signs, toward **Sissinghurst.**

(**Note:** If you would prefer to spend another day in the countryside, rather than going up to London tomorrow, a detour to Canterbury is described in Diversions below.)

Sissinghurst Castle Garden is actually not a castle at all, but the remains of a sixteenth-century manor house. It is, however, most certainly a garden, probably the finest flower garden in all of England, the creation of the writer Vita Sackville-West and her husband Harold Nicolson during the 1930s. It is a garden of barely contained exuberance, best described by Sackville-West herself: "profusion... within the confines of the utmost severity." As if in some giant cottage garden, wildflowers and formal varieties cohabit luxurious borders. Colors mass and flow within frames established by archways, hedges, walls, and doorways as you move through a succession of clearly delineated "rooms." It is at once stunning and comprehensible, unlike many of the vast estates of the largest stately homes. Visiting Sissinghurst will be one of the most memorable events of your trip (open April through mid-October, Tuesday through Friday 1:00 P.M. to 6:30 P.M. and Saturday and Sunday 10:00 A.M. to 6:30 P.M.).

The other end of the English gardening spectrum is the landscape garden—sculpting a landscape with trees and flowering shrubs to create scenery that is artfully artless. One of the finest examples of this kind of gardening is just up the road at **Scotney Castle.** From Sissinghurst Castle, turn **right** onto the A262 again and head west through Sissinghurst village toward **Goudhurst,** through a High Weald landscape punctuated by the white tips of oast-houses. Follow the High Weald Country Tour signs through several turns entering Goudhurst and then, roughly 7 miles (11.3 kilometers) farther on, turn **left** onto the **A21** into **Lamberhurst,** yet another lovely Kentish village of Tudor half-timber and tile-hung houses. Go straight through the village, fol-

This page and opposite: *Scenes from Sissinghurst Castle Gardens*

Among the Gardens of the Garden of England 223

lowing signs for Scotney Castle, just ahead on the left.

Where Sissinghurst ravishes you with its color, Scotney Castle captivates with drama (diminished only slightly by the ancient trees toppled by the great hurricanes of 1988 and 1989). From the car park you walk past a handsome nineteenth-century manor house that overlooks a peaceful vale. At the bottom, the wildly romantic ruin of a turreted fourteenth-century tower and the crumbling walls of its adjoining castle, both partially cloaked in roses and flowering vines, sit on a tiny island within a moat edged with great clouds of daffodil and narcissus. Rhododendron the size of small cottages flank the ruined gatehouse and flourish, along with azalea and ornamental cherry, in clusters arrayed carefully across the hillside. At every turn the view ahead has just the right proportion of color, shape, and texture—bits of stone, patches of water, and a pleasing array of foliage so varied you wonder how there could be so many colors of green. There is even an oriental grotto, immediately below the manor house in what appears to be the quarry from which the stone for the house was taken.

From Scotney, backtrack north along the A21, which becomes a divided highway beyond Lamberhurst, and take the exit for the A264 to **Royal Tunbridge Wells**—Bath "Master of Ceremonies" Beau Nash's other client city. As you enter the town, watch for signs for the **A26** north and turn **right,** heading in the direction of London. After you've left most of the built-up area of the town behind, watch for the **B2176** and turn **left** toward **Penshurst.**

The western reaches of the Weald of Kent, south of London, are crammed with ancient manor houses and stately homes, far too many to visit in the few hours left this afternoon. While the itinerary takes you past several of them, you'll have to choose among them if you're going to make London this evening. Penshurst forces your first decision. The B2176 runs along the leafy top of a ridge, overlooking the valley formed by the headwaters of the River Medway. Then you drop down the slope and cross the river by a narrow bridge, and immediately ahead on the opposite slope is the little village of Penshurst, dominated by Penshurst Place, sheltering behind its massive walls. The house was begun in the fourteenth century by the lord mayor of London and substantially expanded in the sixteenth century by the Sidney family (the poet Sir Phillip Sidney was born here). The house (open Tuesday through Sunday, April through October, 12:30 P.M. to 5:00 P.M.) sits in a vast parkland surrounded by a formidable wall, but the little village, with its secretive enclosed square, is in many ways more interesting.

Continue in the same direction, then turn **left** onto the **B2027.** Soon afterward, turn **left** again onto a minor road (the Weald is a maze of unclassified roads) signposted for **Chiddingstone.** This tiny little village, a masterpiece of Tudor half-timber cottages managed today by the National Trust, takes its name from a stone where, according to local tradition, troublesome wives were taken to be chided (skip the castle, a mock-medieval nineteenth-century reproduction built on the remains of the seventeenth-century original). From the village center, follow signs roughly southwest along minor roads to **Hever Castle,** a magnificent little castle surrounded by a moat and dating from the thirteenth century. The castle was the birthplace and home of the ill-fated Anne Boleyn; after her execution Henry VIII appropriated it and, in the cruelist of ironies, gave it to his fourth wife, Anne of Cleeves. Restored by American millionaire William Waldorf Astor, the castle has a maze,

Scotney Castle Gardens

formal gardens, and a superb collection of furniture and paintings. You arrive to see it at perhaps the best time of day, when the soft light of late afternoon gilds the ancient stone and casts long shadows across the manicured lawns (open daily, April through October, 11:00 A.M. to 6:00 P.M.).

From Hever Castle, head north on the minor road until you reach the **B2027**. Turn **left**, then a bit farther on turn **right** onto the **B269**. Drive through the village of **Four Elms** and then turn **right** again onto a minor road signposted for **Chartwell,** Winston Churchill's splendid home and refuge. It is filled with memorabilia, from his paintings to the brick wall he built to keep himself sane during his "years in the wilderness."

Finally, after a long day of castles, gardens, and stately homes, it's time to head for London—or at least close to it.

ESTABLISHING YOUR LONDON BASE

This itinerary assumes you'll want to spend at least a day at the end of your trip sightseeing in London (for a countryside alternative, see Diversions below). But unless you rented your car in the city and have to return it there, you need not actually drive into the city—a nightmare even for Londoners, except on weekends. There are two attractive alternatives: book yourself into a hotel or B&B near one of the many railroad stations in the suburban countryside south of London, then drive to the airport the morning of your return flight; or drive to the area near your airport this afternoon, book into a hotel or B&B, return your car, and use the train or the subway to get into and out of the city tomorrow. The marginal cost of either of these alternatives can be small, compared to the hassle and cost of staying in the city. Here are the options:

DRIVE INTO LONDON: From Chartwell, drive west to the **B2026,** turn **right,** and drive north to the **A25.** Turn **left** and follow the A25 to the roundabout east of **Godstone.** Follow signs for the **A22** north to London, which eventually merges into the **A23** and continues north into Brixton. Then, using your BTA official London map, simply follow signs for whichever bridge across the Thames will take you closest to the neighborhood in which you plan to spend the next two nights (see Creature Comforts below for suggestions).

STAY IN THE SOUTHERN SUBURBS: If you look closely at your map (the Greater London inset of the Michelin Map #404 or similar) you'll notice, south of the M25, a web of thin black lines interupted by little white rectangles. The lines are railroads, the rectangles stations. The accommodation guides in Further Reading list a number of B&Bs, inns, and hotels in villages near these rail lines. Stay the next two nights here in the south, commute into the city tomorrow morning after the rush hour (thus saving with a day excursion ticket), then come home after dinner or theater in town. In addition to avoiding the annoyance of driving and parking, the money you save on lodging (often in nicer accommodations than in London) will far outweigh the additional cost of the train ticket and the cost of paying for a car you won't use.

STAY NEAR YOUR AIRPORT: If you are flying out of Gatwick, Chartwell and Hever Castle are only about a half-hour away, depending on traffic. Stay near the airport, then, tomorrow morning, take the Gatwick Express from the airport into the city, returning in the evening. If you're flying out of Heathrow, follow the directions to London above, but at Godstone get on the **M25** west and in about **45 minutes** you'll be at Heathrow. Stay at an airport hotel (and return your car) or at a B&B or guesthouse a few miles west on the M4 in Windsor (and get the castle as a bonus), then drive to the airport in the morning and take the Tube (Underground) into the city. Go after the rush hour, buy a day pass, and travel free on the Tube all day.

DIVERSIONS
Detouring to Canterbury

Who will deliver me from this turbulent priest?
—Henry II, of Thomas Becket

Ancient Canterbury, founded more than three centuries before the Roman invasion, the cradle of Saxon Christianity, the destination of Chaucer's pilgrims, and seat of the Church of England, took a terrible drubbing during World War II. Yet somehow, it has managed to retain its medieval soul. As an alternative to a day in London, and an excuse to spend another day among the orchards and hop fields of the Kentish countryside, Canterbury and its cathedral make a wonderful final diversion.

From the village of **Biddenden** in the High Weald (see earlier itinerary), head north on the **A274** in the direction of **Maidstone**, but turn **right** just outside of town onto the **B2077**. Ahead is a chain of gorgeous Kent villages filled with wonderful medieval half-timbered buildings—more than 100 of tiny **Smarden**'s buildings alone are "listed" as historic properties. The road climbs out of the valley of the River Beult to **Pluckley**, then dips down into the valley of the Great Stour River and up again to **Charing**, its main street lined with a handsome mix of Tudor and Georgian houses. At Charing turn **right** onto the **A252** through **Chilham**, where you get on the **A28** for the remaining 6 miles (9.7 kilometers) to Canterbury. As you approach the city, simply follow signs to the City Centre. When the A28 becomes Castle

Street, watch for the blue-and-white "i" signs; the Tourist Information Centre is at 13 Longmarket. Plan not just to visit the cathedral (and Becket's shrine) but to wander awhile within the confines of the thirteenth-century city walls as well. Spend the night in the old city or out in the countryside. Use the guides in Further Reading or contact the Tourist Information Centre, 13 Longmarket, Canterbury, Kent CT1 2JS, telephone (0227) 766567, for advance booking help.

Tomorrow morning, head west on the **M2** to **Exit 5,** then south on the **A249** to Maidstone, and south to Sissinghurst on the **A229,** picking up today's itinerary. Spend tomorrow night near your departure airport (see Establishing Your London Base, above).

CREATURE COMFORTS
Daily Bed

There are dozens of guidebooks to London, packed with accommodation listings in every neighborhood and price range (some are listed in Further Reading). If you plan to stay in London, book your accommodations before you leave home, either on your own or through your travel agent. The London Tourist Board Information Centre in Victoria Station will be happy to help you find a room (for a small fee) if you haven't booked in advance, as will the British Travel Centre at 12 Regent Street, but it's a shame to waste time doing that at the end of a long day.

An attractive alternative to conventional City Centre hotels is staying in one of London's pretty outer neighborhoods. An association of private home B&Bs in these areas, all close to Tube stations, will find you a room at prices well below the range for even modest hotels. Write **London Home-to-Home,** 19 Mount Park Crescent, Ealing, London W5 2RN for their brochure, or call 81-567-2998.

Daily Bread

If you stay south of the city, your best bet for dinner is one of the many restaurants that have sprung up to serve commuting "yuppies" and pubs that take dinner seriously. For the latter, check the pub guide in Further Reading. For the former, check with your hosts tonight; they'll know the surrounding neighborhood better than any guidebook. Then, tomorrow night, splurge and have dinner in the city before you come home.

Note: Remember to confirm your return flight reservations tomorrow morning; call Directory Enquiries for the phone number of your airline (airline reservations and information offices in Europe are generally open only during regular office hours).

♦DAY FIFTEEN

A Flirtation with London

- ♦ How to get around town
- ♦ What to see, what to skip
- ♦ An afternoon window-shopper's walk

I believe the parallelogram between Oxford Street, Piccadilly, Regent Street, and Hyde Park encloses more intelligence and human ability, to say nothing of wealth and beauty, than the world has ever collected in such a space before.

—Sydney Smith
Memoirs, 1855

The trouble with London is that once you spend an hour you want to spend a lifetime. The museums, galleries, monuments, parks, shops, restaurants, pubs, neighborhoods, and passing scene offer almost limitless fascination. Alas, unless you extend this itinerary, lingering in London is not an option. So the challenge is to capture both its principal "sights" and, more important, its essence. Happily, this is an achievable goal, one which is delightful in the execution. The key is to know how to get around efficiently.

Visitors from cities laid out in sensible grids will find London a bewildering maze. Established as *Londinium* by the Romans in A.D. 43, it has been growing willy-nilly ever since. The Great Fire of 1666 leveled much of what was then central London, but the city was already such a hopeless tangle that it was rebuilt along much the same lines. So even though few buildings are older than mid-seventeenth century, the layout is still medieval. One result is that place names can be comically outdated: the church of St. Martin-in-the-Fields, for example, quite clearly *isn't;* it presides over the traffic swirling around Trafalgar Square.

London is best understood as a city of villages, which of course the neighborhoods once were before the city grew to engulf them. Over the centuries, many of these neighborhoods became occupationally specialized. The square mile where London was born, known as the City, is Britain's Wall Street. For most visitors, and most Londoners as well,

230 ITINERARY: DAY FIFTEEN

Tower Bridge from the upper deck of the London Transport Sightseeing Tour bus

the West End is nothing of the sort; it's the very heart of town, the throbbing center of the arts and theater. Farther west still, but nevertheless the political center of town, is Westminster, home of the Parliament and many of the government ministries. Covent Garden was the *convent* garden for the monks at Westminster Abbey, and gradually became the city's fruit and vegetable market (today it's a shopping arcade). Mayfair, Kensington, Knightsbridge, and Chelsea, among London's most fashionable addresses, were distant country villages. Writers in every century exclaimed that further growth was unsupportable, yet on and on the city grew, north and south of the river, upstream and down. As it does yet today.

GETTING AROUND TOWN

Unless you've already done so, buy the **British Tourist Authority**'s *Official London Map* before you do anything else. Accept no substitutes. Send away for it in advance, buy a copy at the information desk when you arrive at the airport (see Day One), or head for either the British Travel Centre at 12 Regent Street, south of Piccadilly Circus (open Monday through Saturday 9:00 A.M. to 6:30 P.M., Sunday 10:00 A.M. to 4:00 P.M.), or the London Tourist Board Information Centres at Victoria Station (similar hours) and the basement of Harrods (Kensington) and Selfridges (Oxford Street) department stores, during normal store hours. In addition, you may want to pick up the tourist authority's "Guide to London," a slim brochure (75p) with descriptions, locations, times, and phone numbers for every major attraction in the city, plus other helpful information.

For getting from place to place you have four alternatives:

TAXI. If you're traveling with several people, take cabs. They're roomy and the drivers are unfailingly friendly, helpful, and polite (always say "please" when giving directions). They spend up to two years, full time, roaming around London by bicycle or on mopeds to learn "the Knowledge" required to obtain a license, so you can trust your driver to know precisely how to get where you want to go by the quickest route, no matter how circuitous it may seem. The fare, when split among three or four riders, will be competitive with the Tube, except over very long distances or in rush hour. Look for one with its roof light on and wave it down. Tip 10 to 15 percent.

BUSES. The advantage of London's great bus system is that you get to see everything along the way. The disadvantage is that the system is impenetrably complex. If you're only in London for a day or two, opt for another form of transportation.

YOUR RENTAL CAR. Driving in London makes sense if you know the city well, have a gifted navigator, relish the strategic challenge of gridlock, and view driving as a blood sport. These details aside, there is this to say about driving in London: the signage is terrific. If you know what neighborhood your destination is in, and roughly what part of town that is, just follow the signs to that neighborhood, then use your London map to find the specific location. If you suddenly find yourself going in a direction apparently away from your target, don't panic, just keep following the signs. They're designed to steer you away from chronically congested areas and one-way traffic traps between you and your destination. As for parking, look for garages, or, if you won't be long, metered spaces. If you lead a particularly charmed life, you may be able to find unrestricted parking in some residential areas, but don't count on it. Under no circumstances park next to a double yellow line.

TUBE. There's almost nowhere in London that isn't a few blocks from a Tube station (look for the red circle bisected by a horizontal blue line that says UNDERGROUND). The route map is in your BTA London map (and on the wall in each station). Each line has its own name and color code. You buy your ticket from an agent in the station (or a vending machine) and *keep it* to hand to another agent (or run through an exit machine) at your destination. In stations where two or more lines intersect, follow signs on the wall for the line with which you want to connect. Many platforms have electronic signs that tell you how soon the next train will come and, if the line splits somewhere, which branch the next train will take. You can zoom across town quickly (in most cases faster than by cab) and the fares are relatively cheap. If you're planning on doing a lot of "Tubing," buy a one-day pass, valid after 9:30 A.M. or anytime weekends and public holidays. The Tube is open Monday through Saturday, 5:30 A.M. to midnight, and Sundays 7:30 A.M. to 11:30 P.M. Safe, clean, reliable, and affordable, the Tube is really your best bet.

What to See, What to Skip

Victorian-era Prime Minister William Gladstone once told a group of visitors that the best way to see London was from the top of a double-decker bus, and that is still the case today. **The Original London Transport Sightseeing Tour,** run by the city bus company, is a terrific 90-minute orientation on the best of the sights with great running commentaries. Distinctively painted double-decker buses leave from **Victoria Station, Piccadilly Circus** (from the corner of Haymarket), **Baker Street** (corner of Marylebone), and **Marble Arch** (at Speaker's Corner), roughly every half-hour from 10:00 A.M. to 5:00 P.M. daily (ending later in summer at Victoria and Piccadilly). Fight for seats on the open top deck. Tickets are cheaper if purchased at the Regent Street Travel Centre, the London Transport Tours Office at Piccadilly, or at the Piccadilly, Oxford Circus, and Heathrow Tube stations. No reservations are needed (for details, call 227-3456).

What you do next depends, of course, on your interests, but given the short time available, you're going to have to be brutally selective. Here are some tips:

♦ **DON'T bother with the changing of the guard at Buckingham Palace.** It's dull, time-consuming, and off the beaten track, and, unless it's the dead of winter or you are very tall, the crowds will block your view anyway.

♦ **DON'T try to see the Crown Jewels.** See the Tower of London by all means, but the line for the jewels is often hours long and the finale is disappointing. Buy a booklet or a postcard of the jewels instead.

♦ **DON'T try to get into the Houses of Parliament.** It's only open for tourists in the afternoon when the House of Commons is in session and the lines are very long.

♦ **DON'T go into the splendid British Museum unless you plan to spend all day.** This monument to imperial sticky fingers has some 90 different galleries, each one more fascinating than the next. You never get out before dark (open Monday through Saturday 10:00 A.M. to 5:00 P.M., Sunday 2:30 P.M. to 6:00 P.M.).

On the other hand:

♦ **DO visit a cathedral, preferably St. Paul's.** Westminster Abbey tends to be crowded, noisy, and uninspiring compared with St. Paul's, Christopher Wren's awe-inspiring masterpiece (he used to come to marvel at his own handiwork). Whichever you choose, take the "Supertour" led by the vergers to really understand these extraordinary monuments to faith.

♦ **DO visit the Tate Gallery.** A short walk upriver from the Houses of Parliament along the banks of the Thames, the newly rehung Tate houses primarily (but not exclusively) British artists and has the largest exhibit of J. M. W. Turner anywhere. It also has an excellent restaurant. (Gallery open Monday through Saturday 10:00 A.M. to 5:30 P.M., Sunday 2:30 P.M. to 5:30 P.M.)

♦ **Most of all, DO walk through some of London's old neighborhoods.** If you have time to do only one thing, after you've taken the

London Transport bus tour, walk. Skip the "must see" sights and take the walk outlined below. Or simply choose a neighborhood that intrigues you (see London guides in Further Reading). Walk slowly, take in the extraordinary architectural details, stroll through a park and feed the ducks, duck into a pub for a pint. This is the real London.

🚶 THE PALACES OF ST. JAMES'S AND THE PURVEYORS OF MAYFAIR: A LONDON WALKING TOUR

Distance: As long as you want
Difficulty: Many pubs hard to pass up
Total Elevation Gain: Some irresistible two-story shops
Gear: Comfortable shoes, credit cards
Map: BTA London Map

This afternoon's walk is a delightful combination of the pomp of monumental London and the smaller pleasures of the Victorian-era shops tucked away into the narrow old streets in and around St. James's and Mayfair. From wherever you leave the bus tour, take the Tube to the **Westminster** stop (on the Circle line). Walk across **Westminster Bridge,** turn around, and gaze back on the view that obsessed Monet and about which Wordsworth said, "Earth has not anything to show more fair." Ahead is **the Palace of Westminster** (the official name of the Houses of Parliament), the home of English Kings from Canute to Henry VIII. The buildings are recent, despite their Gothic façades; only the eleventh-century Great Hall survived a nineteenth-century fire. At the end of the bridge is **Big Ben** (not the name of the clock tower, as most people think, but of the 13-ton bell inside it).

Then walk back to the corner and look across the street to Parliament Square and Ivor Roberts-Jones's statue of **Winston Churchill**—his aging body all but engulfed in his voluminous greatcoat, bent under the weight of the nation and leaning heavily on his stick, but with his jaw still set with iron determination.

Turn **right** up **Parliament Street;** the second street on your left is block-long **Downing Street,** site of the prime minister's residence and office. Ahead, Parliament Street becomes **Whitehall,** site of many of Britain's most important ministries, and on the right above the **Horse Guards** is **Scotland Yard,** site of many of Britain's most important mysteries.

At the top of Whitehall is **Trafalgar Square,** with its fountains, pigeons, and **Nelson's Column.** Turn **left** at Trafalgar, passing under **Admiralty Arch** and down **the Mall.** Enter lovely **St. James's Park** and walk west through its leafy paths past the lake and bandstand to

A Flirtation with London **235**

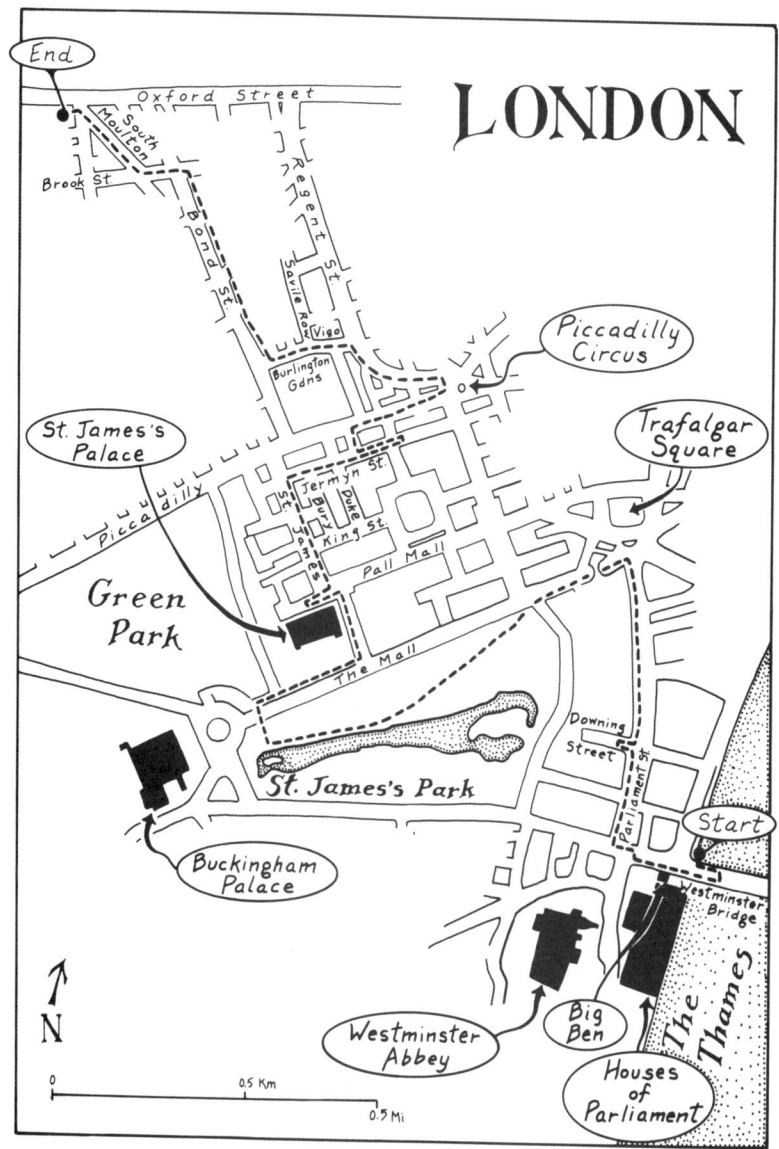

Buckingham Palace, massive and austere in its barren forecourt. Then turn **right,** walk back down the left side of the Mall, and turn **left** into **Marlborough Road.** To your right at the next intersection is **Pall Mall,** named after a popular croquetlike game played here in the seventeenth century when this was a broad lawn. Across Pall Mall is a tiny, narrow alley called **Crown Passage,** which houses one of the city's wonderful little pubs, the Red Lion. Farther down Pall Mall are several prestigious private clubs. Descendents of seventeenth-century coffee houses, most—like the **Travellers**—were established in Queen Victoria's time. In the other direction, marked by a sentry box with one of those unflinching fur-helmeted guards tourists love, is **St. James's Palace,** the remarkably unpretentious brown brick building that was the home of English kings and queens from Henry VIII to Victoria (ambassadors to Britain are still posted to "the Court of St. James"). Today the palace is the home of the duke and duchess of Kent.

A **right** turn opposite the palace takes you up **St. James's Street,** home of several more clubs (**Boodle's** and **Brooks's**) and of three of London's oldest shops—the wine merchants **Berry Bros. and Rudd,** the hatter **Lock and Co.,** and the shoemaker **Lobb's**—all three with splendid old eighteenth-century interiors.

The next street on the right is **King Street,** home of **Christie's** and other famous art auctioneers. Farther up St. James's Street, just past the handsome bow-front façade of Boodle's, turn right at the tobacconist

Changing the guard at St. James's Palace

Davidoff onto **Jermyn Street,** world renowned for its custom shirtmakers, but dotted also with many of London's most atmospheric Victorian shopfronts. On the right at **Bury Street** is the cherub-decorated front of **Turnbull and Asser,** shirtmakers, its windows filled with the loudly striped shirts English gentlemen favor under their somber business suits. Continue along the right side of the street to the **Cavendish Hotel,** upon which the television series "The Duchess of Duke Street" was based. Just ahead is **J. Floris,** founded in 1730, its shopfront capped by the royal crest and its brass and wood interior redolent of the soaps, powders, perfumes, and badger-bristle shaving brushes of a gentleman's (and, lately, ladies) dressing room. You expect Jeeves or Bunter to appear at any moment. Next door is an olfactory experience of another kind, the richly aromatic premises of **Paxton & Whitfield,** cheesemongers. There's sawdust on the floor and hundreds of cheeses climb to the ceiling in this classic Victorian-era shop.

Now turn and walk back along the other side of Jermyn Street, past **Bates** the hatter (with its beloved cat now stuffed and mounted in a glass cabinet inside) and the ornate plumbing supplies at **Czech & Speake.** At **Duke Street,** turn in the back door of **Fortnum and Mason:** grocer to the queen, caterer to the Crimean War, and home of perhaps the finest selection of teas anywhere on earth. The main floor on Piccadilly is packed with gourmet foods and overseen by salespeople in cutaway formal suits. You can fortify yourself with tea and ludicrously rich tea cakes in the restaurant up the central stairs from the main floor.

Next, go out Fortnum's ornate main entrance, turn **right,** and walk along Piccadilly to **Piccadilly Circus** (circle)—London's own Times Square, complete with suggestive billboards and statue of Eros. London's "West End" theater district stretches from here to the east. (**Note:** Three blocks east of the Circus, at **Leicester Square,** is the half-price ticket booth for West End theater performances that have unsold seats. For last-minute seats to sold-out shows, go to the individual theater box office two to three hours before curtain time and ask when returned and unclaimed tickets are sold.)

From Piccadilly, turn sharply **left** into **Regent Street,** with its broad sweep of neoclassically fronted department and specialty stores. You may want to stroll the full length of Regent Street (famous **Liberty's** fabric store is uphill on the right). Otherwise, turn **left** into **Vigo Street.** The first street to your right is **Savile Row,** home of London's most prestigious "bespoke" (custom) tailors. Continue past Savile Row and into **Burlington Gardens,** with shop-filled **Burlington Arcade** (built originally to keep passers-by from throwing trash into the garden of adjacent Burlington House!) on the left. At the end of the block, turn **right** into **Bond Street,** lined with some of London's most chic designer shops. At **Brook Street** turn **left,** then **right** into the

South Moulton Street pedestrian mall, with several of the city's contemporary designer clothing and accessory shops.

At the end of South Moulton is **Oxford Street,** London's principal shopping thoroughfare and home of two of its largest department stores, **Selfridges** and **Marks and Spencer,** the latter known for inexpensive but high-quality woolens.

If no trip to London would be complete for you without seeing **Harrods,** take the Jubilee (silver) Tube Line from the Bond Street station at the corner of Oxford and South Moulton to the Green Park stop, then change to the Piccadilly (navy blue) Line, going two stops to **Knightsbridge.** The exit is right next door to Harrods. The truth is, in these days of huge shopping malls, Harrods isn't as remarkable as it once was, with one spectacular exception: its **Food Halls**—cavernous, fan-vaulted, tiled, and muraled halls of fish, game, fruit and vegetables, sausage and smoked meats, baked goods, and candy that seem to stretch for blocks. There's nothing like it in the world, either for sheer size or artistry.

Then, if your feet are up to it, stroll down **Brompton** and **Fulham roads** for more of London's finest shops, including Terrence Conran's housewares emporium built within a magnificent, tiled art-deco building, formerly a Michelin tire garage.

Then, as your last day in Britain draws to a close, head back to your hotel or B&B, have an early dinner, and begin the depressing job of packing for your return home.

A window-shopper's sampler

♦ DAY SIXTEEN

Home

The toughest thing about leaving England—besides the leaving—is coping with the chaos at the airport without squandering in a single morning all the rest and relaxation you've gained during the past two weeks. International flights all tend to depart in roughly the same fashion in which they arrived: all at once. Flights to the States, for example, leave between midmorning and early afternoon. This means there's going to be a huge crush of folks all trying to check in at once.

You can keep the craziness to a minimum by knowing your options in advance; here are some tips.

GETTING TO THE AIRPORT

If you decided to spend the last two nights in the countryside somewhere near your airport, your life this morning will be fairly simple. All international travelers are expected to be *checked in* two hours before departure time. But security checks, while better than they used to be, are also longer, so to be safe plan to arrive three hours before your flight.

If you have not checked in before the deadline, the airline is free to give your seat away. With a fully booked flight and a ticket restricting your ability to reschedule, being late will be more than just inconvenient—you'll take a financial bath. If you check in *before* the deadline and are denied boarding because the airline overbooked, most U.S. carriers follow U.S. Department of Transportation rules governing domestic flights and outbound international flights. These rules require the airlines to (1) ask someone who has a seat to yield it to you or (2) book you on another flight that will get you home within two hours of your original flight. Failing that, you may be entitled to cash compensation of up to $400 per person, for the delay. While the rules on return flights are hazy, your ticket is a contract and your bargaining power considerable.

Between seasonal fog, occasional strikes (usually at peak travel times), and other vagaries of air travel, it pays to check in with your airline the morning of your flight to determine its status. Your airline's number is either on your ticket envelope or in the phone book (or call Directory Enquiries, 142).

GETTING TO HEATHROW FROM LONDON. If you spent last night in London you have three options for getting to Heathrow this morning. A **taxi** will cost nearly £40 from the center of the city, but if you have a lot of baggage, door-to-door taxi service is hard to beat. If your budget is tight, consider the **Tube.** Take the Piccadilly (blue) Line to Heathrow (*not* Rayners Lane or Uxbridge). It takes about an hour and costs less than £3. Baggage carts are available at the other end, so you'll only have to lug your bags once. If your hotel is near an **Airbus** stop (check with the front desk or call London Transport), the bus is an attractive alternative. It also takes about an hour and costs about £5.

GETTING TO GATWICK. No contest; take a cab or the Tube to Victoria Station and the BritRail **Gatwick Express** to the airport. Departures are every 15 minutes; the trip takes roughly 30 minutes (delays en route are not uncommon, however, so don't cut it too tight).

RETURNING YOUR RENTAL CAR

If you've kept your car until now, here's the most efficient way to return it: assuming you're traveling with someone else, drop them off at the departure terminal with the baggage, tickets, and passports. Then take the car to the rental agency, stopping at a petrol station to top off the tank if you're expected to return it full. After completing the formalities, save your receipt (you'll need it if billing discrepancies arise, which they frequently do), and return to the terminal. Then you and your companion(s) can clear security and check in.

If you've spent last night some distance from the airport, leave plenty of extra time. Traffic around the airports is predictably heavy and delays are common, except on weekends. The signs to terminals, on the other hand, are clear, so you're unlikely to get lost.

VAT REFUNDS

Like many European countries, Britain wants to encourage you to shop. So they have a **Retail Export Scheme** by which the 17.5 percent value added tax (VAT) levied on purchases of goods you take out of the country can be refunded (thus, things you consumed in England—food, hotel, car rental—don't qualify). At least that's the theory. First, you have to be sure the firm you buy from participates (most, but not all, do). Some (but not all) stores require you to spend above a certain minimum (often £50). Then you have to remember to request a VAT

refund form from the store (they don't volunteer them), show your passport, have them complete and sign the form on the premises, and get a self-addressed (but sometimes not stamped) envelope by which the form can be returned after customs validates it at the airport.

Then there's the little matter of getting the airport VAT officials to stamp the forms. They'll want to see the goods you purchased, the receipts, your ticket, and your passport, all of which is reasonable enough. What isn't reasonable is that these officials are located *inside* security, which you reach *after* you've checked your baggage through. This means that you have to pack your purchases in your carry-on baggage—not a problem if you've purchased a dress, perhaps, but a bit awkward if you've just acquired a nice twenty-piece set of English china. After the customs people have stamped the form you simply slip it into the envelope and mail it back to the store, assuming you've got a stamp. Otherwise you have to find a stamp machine somewhere. You can do this *after* you get home, but customs people find this all very mysterious.

Then, several weeks (sometimes months) later, a check will arrive (or, sometimes, not). It will, of course be in pounds, which your bank will charge you a small fortune to cash—typically almost exactly what you hoped to save. The way to get around this is to request that the refund be credited directly to your credit card, a solution which is beginning to catch on at last. Under a new program, in which some 12,000 stores participate, you send a single form to Tourist Tax Free Shopping, Europa House, 226 Upper Richmond Road, London SW15 6TQ. They will respond within five days, by check in your own currency or by credit card credit, however you wish. It's still awkward, but 17.5 percent is nothing to sneeze at.

DUTY FREE SHOPS

In case you've somehow failed to spend enough money during your holiday, airport authorities offer you a chance at redemption: the Duty Free Shop. The emphasis is on liquor and tobacco, but perfume, electronic gadgets, and gift clothing are also featured. Look around for monthly specials and the discount coupons Duty Free staff distribute in the waiting area for the best deals. If the pound is weak compared to your own currency, you may find significant bargains. Since you won't be able to exchange coins when you get home, dispose of them here. This is how the magazine and candy shop stays in business—but better yet, look for charity donation boxes that will turn your soon-to-be-worthless change into good works.

HEADING HOME

One last tip: don't press your luck lingering in the Duty Free Shop at departure time. Gates at both Heathrow and Gatwick seem miles from the departure waiting lounge (you may have to take a shuttle train at Gatwick). The plane *will* leave without you if you're late.

Then sit back, relax... and begin planning your next two weeks in the incomparable British countryside.

Further Reading

Backgrounders

Of the comprehensive guides to Britain or Wales, the *Insight Guides* series is the most imaginative and the most lushly illustrated. Separate books on *Great Britain, Scotland,* and *Wales* (published by APA Publications and distributed by Prentice-Hall Travel).

The finest regional guidebooks (with first-rate road maps) are the *AA/Ordnance Survey Leisure Guide Series.* Editions applicable to this itinerary include *East Anglia, Peak District, Snowdonia and North Wales, Brecon Beacons and Mid Wales, Forest of Dean and Wye Valley,* and *Cotswolds.* Published jointly by the Automobile Association and the Ordnance Survey.

Best book on natural history and wild areas: *Discovering Britain.* London: Drive Publications (for the Automobile Association) was published last in 1986. Check your local library.

Best books on London: *Insight Guides: London* (see above), and *London Access,* by Richard Wurman. New York: Access Press, 1993.

Accommodations Guides

FOR INNS AND SMALL HOTELS:

Brown, Karen. *English, Welsh, and Scottish Country Hotels and Itineraries.* Chester, Conn.: Globe Pequot Press, 1994.

Levitin, Jerry. *Country Inns and Back Roads: Britain and Ireland.* New York: Harper and Row, 1992.

Rubenstein, Hilary. *Europe's Wonderful Little Hotels and Inns: Great Britain and Ireland.* New York: St. Martins Press, 1994.

Stay at an Inn. London: British Tourist Authority, 1994.

FOR SELECT B&BS:

Country Lodging on a Budget: The Official Guide of the Farm Holiday Bureau U.K. 1991. London: William Curtis Limited, 1991. **Far and away the best B&B guide for the countryside.**

Brown, Karen. *English Country Bed & Breakfast.* Chester, Conn.: Globe Pequot Press, 1992. An excellent selection.

The Bed & Breakfast Guide to Great Britain. New York: Consumer Reports Books, 1992.

Welles, Sigourney. *The Best Bed and Breakfast in the World: England, Scotland, and Wales.* Chester, Conn.: Globe Pequot Press, 1994–95.

Good Room Guide. Excellent booklet listing first-rate B&Bs, published privately by Guestaccom, 190 Church Road, Hove, East Sussex, BN3 2DJ, or phone (0273) 722833.

YOUTH HOSTELS:

YHA 1992 Accommodation Guide. Available through Hostelling International/American Youth Hostels, P.O. Box 37613, Washington, D.C. 20013-7613, or phone (202) 783-6161.

Books on Food

FOR RESTAURANTS:

Jaine, Tom. *The Good Food Guide 1993.* London: Hodder and Stoughton (for the Consumers' Association), 1993.

FOR PUBS:

Aird, Alisdair. *The 1992 Good Pub Guide.* London: Ebury Press, 1992.

Hanson, Neil. *The Best Pubs of Great Britain.* Chester, Conn.: Globe Pequot Press (compiled by the Campaign for Real Ale), 1989.

Useful Addresses

British Tourist Authority Overseas Offices

UNITED STATES:

551 5th Avenue
Suite 701
New York, NY 10176
1-800-462-2748
In NYC: (212) 986-2266

CANADA:

111 Avenue Road
Suite 450
Toronto, Ontario M5R 3T8
(416) 925-6326

AUSTRALIA:

210 Clarence Street
Sydney, NSW 2000
(02) 267-4555

NEW ZEALAND

Dilworth Building
Third Floor
Cnr. Queen and Customs Street
Auckland 1
(09) 3031 446

National Tourist Boards

English Tourist Board
Thames Tower, Black's Road
Hammersmith, London W6 9EL
(071) 846 9000

Welsh Tourist Board
Brunel House, 2 Fitzalan Road
Cardiff CF2 1UY
(0222) 499909

Scottish Tourist Board
23 Ravelston Terrace
Edinburgh EH4 3EU
(031) 332 2433

National Parks Covered in This Book

Exmoor National Park
Exmoor House, Dulverton
Somerset TA22 9EN
Tel.: Dulverton 23665

Dartmoor National Park
Parke, Haytor Road, Bovey Tracey
Devon TQ13 9JQ
Tel.: Bovey Tracey 832093

Other Helpful Organizations

The National Trust
36 Queen Anne's Gate
London SW1H 7AS
(071) 222 9251

Countryside Commission
John Dower House
Crescent Place, Cheltenham
Gloucestershire GL50 3RA
(0242) 521381

Ordnance Survey
Romsey Road, Maybush
Southampton SO9 4DH
(0703) 792763

Ramblers' Association
1/5 Wandsworth Road
London SW8 2XX
(071) 582 6878

Automobile Association
Fanum House
Basingstoke, Hants. RG21 2EA
(0256) 20123

Index

Abbotsbury 158–59, 161–68
   Castle 166–67
   St. Catherine's Chapel 165
   Swannery 163
accommodations 30–32. *See also*
   "Daily Bed" in each chapter
   booking in advance 22
   guides 245–46
airports (London) 43–44
   arrival procedures 43
   departure procedures 240–41
   transportation to, from 44, 241
Alfriston 197, 205–206, 213
Athelhampton Hall 179
automobile. *See* cars
Avebury 175–76, 185, 186–93
   museums 193
   Silbury Hill 189
   West Kennet Long Barrow 191
   Windmill Hill 189
Barnstaple 108
Barrington, Great 62
Barrington, Little 62
Bath 80–82, 84–93
   Abbey 91
   history 88–92
   Roman Baths 86–88
   Royal Crescent 92
   walking tour 88–93
Battle 211
Bed and Breakfast 30–32
Bedruthan Steps 126
Beeny Cliff 118
Berkshire Downs 51
   Ridge Way 51
   Wayland Smithy 51
   White Horse Hill 51–52
Bibury 79–80
Blenheim Palace 82–83
Bodiam Castle 219
Bodmin Moor 125–26

Boscastle 112, 115–17
Boulter's Lock 47
Bourton-on-the-Water 62
Bovey Tracey 145, 146, 147
Bridport 158
Brighton 197
British Tourist Authority 228, 231, 247
Broadway 63
Burford 54, 57
Cadgwith Cove 132, 137
canal travel 48
Canterbury 227–28
Carn Euny 135
cars
   insurance 19, 29
   rental 18–19, 43–44, 241
Cerne Abbas 179
Cerne Giant 178
Chartwell 226
Chesil Bank 165
Chewton Mendip 100
Chiddingstone 224–25
Chipping Campden 63–65
Church Cove (Landewednack) 131
Chysauster 133–34
Cliveden House 48–49
clothes 21
   walking gear 21–22
Clovelly 108–10
Cookham 48
Corfe Castle 171–72
Cornwall 114–47
   Coast Path 117–21
Cotswold Farm Park 67
Cotswolds 53–79
Cotswold Way 69–74
Cotswold Woolen Weavers
   Exhibition and Mill 54, 56
Crackington Haven 112, 113, 119–21

Crowlink 203
currency 35–36
Dartington Glass Works 110
Dartmoor National Park 144–56
    guided walks 151
    park headquarters 146
    talks, slide shows 146
Devil's Frying Pan 132
Dorchester 171
    Dorset County Museum 171
Dorset 160–74
driving 27–30
    terms defined 30
    license 20
    parking 29
    road classifications 27–29
    speed limits 29
Dunster 105
    Castle 105
duty free shops 243
Eastbourne 208–209
East Sussex 208–13
Exmoor National Park 101–102, 105–108
food 32, 35. *See also* "Daily Bread" in each chapter
    cheddar cheese 100
    Cornish pasties 124
    Devon cream tea 151
    marmalade, history of 67
Fosse Way 62
Fowey 143, 144
Friston Forest 204, 207
gardens 65, 140, 143, 166, 221
Glastonbury 97–99
    Abbey 97–99
Glastonbury Tor 93
Godmanstone 176
Great Dixter 219
Grey Mare and Her Colts 168
Grimspound 155
Hardy Monument 168
Hartland Quay 110
Hastings 216
hedgerows 52–53
Helford 137, 140
Henley-on-Thames 49
Herstmonceux Castle 211
Hever Castle 225–26
Hidcote Manor Gardens 65
High Cliff 119
Hound Tor 153, 154–55
jet lag 23
Kent 220–28
Kentish Weald 220–21, 224
Kynance Cove 130
Lamorna 136, 137
Land's End 125, 135
language, British-U.S. equivalents 25–26
Lanyon Quoit 134–35
Lechlade 54
Lewes 197
Litlington 205
Lizard, the 125–37
    Lizard Point 130–31
London 44, 226–27, 228, 229–39
    British Museum 233
    bus tour 232–33
    cathedrals 233
    Jermyn Street 237
    sightseeing 232–34
    Tate Gallery 233
    theaters 237
    transportation, airport 44, 241
    transportation, in-city 231–32
    Tube 44, 227, 232
    walking tour 234–39
Long Man of Wilmington 206–207, 213
Looe, East 144
Looe, West 144
Lulworth Cove 172
Lynmouth 106
Maiden Castle 169–71
Manaccan 137
Marlborough 184, 185
Marlow 49
Men-an-Tol 135
Merry Maidens 136
Michelham Priory 212–13
Midhurst 195
Minster Lovell Hall 74
money 20–21, 35–36
Mullion 137
North Bovey 155
Northleach 62
oast-houses 220

Old Sarum 182–83
Oxford 83
Padstow 126
Penshurst Place 224
Pentargon Falls 118
Penwith 133–36, 137
Penzance 137
Petworth House 195
Pevensey 211
phones 36
Polperro 144
Porthcurno 135
Port Isaac 112–13
prehistoric sites 51–52, 71, 133, 135, 136, 144, 155, 166– 67, 168, 169–171, 175–76, 178, 182, 183, 184, 185, 186– 93, 206
pubs 33–35
    hours 35
Reading 49
restaurants 246. *See also* "Daily Bread" in each chapter
Romney Marsh 215
Royal Greenwich Observatory 211
Rye 214–15, 216, 218–19
safety 38
St. Mawes Castle 140–143
Salisbury 179–82
Scotney Castle 221, 224
Selworthy 105–106
Seven Sisters 200, 203
    Country Park 203
Sissinghurst Castle Garden 221
Slaughter, Lower 62–63, 76
Slaughter, Upper 76–77
Snowshill 74
Somerset 97, 99–100
Somerset Levels 97
South Downs 200–208
South West Peninsula Coast Path 117–18
Stanton 71

Stanway 72
Stonehenge 183
Stow-on-the-Wold 63
Streatley 49
Sussex "trugs" 212
Tavistock 144
Thames, River 45, 48
thatched roofs 107
Tintagel 112, 122
Tintagel Island 122–24
tourist information centres. *See* "Creature Comforts" in each chapter
traveler's checks 20–21
Trelissick Garden 140
Tube (London Underground). *See* London
Uffington 53–54
Uffington Castle 51–52
Vale of Pewsey 183–84
Value Added Tax (VAT) 19, 241–43
Veryan 143
walking 37–39
Wansdyke 184
Warwick Castle 65–66
Watersmeet 108
Weald and Downland Open Air Museum 196
weather 18
Wells 93–97
    Bishop's Palace 96–97
    Cathedral 94–96
    Vicars' Close 96
West Bexington 166
Widecombe-in-the-Moor 145
Winchelsea 216–17
Winchester 194
Windsor Castle 45
Wistman's Wood 155–56
Woolstone 53
youth hostels 20. *See also* "Daily Bed" in each chapter

ABOUT THE AUTHORS

Bill North is a writer and independent public policy consultant. **Gwen North** is a consultant in fashion merchandising. Maryland residents, the Norths are avid travelers who visit Great Britain several times a year. For years they have been developing travel itineraries for their friends, tailored for independent, sophisticated travelers with wide interests but limited vacation time. The increasing demand for these itineraries led to *The Two-Week Traveler Series*.

N. M 23.
E M 25